TOP **10**
GREEK ISLANDS

CAROLE FRENCH

D0897385

DK

EYEWITNESS TRAVEL

Left **Colourful ceramics, Páros** Centre **Street vendor, Crete** Right **Limestone cliffs, Kefalloniá**

LONDON, NEW YORK,
MELBOURNE, MUNICH AND DELHI
www.dk.com

Printed and bound in China

First American Edition, 2011

15 16 17 18 10 9 8 7 6 5 4 3 2 1

Published in the United States by
DK Publishing, 375 Hudson Street,
New York, New York 10014

**Copyright 2011, 2015 © Dorling Kindersley
Limited, London, A Penguin Company**

Reprinted with revisions 2013, 2015

Published in the UK by
Dorling Kindersley Limited

ISSN 1479-344X

ISBN 978 1 4654 2918 6

Within each Top 10 list in this book, no hierarchy
of quality or popularity is implied. All 10 are, in the
editor's opinion, of roughly equal merit.

MIX
Paper from
responsible sources
FSC
www.fsc.org   FSC™ C018179

Contents

Greek Islands' Top 10

The information in this DK Eyewitness Top 10 Travel Guide is checked regularly.
Every effort has been made to ensure that this book is as up-to-date as possible at the time of
going to press. Some details, however, such as telephone numbers, opening hours, prices,
gallery hanging arrangements and travel information are liable to change. The publishers
cannot accept responsibility for any consequences arising from the use of this book, nor for
any material on third party websites, and cannot guarantee that any website address in this
book will be a suitable source of travel information. We value the views and suggestions of
our readers very highly. Please write to: Publisher, DK Eyewitness Travel Guides,
Dorling Kindersley, 80 Strand, London WC2R 0RL, UK, or email travelguides@uk.dk.com

Left **Blue-domed church, Santoríni** Right **Boats in Vathý harbour, Itháki**

Contents

Left **Stunning Navagio beach, Zákynthos** Right **Archaeological site, Delos**

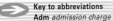

Key to abbreviations
Adm admission charge

3

GREEK ISLANDS' TOP 10

GREEK ISLANDS' TOP 10

⏉⏉10 The Greek Islands' Highlights

Comprising over 6,000 islands and islets, spread across several archipelagos, the Greek Islands offer a fabulous choice of holiday destinations. Some host bustling holiday resorts, while others consist solely of rural communities. In others, ancient temples sit amid cosmopolitan towns. Add beaches, pine forests, olive groves and coastlines indented with spectacular coves and bays, and the result is a collection of islands just begging to be explored.

1 Corfu Old Town
The arcaded terraces of the Listón, the ancient fortresses of Palaió Froúrio and Néo Froúrio, and Plateía Spianáda, with its Venetian architecture, all combine to give Corfu Old Town its infinite charm. Museums include the Antivouniótissa Museum *(see pp8–9)*.

2 Rhodes Old Town
This city was occupied by the Knights Hospitallers (1309–1522) who left such magnificent treasures as the Palace of the Grand Masters and the Street of the Knights *(see pp10–11)*.

3 Monastery of St John, Pátmos
Dedicated to St John, who reputedly wrote the *Book of Revelation* nearby, this 11th-century monastery is a UNESCO site *(see pp12–13)*.

5 Néa Moní, Híos
Containing one of Greece's finest collections of mosaics, this 11th-century monastery was built by Emperor Constantine IX Monomachos *(see pp16–17)*.

4 Delos
According to Greek mythology, this tiny uninhabited island was the birthplace of Apollo and Artemis. An important place of worship, it also has remains of civilizations dating from the 3rd century BC *(see pp14–15)*.

Phaestos Palace, Crete
The remains of this palace, one of two from the Minoan period, were found at what is now one of Crete's most important archaeological sites *(see pp20–21)*.

Pythagóreio and Heraion, Sámos
he remains of Pythagóreio, an ncient Greek and Roman fortified ort, and Heraion, a Neolithic emple, have put Sámos on the eritage map *(see pp18–19)*.

Palace of Knossos, Crete
The largest Bronze Age archaeological site on Crete, the remains of the Minoan Palace of Knossos give an incomparable insight into this ancient civilization *(see pp22–5)*.

(map of Greek Islands)

50 ⊢——— miles ⌐0 ⌐ km ———⊣ 50

Évvia
This long, narrow and largely mountainous island lies off the coast of mainland Greece. Évvia has been ruled in turn by the Macedonians, Romans, Venetians and Ottoman urks. Their influence gives the island ts inimitable character and distinctive rchitecture *(see pp28–9)*.

Temple of Aphaia, Égina
A well-preserved Doric temple dedicated to Aphaia, the ancient Greek goddess of fertility, this structure dates from around 480 BC. It stands on a hilltop covered with pine trees on the island of Égina *(see pp26–7)*.

🔟 Corfu Old Town

With its cobbled plazas and tiny alleyways dating back to ancient times, Corfu Old Town continues to retain its old-world charm. Palaces, museums, fortresses, gourmet restaurants, traditional tavernas, cultural venues and a lively harbour combine to give the town its inimitable character. It has beautiful arcades reminiscent of the finest in Paris, along with elegant Venetian mansions, which line the town's main thoroughfare, the Kapodistrou. Add Greek, Italian and British influences and you have an eclectic architectural anthology.

Cafés lining the arched Listón, Corfu Old Town

🔵 Watch the world go by while you enjoy a coffee at the chic cafés at the Listón.

• Map B5
• Palaió Froúrio: Palaió Froúrio Islet; 26610 48310; open summer: 8am–7:30pm daily; winter: 8am–3pm; adm €3, concessions €2
• Néo Froúrio: Plateía Solomoú; summer: 8am–7:30pm daily; winter: 8am–3pm; adm €3
• Church of Ágios Spyrídon: Agíou Spyrídonos; open 6:30am–8pm (tourist visits discouraged during church services)
• Palace of St Michael and St George and Museum of Asiatic Art: Plateía Spianáda; 26610 30443; open summer: 8am–7:30pm Tue–Sun; winter: 9am–3pm; adm €3, concessions €2; gardens 8am–dusk daily
• Antivouniótissa Museum: Prosfórou 30; 26610 38313; open 8:30am–3pm Tue–Sun; adm €3, concessions €1

Top 10 Features

1. Palaió Froúrio
2. Néo Froúrio
3. Plateía Spianáda
4. The Listón
5. Maitland Rotunda
6. Church of Ágios Spyrídon
7. Palace of St Michael and St George
8. Dimarchío
9. The Old Port
10. Antivouniótissa Museum

Palaió Froúrio
A landmark of Corfu, the Old Fortress was built in the 16th century on a tiny islet to protect the city from invaders. Its interiors have been restored and it has become a popular venue for cultural events. At its base stands St George's Church.

Plateía Spianáda
One of the largest squares in Greece, the Plateía Spianáda *(right)* is always bustling. Its Venetian and French architecture give it an elegant feel. The labyrinth of alleyways off the square, Campiello, is one of the town's oldest parts.

Néo Froúrio
The Venetians built this mighty fort *(left)* in the 1500s to strengthen the town's defences. Despite its name, the New Fortress was completed only a few years after the Old Fortress. With a maze of tiny medieval walkways to explore, the former naval garrison is now open to the public.

↪ Corfu Old Town was designated a UNESCO World Heritage Site in 2007.

The Listón

The Listón was built by the French in the early 1800s, inspired by the grandiose buildings along the Rue de Rivoli in Paris. Its arcaded terraces were once used solely by Corfu's aristocrats, but are now full of stylish cafés where locals and visitors chill out.

Maitland Rotunda

Built to commemorate the life of Sir Thomas Maitland, the first Lord High Commissioner of the Ionian Islands during the British administration, this 19th-century monument *(above)* dominates the southern end of Plateía Spianáda.

Church of Ágios Spyrídon

Named after Corfu's patron saint, St Spyrídon, whose remains lie here in a lavish silver coffin, this 16th-century church is an Old Town landmark. It has a distinct red-topped campanile with bells that ring out at regular intervals.

Palace of St Michael and St George

Dating from the British period, this imposing Georgian-style palace has been the home of the Greek royal family, the British High Commission and the island's treasury. It now houses the Museum of Asiatic Art.

Dimarchío

The Dimarchío, or Town Hall, is a classic Venetian-style building that was once the San Giacomo Theatre, a favourite haunt of the island's nobility.

Antivouniótissa Museum

With its Byzantine and post-Byzantine icons and ecclesiastical artifacts collection, this museum *(above)* is located in the Church of Panagía (Our Lady) Antivouniótissa, one of the city's oldest religious buildings.

The Old Port

While cruise ships tend to head for the New Port these days, in ancient times the Old Port *(below)* would have been a hive of nautical activity. It is located between the fortresses and is in one of the most picturesque parts of the Old Town.

The Mános Collection

One of the key exhibits at the Museum of Asiatic Art in Corfu Old Town is the Mános Collection, which comprises about 11,000 items. Corfiot diplomat Grigórios Mános (1850–1929) had a passion for Japanese, Chinese and Korean art, furnishings, ceramics and weapons. He amassed a fabulous private collection and donated it to the government to establish a museum in Corfu. Mános was alive to see the opening of the museum in 1927.

Rhodes Old Town

The citadel at the heart of Rhodes Town, the capital of Rhodes island, is a "living museum" showcasing the ancient and the medieval areas of the city. The Knights Hospitallers occupied the city from 1309 and transformed it into a formidable stronghold, but in 1522 Suleiman the Magnificent, Sultan of the Ottoman Empire, conquered the Knights. The UNESCO World Heritage Site walled city boasts outstanding buildings from both periods, including the Palace of the Grand Masters, Street of the Knights, mosques and hammams.

Floor mosaic, Palace of the Grand Masters

🗝 A special combined ticket allows entry to some of the churches and museums here.

🍴 Head for the Plateía Ippokrátous, Plateía Martýron Evraíon and Sókra tou Sokrátous for the best choice of cafés.

• Map V4
• Palace of the Grand Masters: Ippotón, Rhodes Old Town; 22413 65270; open 8am–8pm daily; adm €6, concessions €3
• Archaeological Museum, Rhodes: Hospital of the Knights, Plateía Mouseíou; 22410 25500; open summer 8am–7:40pm daily (from 1:30pm Mon); adm €3, concessions €1
• Municipal Museum of Modern Greek Art; Symi Square, Rhodes Old Town; 22410 23776; open 9am–2pm Mon–Fri (winter to 1pm); adm €3, concessions €1
• Temple of Venus, Rhodes Old Town; free

Top 10 Features

1. Palace of the Grand Masters
2. Hóra
3. Street of the Knights
4. Medieval City Walls
5. Archaeological Museum, Rhodes
6. Jewish Quarter
7. Mosque of Suleiman the Magnificent
8. Marine Gate
9. Temple of Venus
10. Municipal Museum of Modern Greek Art

Palace of the Grand Masters

Located in the citadel in the Collachium area, this is a replica of the original Knights' palace destroyed in 1856. The Italians rebuilt it and it is a museum now *(above)*.

Hóra

The citadel is divided into two main areas, the Collachium and the larger Hóra (Bourg), home to some of the city's busiest streets. Cafés vie for attention with markets full of stalls.

Street of the Knights

A cobbled street *(below)* crossed by arched bridges and lined with the Inns of the Tongues, this famous site dates from the 14th century. Although remodelled, it is recognized as one of the world's finest examples of Gothic urbanism.

4 Medieval City Walls
The Knights built the walls *(above)* on Byzantine fortifications to completely encircle and thus protect their city. The 4 km- (6 mile-) long walls contain a labyrinth of tiny alleyways.

5 Archaeological Museum, Rhodes
Known for its amphorae collection and artifacts *(left)*, this museum is housed in the Hospital of the Knights. Its infirmary is the main exhibition hall.

6 Jewish Quarter
This area dates from the 1st century AD. The Plateía Martýron Evraíon *(left)* has a very moving monument to the Rhodian Jews who died in WWII concentration camps.

7 Mosque of Suleiman the Magnificent
Erected as a triumphal mosque by Suleiman in 1522, the present structure *(above)* was built in 1808 using materials from the original.

9 Temple of Venus
I thought to date from the 3rd century BC, this temple was identified as dedicated to Venus due to the nature of the votive offerings found by archaeologists. The remaining columns and fragments demonstrate that Rhodes was of major importance during the Hellenistic period as well as during medieval times.

Municipal Museum of Modern Greek Art 10
This impressive collection features a permanent exhibition of important contemporary Greek art as well as several special themed exhibitions throughout the year.

8 Marine Gate
Dominating the Plateía Ippokrátous, Pýli Agías Aikaterínis, known as Marine Gate, is a mighty bastion of two towers and is the most magnificent of all the gates leading to the inner Old Town *(below)*.

Inns of the Tongues

The Knights Hospitallers, Order of St John of Jerusalem, were divided by nationality into groups known as "Tongues". Each had their meeting place (inn), with their Coat of Arms, and these lined the Street of the Knights. The Inn of Provence and Chapelle Francaise are on the street's north side, while on the south is Spain, one of the largest inns.

 Rhodes Old Town was declared a UNESCO World Heritage Site in 1988.

🔟 Monastery of St John, Pátmos

The island of Pátmos is reputedly where St John wrote the Book of Revelation, *or the* Book of the Apocalypse, *in AD 95. This book is the last of the* New Testament. *John is said to have lived the life of a hermit in a cave in ancient Hóra, where he received apocalyptic visions from Jesus Christ that compelled him to write the work. The Cave of the Apocalypse lies close to the monastic complex of the Monastery of St John, built in 1088 in the saint's honour. Hóra, the cave and the monastery are a UNESCO World Heritage Site.*

Icon showing the Annunciation of the Virgin

🕐 Aim to arrive in the early morning or late afternoon to avoid the tour crowds and the heat of the midday sun.

🍴 Hóra has a few small cafés and tavernas where you can purchase refreshments. Be sure to take bottled water with you.

• Map F4
• Monastery of St John, Hóra: 22470 31234; open 8am–1:30pm Mon–Sat, 4–6pm Tue & Thu, 10am–1pm & 4–6pm Sun
• Treasury: 22470 20800; open 8am–1.30pm Mon–Sat, 4–6pm Tue & Thu, 10am–1pm & 4–6pm Sun; adm €6

Top 10 Features

1. Hóra
2. Monastery of St John
3. The Walls
4. Chapel of the Holy Cross
5. Icon of St John
6. Hospitality of Abraham
7. The Chapel of Christodoúlou
8. The Treasury
9. Cave of the Apocalypse
10. Chrysobull

Hóra
This ancient settlement has over 40 monasteries and chapels and is one of the few places where early Christian ceremonies are still practised. The town is famous for its Byzantine architecture, including *mantómata* – window mouldings with a decorative cross.

Monastery of St John
An imposing 11th-century fortification dominating the skyline above Hóra *(below)*, this monastery is one of the most sacred Christian sites in the world. Fabulous icons and treasures are on display.

The Walls
The fortified walls of the monastery were built because of the threat of invasion. In some places they are said to be very deep and to contain fragments of the ancient Temple of Artemis that stood on the site before being destroyed in the 11th century.

St John is said to have been one of the 12 apostles of Jesus Christ.

Chapel of the Holy Cross
Many small chapels were built in the monastery because law dictated that prayer could be heard in a chapel only once a day. Among them are the chapels of the Holy Cross (above), Holy Apostles and John the Baptist.

Icon of St John
The most sacred treasure is the Icon of St John, housed in the inner narthex of the monastery. Dating from the 12th century, it shows the saint holding his work.

Hospitality of Abraham
A fabulous work of art, this 12th-century fresco (above) from the Chapel of Panagía depicts three angels receiving hospitality from the patriarch Abraham. It was painted over once and was only discovered after an earthquake in 1956.

The Chapel of Christodoúlou
Ioánnis Christódoulos, the Blessed, was the monk who had the Monastery of St John built. It took three years to complete. This chapel is dedicated to him and houses his remains in a marble sarcophagus.

The Treasury
Thousands of manuscripts, parchment documents, books, ecclesiastical art, gems and a fabulous silverware collection (below) are exhibited for the public.

Cave of the Apocalypse
The cave (below) contains a rock where Revelation was written, and a crack in the wall through which St John heard a voice and saw a vision. He lived here in exile during the reign of Roman Emperor Domitian (AD 51–96).

Chrysobull
The Chrysobull is the Treasury's star exhibit. A parchment scroll, it is a deed sealed in gold by the Byzantine Emperor Aléxios Komnínos, commissioning Ioánnis Christódoulos to found the monastery in 1088.

Book of Revelation
One of the most important books of the New Testament, the Book of Revelation says that there were seven early Christian communities in Asia Minor that received a letter from St John following his vision. It is believed St John was from Ephesus in modern day Turkey. He is known by a number of names, including John of Pátmos, John the Divine, John the Apostle and Saint John the Theologian, although a modern theory says that these were different people.

UNESCO awarded Hóra, the Monastery of St John and the Cave of the Apocalypse World Heritage status in 1999.

🔟 Delos

The island of Delos, home to civilizations as far back as 2500 BC, is one of the world's most important archaeological sites. As the mythological birthplace of the sun god, Apollo, and his twin, Artemis, the goddess of the moon and the hunt, it was the most sacred place of worship in ancient Greece. The old port, with its magnificent sanctuary, amphitheatre and dwellings, can be explored.

Detail of a marble pillar

Statues of Cleopatra and Dioscourides

⚠ Take bottled water to avoid dehydration. Wear sunscreen and a hat to guard against the sun, as there is little shade at the site.

🍴 The Sanctuary of Apollo has a small restaurant for refreshments.

• Delos Archaeological Museum, Delos
• Map P6
• 22890 22259
• Open 9am–3pm Tue–Sun
• Adm €5; concessions €3

Top 10 Features

1. Sanctuary of Apollo
2. Theatre Quarter
3. Sacred Lake
4. Temple of the Delians
5. Terrace of the Lions
6. Agorá of the Competaliasts
7. Hall of the Poseidoniasts
8. Maritime Quarter
9. House of Dolphins
10. Sanctuary of Dionysos

1 Sanctuary of Apollo

With its three temples, Pórinos Naós (6th century BC), the Great Temple of Apollo (477 BC) and the later Temple of Athenians, this sanctuary would have been at the heart of Delos culture.

3 Sacred Lake

According to legend, this lake *(above)* was where Apollo and Artemis were born to Leto. Though dry now, a wall denotes its boundaries.

2 Theatre Quarter

The remains of lavish homes, many with colonnaded courtyards, suggest that the Theatre Quarter was a small but exclusive residential area. Its key feature is a spectacular amphitheatre *(main image)* which was designed to hold over 5,000 spectators.

4 Temple of the Delians

The classic Doric-style Temple of the Delians *(below)* is one of the many excavated, along with the Roman-era Temple of Isis and the 5th-century Temple of Hera.

5 Terrace of the Lions
This row of lions *(above)* is one of the iconic images of Delos. Dating from the 7th century BC and carved of Naxian marble, they overlook the Sacred Lake. Now replaced by replicas, the original statues are housed in the Delos Archaeological Museum.

6 Agorá of the Competaliasts
The remains of shops and potholes for awnings *(above)* can be seen in the Hellenistic-era marketplace near the Sacred Harbour. The stone-paved ground is heavily worn.

7 Hall of the Poseidoniasts
The cultic hall *(above)* housed meeting rooms and shops belonging to Beirut merchants who worshipped Baal (known as Poseidon) here.

8 Maritime Quarter
Revolving around the Sacred Harbour, the Maritime Quarter was the main residential area of Delos. Among the ruins are floor mosaics of the mansions built by wealthy merchants.

9 House of Dolphins
With its floor mosaic of dolphins at play *(above)*, this house to the amphitheatre's north, is very well preserved. Dating from the 2nd century BC, it gives an insight into the fashion of the day.

Sanctuary of Dionysos 10
Dedicated to Dionysos, god of wine and ecstasy, and Zeus's son, this sanctuary *(right)* was used for ritual worship and is known for its 2,300 year-old phallic monuments.

People of Delos

Delos is uninhabited today, but this was not always so. In 426 BC, the Athenians decided to "cleanse" Delos and its thousands of inhabitants were exiled. It was declared that no one would ever be born, die or be buried on the holy island. Graves were opened and the remains removed. As a result, the buildings and the island were abandoned.

Néa Moní, Híos

Considered one of the finest examples of architecture from the Macedonian Renaissance, this UNESCO World Heritage Site is famous for its golden mosaics. Located just west of Híos town, the 11th-century Néa Moní, meaning New Monastery, was built by Byzantine Emperor Constantine IX Monomachos and Empress Zoe (r.1042–1050). According to legend, three monks found a miraculous icon of the Virgin Mary here. It became an influential and wealthy monastery but its decline began when the Ottomans plundered Híos in 1822.

A cross at Néa Moní

🔾 Néa Moní is undergoing an extensive restoration programme and some areas of the complex may be closed to visitors.

🔾 The monastery is surrounded by small villages that have tavernas and coffee shops for refreshment.

- Híos
- Map K5
- Monastery open dawn to sunset daily, but closes 1–4pm; museum open 9am–1pm Tue–Sun
- Adm €2 (free on Sun)

Top 10 Features

1. The Narthex
2. St Luke's Chapel
3. Cistern
4. Mosaics
5. Skull Cabinet
6. The Belfry
7. Monks' Cells
8. Trapeza
9. The Catholicon
10. Churches

The Narthex
The esonarthex (inner narthex) and the exonarthex (outer narthex) entrances *(above)* feature some of the monastery's most prized mosaics. There is also a marble inlaid floor, which was a sign of wealth in Byzantine times.

Cistern
A key part of the monastery's infrastructure, the cistern, or *kinsterna*, is a well-preserved underground complex of marble columns, arches and vaults, designed to collect and hold rain water. This water was supplied to the monks.

St Luke's Chapel
This small chapel, *(below)* dedicated to St Luke, the early Christian author of the *Gospel of Luke*, is near the monks' cemetery, just outside the monastery's boundary wall. Its architecture is typical of the 11th-century ecclesiastical style.

Mosaics
Worked in marble on a gold background, the mosaics depict biblical scenes and figures. The works include the famous *Anástasis* (Resurrection), showing Christ's rescue of Adam and Eve from Hell *(above)*.

Skull Cabinet
A macabre sight, this cabinet contains skulls and bones of the islanders massacred by the Ottomans in 1822. The dead included 600 monks from Néa Moní.

The Belfry
The original majestic belfry was built in the early 16th century. It collapsed during the 1881 earthquake and was rebuilt in 1900.

Monks' Cells
The Venetian-period cells *(above)*, known as Keliá, are where the monks would have slept. Though most are in a ruined state, one has been renovated and houses a small museum.

Trapeza
The dining hall, or refectory, is where the monks would have met for meals. A once-massive structure, it was damaged in 1822 by the Ottomans and again by the 1881 earthquake. Its remains can be visited.

The Catholicon
The Catholicon, or Katholikón, is the main part of the church between the esonarthex and exonarthex. Dedicated to the Virgin Mary, it is a rare early example of insular octagonal architecture and is dominated by its dome.

Churches
The monastery has two small churches. One is dedicated to the Holy Cross *(right)*. The other, Pandeleimon, is named after the saint who, according to legend, became a martyr during the Roman persecution of Christians in AD 303.

Macedonian Renaissance Art
The Macedonian Renaissance, a period of Byzantine art, began in the late 9th century and continued till the mid-11th century. During this time, cross-in-square and octagonal churches with fabulous frescoes, icons and mosaics were commissioned. The use of marble and ivory, often on gold and black backgrounds, became fashionable. The finest examples from the period are Ósios Loukás Moní and Dafní Moní on the Greek mainland, which share UNESCO status with Néa Moní.

Pythagóreio and Heraion, Sámos

Pythagóreio, named after the ancient philosopher Pythagóras, and the Sanctuary of Heraion are two treasures of Sámos. Pythagóreio, now a bustling holiday resort, was an important port in antiquity, its fortifications acting as a stronghold against invasion. Remains of the town's citadel, along with Roman baths, the harbour and an extravagant aqueduct, Tunnel of Efpálinos, can be seen. Nearby, Heraion is a sanctuary where Hera, the Greek goddess of fertility, was cult worshipped. Its architecture is among the finest from the period.

Wild flowers in Pythagóreio, Sámos

🌳 Just a few trees provide shade at the Sanctuary of Heraion and some of the other remains around Pythagóreio, so be sure to wear a hat and carry water if visiting in the hot summer months.

💬 When visiting the ancient site at Pythagóreio and the nearby Sanctuary of Heraion, visitors can stop for refreshments at Pythagóreio's many tavernas and restaurants.

• Map F4
• Archaeological Museum of Sámos: Kapetán Gymnasiárchou Katevéni, Vathý, 22730 27469; open 8:30am–3pm Tue–Sun; adm €3; concessions €2

Top 10 Features

1. Tunnel of Efpálinos
2. Statue of Pythagóras
3. Castle of Lykoúrgos Logothétis
4. Ancient Port
5. Ancient Harbour
6. Ancient Fortification
7. Sanctuary of Heraion
8. Temple of Hera
9. Greek and Roman Remains
10. Treasures from Pythagóreio and Heraion

Tunnel of Efpálinos
Built in the 6th century by ruler Polykrates to provide his people with water, this aqueduct *(above)* is an engineering marvel. It is notable as one of the first to be excavated from both ends.

Statue of Pythagóras
Standing on the harbourside at Pythagóreio, this 3 m (9 ft) tall statue celebrates the life of Pythagóras the Samian, who was born on the island in 570 BC. The town is named after him.

Castle of Lykoúrgos Logothétis
This castle *(left)* and tower was built by a local hero, Lykoúrgos Logothétis, three years after his heroic part in the War of Independence of 1821. It is believed to stand on the site of the ancient acropolis.

Together, Pythagóreio and Sanctuary of Heraion share UNESCO World Heritage status, granted in 1992.

Ancient Port

Sámos was a major naval and mercantile power in the 6th century BC. Its port *(above)* was once bustling with ships and merchants, through which produce, materials and grain were loaded. It brought great wealth to the island.

Ancient Harbour

Pythagóreio's harbour is considered the oldest manmade maritime installation in the Mediterranean. Dating from the 6th century BC, it is now silted up and can be crossed by a causeway.

Ancient Fortification

The city walls *(above)* of Pythagóreio, known as Polykrates Wall, date from the 6th century BC and surround the ancient town and its harbour. They run from the Lykoúrgos Logothétis tower to the Tunnel of Efpálinos.

Sanctuary of Heraion

Within the grounds of this sanctuary, dedicated to Hera, are the archaeological remains of an early Christian basilica and the Temple of Hera. There are statues *(main image)* on the Sacred Way path leading to the temple.

Temple of Hera

A single column *(left)* is all that remains of the temple, but evidence indicates that it was once among the largest in antiquity. The goddess Hera is said to have been born, raised and worshipped here.

Greek and Roman Remains

A wealth of Roman remains lie around Pythagóreio, including an amphitheatre and an acropolis located in the castle grounds *(below)*.

Treasures from Pythagóreio and Heraion

Many Pythagóreio and Heraion treasures, including Koúros, a 5 m- (16 ft-) tall marble statue dedicated to Apollo and dating to 580 BC, are displayed in the museum in Vathý.

Pythagóras

Pythagóras was a 5th-century BC Greek philosopher, mathematician and scientist, known for his theorem of the geometry of triangles. He is also credited with Pythagórean tuning, a system whereby musical instruments are tuned to intervals on a 3:2 ratio. According to legend, he was the son of Apollo. He was also the founder of an ancient religious movement, Pythagóreanism.

🔟 Phaestos Palace, Crete

Phaestos, one of the great cities of ancient Greece, is believed to have been founded by the mythological King Minos of Crete. Overlooking Crete's Messára Plain, this remarkable archaeological site was discovered in the 1880s. Comprising the remains of a palace built in the late Bronze Age, this well-preserved site provides a fascinating insight into Minoan life. Another palace occupied the location before being destroyed in an earthquake, and fragments of it remain.

Main Hall
This hall *(above)*, with 10 storage rooms, is where artifacts such as clay seals from the Protopalatial period were discovered.

The Grand Staircase

⊘ Care should be taken by anyone using a wheelchair as the site is uneven and has many steps to negotiate.

❍ There is a small cafeteria for refreshments, but do carry bottled water to avoid dehydration in the summer months.

* Phaestos, Míres
* Map E6
* 28920 42315
* Open summer: 8am–8pm daily; winter: noon–5pm Mon, 8:30am–3pm Tue–Sun
* Adm €6; concessions €2
* Special ticket available to see Phaestos Palace, the Royal Villa at Agia Triada (see pp98–9) and Irákleio's Archaeological Museum (see p97); adm €10, concessions €3

Top 10 Features

1. Main Hall
2. Grand Staircase
3. West Courtyard
4. Church of St George of Falándra
5. Archives Room
6. Central Courtyard
7. The Peristyle Hall
8. Northeast Quarter
9. Royal Apartments
10. First Palace

Grand Staircase
This immense flight of stone steps leading to the propylon (porch) was the main entrance to both the new and the old palaces, and linked the lower and upper levels of the west courtyard.

West Courtyard
Dating from around 1900 BC, this courtyard *(below)* was used for plays, religious rituals and ceremonies. To the north are eight rows of stone seats once used by spectators.

Church of St George of Falándra
This small 16th-century church, to the west of the palace, has served the local community since Venetian times. It has an elaborate façade.

The Prepalatial period ran from 3500 to 1900 BC, while the Protopalatial period ran from 1900 to 1700 BC.

Archives Room
Best known for being where the Phaestos Disc *(see box)* was discovered in 1903, the archives room consisted of chambers constructed with sun-dried bricks made from mud, clay and sand. Valuables would have been kept here.

Central Courtyard
This monumental paved courtyard *(left)*, once flanked on two sides by covered walkways, may have been a parade ground. Recesses in the walls by the main entrance are believed to have been sentry boxes.

The Peristyle Hall
This hall comprised a covered walkway and private courtyard *(above)*, which would have led to the royal apartments. The courtyard probably contained a small garden.

Northeast Quarter
This quarter housed the artisans' workshops where crafts included weaving and the making of clay pots. In the courtyard the remains of a furnace used for smelting metal can still be seen.

Royal Apartments
Comprising the King's and the Queen's Megarons (chambers), these rooms *(right)* would have been highly ornate. The floors were alabaster-lined. One of the finest lustral basins on Crete was found here.

First Palace
The original palace was built during the Protopalatial period but was damaged by earthquakes and rebuilt many times. The oldest palatial ruin on Crete, it lies to the site's southeast *(left)*.

The Phaestos Disc

This 17th-century BC clay disk, 16 cm (6 inches) in diameter, has the finest example of Minoan script ever discovered. It is now in the Irákleio Archaeological Museum *(see p97)*. The inscription uses 45 pictorial words, thought to be religious text. Spiralling from the outer edge to the centre, the signs, stamped on clay, are the earliest known form of typography.

Palace of Knossos, Crete

Knossos, inhabited since Neolithic times, became a powerful commercial and political centre when the legendary King Minos built his palace here in around 1900 BC. The first palace was destroyed in around 1700 BC but this seat of royalty and hub of Minoan life was quickly rebuilt. Discovered in 1878, the second palace comprises a maze of apartments, workrooms and courtyards, many with replica frescoes – originals are in Irákleio Archaeological Museum (see p97) – showing Bronze Age life. Knossos is the world's largest Minoan site.

Pillared gateway with replica of a fresco

⊙ Guided tours of the site are available in different languages, along with books on sale at the bookshop.

⊖ A café serves light snacks and beverages, and there are several tavernas nearby.

• Knossos, south of Irákleio
• Map E6
• 2810 231940
• Open Apr–Oct: 8am–8pm daily, Nov–Mar: noon–5pm Mon, 8:30am–3pm Tue–Sun
• Adm €6; concessions €3
• Special ticket package available for entry to the Palace of Knossos Archaeological Site and the Irákleio Archaeological Museum (see p97); adm €10, concessions €5

Top 10 Features

1. The Palace
2. The Royal Apartments
3. The Throne Room
4. Hall of the Royal Guard
5. Corridor of the Procession
6. Horn of Consecration
7. Private Houses
8. Workshops
9. Royal Road
10. Priest-King Fresco

2 The Royal Apartments
Containing the King's Megaron (chamber), known as the Hall of the Double Axes, and the Queen's Megaron decorated with the famous dolphin fresco replica *(above)*, the apartments had the rarity of a private bathroom.

1 The Palace
Built around a central courtyard, the palace complex *(main image)* was arranged with four wings that contained the royal apartments, the throne room, chapels, administration rooms and workshops. Private dwellings dot its periphery. It dates back to 2000–1350 BC.

3 The Throne Room
This imposing room has a carved stone throne copy *(left)*, believed to be in the image of a priestess. The room was probably used for worship. A griffin fresco guards the throne.

The term "palace" meant not only the ruling monarch's home, but the administrative, political and cultural centre of the city.

4 Hall of the Royal Guard

One of several administrative areas, this hall *(above)*, adjacent to the royal quarters, would have been heavily guarded. It is where the King's guardsmen lived and worked. The wall frescoes here depict shields.

5 Corridor of the Procession

This corridor is the main entrance to the site. It has a copy of the original *Procession* fresco, with over 500 figures.

6 Horn of Consecration

Standing about 3 m (9 ft) tall, this restored stone symbol *(above)* is said to represent the horns of a bull, considered sacred in Minoan times.

7 Private Houses

Among the remains of dwellings are the Royal Villa, which is religious in design and probably the home of a priest, and the Villa of Dionysus, where he was cult worshipped.

8 Workshops

The remains of workshops, used for food preparation and crafts such as pottery, are mainly in the east wing. Excavations revealed many *pithoi* (jars), which were used for storage *(right)*.

9 Royal Road

Said to be the oldest paved road in Europe, the Royal Road heads towards the northwest of the site to the town of Knossos. The theatre and the Little Palace, a smaller version of the main building, are located just off the road.

10 Priest-King Fresco

This replica *(right)* of the original brightly coloured fresco of the *Priest-King* wearing a crown of lilies and feathers, is a detail segment from the *Procession* fresco. It is also known as the fresco of the *Prince of Lilies*.

Sir Arthur Evans

Credited with unearthing the Palace of Knossos, deciphering ancient Cretan script and giving the Minoan civilization its name, Sir Arthur Evans (1851–1941) was a rich British archaeologist with a passion for Crete. In 1878, Cretan Minos Kalokairinós had found Knossos but the ruling Ottoman Turks thwarted his excavation. Sir Arthur purchased the site in 1898 and mounted the excavation.

Left **Replicas of frescoes, off the Central Court** Right **Copy of the dolphin fresco**

🔟 Treasures from Knossos

Snake Goddess
A ceramic female figure just over 34 cm (13 inches) tall and decorated with a fine tin glaze, this faïence statuette is considered one of the finest examples of Minoan art. It was discovered in 1903.

La Parisienne Fresco
This fresco of a young girl with large eyes, ruby red lips and long dark curls was christened *La Parisienne* by Sir Arthur Evans because of its beauty. Dating from around 1450 BC, it is one of the oldest examples of Minoan art.

Blue Bird Fresco
A work of vivid colour, this fresco shows a bird on a rock surrounded by flowers. Dating from the late Bronze Age, it is one of the earliest paintings found in the House of Frescoes at Knossos.

Replica of the blue bird fresco

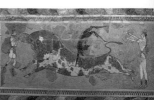

Replica of the *Bull Leaper* fresco

Bull Leaper Fresco
Dating from around 1550 BC, this wall painting depicts bull-leaping, an athletic event held during Minoan times. It shows three figures representing each stage of the feat. An abstract border in shades of blue and red surrounds the picture.

Bull's Head Rhyton
This black steatite jug, used for drinking or pouring, was known as a rhyton. It was fashioned into the head of a bull, the most sacred animal in Minoan culture, and has eyes of rock crystal and eyelashes of jasper.

Dolphin Fresco
Depicting several lavishly coloured blue-grey dolphins swimming with various other sea creatures, this celebrated late-Bronze Age fresco would probably have decorated the Queen's Megaron.

The Bull-Leaping Figurine
Considered one of the earliest examples of chryselephantine art, in which ivory figures are "clothed" in garments of gold

The originals of most of the treasures from Knossos are on display in the Irákleio Archaeological Museum (see p97).

Shield motif, Knossos

Minoan Art

While little Minoan art remains from the Prepalatial period (3500–1900 BC) other than fragments of pottery, there are magnificent examples from the Protopalatial period (1900–1700 BC) and the Neopalatial period (1700–1425 BC), when Cretans are said to have been encouraged to express themselves creatively. Wall frescoes were painted in vivid colours, with figures and animals depicted in great anatomical detail and showing a natural "movement". The La Parisienne and the Bull Leaper frescoes are prime examples. Similar detailing was fashioned into gold and silver jewellery, chryselephantine ivory, gold-leaf figures and faïence objects moulded from clay for making seals. Development of a primitive form of potter's wheel meant potters could produce both practical and decorative pottery. The Kamares style of symmetrical, rounded vases and rhyton jugs with thin walls was typical of the period. Minoan art often included representations of sacred animals.

Top 10 Minoan Archaeological Sites

1. Palace of Knossos
2. City and Palace of Phaestos
3. Palace of Malia
4. Palace at Zakros
5. City of Górtys
6. Royal Villa at Agia Triada
7. Town of Paleókastro
8. Sacred Ideon Cave
9. Settlement at Myrtós Pýrgos
10. Palace of Galatas

Large *pithoi* (jars), used to store supplies

Restored fresco of a griffin in the Throne Room

af, this figurine is in a leaping osition. Dating back to 1550 BC, is famous for its detail.

Priest-King Fresco
This fresco, dating from bout 1550 BC, portrays the *rince of Lilies*, believed to have een the Priest-King. The brightly oloured painting shows a figure ith a peacock feather headdress.

Isopata Ring
Discovered in a grave, the opata gold signet ring, dating om 1600 to 1400 BC, shows

four female figures wearing elaborate costumes and dancing among flowers. Well-preserved, it is famous for its remarkable detailing.

Faïence Plaque Collection
A collection of ceramic plaques, which includes the famous wild goat and kid plaque found in the sacred treasury rooms of the palace, show the use of the faïence technique of tin glazing. These plaques are believed to have been used as inlays.

TOP 10 Temple of Aphaia, Égina

Named for princess Aphaia, who became a Greek goddess of fertility, this magnificent temple is thought to have been built around 480 BC with loot seized from the Persians after their defeat by the Greeks at the Battle of Salamis. It is located on the site of an earlier temple, the remains of which are said to have been used in its construction. Standing majestically on a pine tree-covered hilltop above the Agía Marína resort, this temple is the most important monument in the Sanctuary of Aphaia.

Remains of the priest's house, Temple of Aphaia

🕐 The site offers little shade, so try to avoid the middle of the day during summer when the sun is at its strongest.

🍴 Take bottled water and snacks with you as there are no refreshment outlets near the temple.

• Temple of Aphaia: 13 km (8 miles) from Égina Town; Map L1; 22970 32398; open 8:30am–7:30pm daily; adm €4, concessions €2
• Archaeological Museum of Égina: Égina Town; Map K1; 22970 22248; open 8am–3pm Tue–Sun; adm €3, concessions €2

Top 10 Features

1. Doric Columns
2. Sphinx Statues
3. The Altar
4. Inner Columns
5. East Pediment
6. West Pediment
7. Limestone Architraves
8. Prónaos and Opisthódomos
9. Figurines
10. Cella

Doric Columns
The temple was built according to the hexastyle format of the Doric period, with 12 outer columns along its longer sides and six along its shorter ends as seen in this model *(above)*. They incline to strengthen the building. All the columns were fluted except three.

Sphinx Statues
Four marble sphinx statues would have been positioned at each corner of the temple's roof. With the head and breasts of a woman, body of a lion, a serpent's tail and wings of an eagle, the sphinx was a popular figure of Greek mythology.

The Altar
Remains of Aphaia's altar were discovered at one side of the temple, near the sanctuary's centre. A paved path with a ramp, possibly lined with statues, would have given access to the temple. Offerings to Aphaia were burned at the altar.

Inner Columns
The inner columns *(left)* enclose the cella *(see opposite)*, and are presented in a two-row, two-storey fashion with the lower columns supporting a platform for the upper columns. The fluted design echoes that of the outer Doric columns.

A 5th-century temple dedicated to the god Apollo lies a short distance from the Temple of Aphaia.

East Pediment
The 480-BC sculpture of Greek warrior Telamon fighting the Trojan King Laomedon adorned the temple's east pediment. A re-creation sits there now *(above)*.

West Pediment
The re-creation of the west pediment sculpture depicts the mythological hero Ajax *(below)* fighting in the Trojan War. Dating from the Archaic period (800–480 BC), the figure is intricately carved in white marble mined in Páros in the Cyclades.

Limestone Architraves
Porous local limestone was used to construct the architraves *(below)*, which were plain with a narrow band of plain metopes alternating with carved triglyphs above. They would have been covered with stucco and richly painted.

Prónaos and Opisthódomos
The temple is balanced symmetrically by its portico, *prónaos* (walkways) at its entrance and a small room to its rear, the *opisthódomos*. The cella's façade would have been between these two.

Figurines
Excavated female fertility figurines and pottery dating from the Bronze Age suggest that the temple has been a site of cult worship for more than 4,000 years. Artifacts can be seen in the Archaeological Museum of Égina.

Cella
Traditionally a cella, also known as a naos, is an inner chamber housing a cult sculpture of the deity to whom the temple is dedicated *(left)*. This cella would have had a statue of Aphaia and offerings would have been laid out in front of it.

Aphaia
According to legend, the princess Aphaia was saved after she attempted suicide by jumping into fishing nets in the waters off Égina, while fleeing from an unwelcome admirer. She was much loved by the goddess Artemis, who, relieved that she had been saved, made her a goddess and a sanctuary was built in her name. To the people of Égina she is their legend, but Cretans also claim that the story happened on Crete, where Aphaia is known as Diktynna.

TOP 10 Évvia

This long and narrow island, which is separated from mainland Greece by the Euripus Strait, is the second-largest Greek island. Largely mountainous, Évvia was inhabited in prehistoric times when it was home to two wealthy city-states, Chalcis, on the site of its present capital Halkída, and Erétria. The remains of Erétria can be seen near the modern town of the same name. Évvia has a long commercial history and was known for the Euboian scale of weights and measures used throughout Greece. The island has been inhabited by Sicilians, Macedonians, Venetians and Turks, all of whom left their legacy on its architecture and culture.

Stení

🖈 Évvia can be reached by boat, rail or road. It has a good network of roads linking its capital, Halkída, with other major towns. The mountain roads can be windy and uneven, so care needs to be taken.

🍴 Although largely untouched by tourism, Évvia has a varied selection of eateries. Its tavernas serve traditional food and are a great place to mix with locals.

• Map D3
• Archaeological Museum: Erétria; Map D3; 22290 62206; open 8:30am–3pm daily; adm €2, concessions €1

Top 10 Features

1. Halkída
2. Ancient Erétria
3. Límni
4. Kými
5. Loutrá Edipsoú
6. Évvia's Mountains
7. Stení
8. Kárystos
9. Ochthoniá
10. Prokópi

1 Halkída
Évvia's capital, Halkída has a mix of modern and historic buildings. Its waterfront boasts many tavernas and hotels. Venetian and Turkish influences can be seen in the Kástro quarter.

3 Límni
An attractive town of cobbled streets, a pretty harbour and elegant stone houses that hint at its past wealth, Límni *(below)* was a key maritime port in the 19th century. Today, it is a popular holiday location.

2 Ancient Erétria
Excavations at the site of ancient Erétria began in the late 1890s. Finds, such as a statue of goddess Athena *(left)* and pottery and tools dating back to prehistoric times were unearthed and can now be seen in the Archaeological Museum of Erétria.

➔ *Évvia is also known as Evia or Euboia.*

Kými
Picturesque, with Neo-Classical mansions overlooking the sea, Kými was a wealthy village during the 19th century due to its thriving maritime industry. Today, it is a place to see traditional crafts, such as embroidered household items *(left)*, and visit the "health-giving" natural springs.

Loutrá Edipsoú

With its warm, sulphurous water, which has attracted the rich for centuries, Loutrá Edipsoú is the largest spa town in Greece. Neo-Classical buildings line its harbour, while local fishermen continue to ply their trade in the wide bay *(right)*.

Évvia's Mountains
At 1,745 m (5,720 ft), Mount Dírfys is Évvia's highest peak. It is followed by mounts Óchi, Ólympos, Pixariá and Kandíli, all of which have dramatic rock formations and landscapes of pine forest and grasslands.

Stení
One of the island's many unspoiled mountain villages, Stení lies on the slopes of Mount Dírfys. Affording cooler temperatures than the coastal villages, it is popular with locals and visitors, especially in summer.

Kárystos
The spectacular slopes of Mount Óchi and the village of Mýli form the backdrop to this scenic fishing port and holiday hotspot. Its Neo-Classical buildings and Venetian Boúrtzi fortress *(main image)* are worth a visit.

Ochthoniá
A Frankish castle and Venetian watchtowers adorn Ochthoniá's skyline. Its coast has a series of deserted beaches *(above)* that lead to a dramatic wall of cliffs, known as Cape Ochthoniá.

Geórgios Papanikoláou

Physician Geórgios Papanikoláou (1883–1962) was born on Évvia. A pioneer of the study of human cells, cytology, he invented the cervical smear test, or Pap Test, used worldwide in the detection and prevention of cancer of the cervix. His statue stands in the main square in his birthplace, Kými. His image was used on the 10,000 drachma banknote until 2001.

Prokópi
Head for Prokópi, a sleepy village on the slopes of Mount Kandíli, for fabulous pine forest views. The large village has whitewashed stone houses *(right)*. Pilgrims come here to worship the 18th-century saint St John the Russian.

Évvia is home to Arvanites – descendants of 15th-century Albanian immigrants – who speak their own dialect, Arvanítika.

Left **Napoleon Bonaparte** Centre **Peloponnesian War** Right **Venetian fortress**

Moments in History

1 3000–1000 BC: Cycladic Civilization

The Early Bronze Age civilization that existed in the Cyclades before the advent of the Minoans is thought to be the Greek Islands' earliest. This important period in Mediterranean history is best known for its female icons carved from marble. The Cycladic people were believed to be great fishermen.

Cycladic marble figurine

2 700 BC: Creation of the Dorian Hexapolis

Along with the Ionians and the Aeolians, the Dorians were a tribe of ancient Greece and are mentioned in the *Odyssey*. They created the Dorian Hexapolis, a coalition of six cities, to serve the people and the gods. These were Camirus, Lindus and Lalysos on Rhodes, Cnidus and Halicarnassus in Caria, a region of western Anatolia, and Kos.

3 431–404 BC: Peloponnesian War

A period of unrest between the residents of Corfu, allies of the Athenian empire, and their colonizers, the Corinthians, triggered the Peloponnesian War. It was fought between the Athenian and Spartan empires. A peace treaty was signed in 421 BC but the war resumed six years later. The Spartans eventually triumphed at the mighty battle at Aegospotami.

4 197–146 BC: Roman Invasion

Subjugation by the Romans started in 197 BC and the Roman period began when Corinth was defeated and Greece became part of the Roman Empire in 146 BC. It was a period of change, and Greece, supported by its isles, became the cultural centre of the Roman Empire. Corinth was rebuilt in 46 BC.

5 1204–1797: Venetian Occupation

The Republic of Venice took control of the Ionians from 1204. This was a key period in the history of the islands – it was due to strong Venetian fortifications that they were able to escape occupation during the Ottoman invasion of Greece. As a result, the islands remained Christian.

6 1309–1522: Knights Hospitallers

Knights Hospitallers, Order of St John of Jerusalem, invaded many islands in the 14th century, particularly those in the Dodecanese. They brought much wealth and built strongholds to protect their cities. Their architectural legacy is most notable in Rhodes. The Knights were overthrown in Rhodes by the Ottomans in 1522.

7 Ottoman Rule

There have been several periods of Ottoman rule in the islands, the most notable being

Preceding pages **Mýkonos**

in the 14th, 16th, 17th and 19th centuries. For example, the Sultan of the Ottoman Empire, Suleiman the Magnificent, captured islands in the Cyclades and Dodecanese in the 1500s, while Crete fell in the 17th century.

8 1814–1864: British Protectorate

The Greek Islands came under the protectorate of the British in 1814, and, following the Greek War of Independence waged by revolutionaries from 1821 to 1829, overthrew the last period of rule under the Ottoman Empire. The islands acquired Union with Greece in 1864.

German tanks entering Greece

9 1941: Axis Occupation

During World War II, the Axis alliance, which included Germany and Italy, took control of Greece and, in 1941, many of the islands were ruled by the Italians. In 1943, the Germans evicted the Italians and immediately exerted their power by sending local Jews to their death.

10 1953: Major Earthquake

The most significant event in modern history was the earthquake that hit the Ionian islands in 1953. This major earthquake, measuring 7.1 on the Richter scale, caused massive damage, destroying many towns. Today, all buildings are built to earthquake-proof standards.

Top 10 Historical Figures

1 Hippocrates (460–370 BC)
The ancient Greek physician, known as the "Father of Medicine", was born on Kos.

2 Emperor Aléxios Komnínos (1081–1118)
He ruled during the Byzantine period and was instrumental in building many monasteries.

3 Lámbros Katsónis (1752–1804)
An 18th-century naval hero, Katsónis fought the Ottomans with his small fleet.

4 Napoleon Bonaparte (1769–1821)
Napoleon, later Emperor Napoleon I, conquered the Venetian Republic in 1797.

5 Ioannis Kapodistrias (1776–1831)
The Greek state's first governor after Ottoman occupation in 1827 was from the Ionians.

6 Dionýsios Solomós (1798–1857)
Born in Zákynthos, poet Solomós wrote the Greek national anthem.

7 William Gladstone (1809–1898)
Key UK government figure and later Prime Minister who was instrumental in giving the islands to Greece in 1864.

8 Empress Elisabeth of Austria (1837–1898)
Empress Elisabeth of Austria built the Achílleion Palace in Corfu during the 1890s.

9 Sir Arthur Evans (1851–1941)
Archaeologist who found the Palace of Knossos and identified the Minoan civilization.

10 Duke of Edinburgh (b.1921)
Husband of Queen Elizabeth II and grandson of King George I of Greece was born in Corfu.

Left **Bar sign**, Skiáthos Centre **Ágios Geórgios beach**, Santoríni Right **Pórto Katsíki, Lefkáda**

Bays and Beaches

1 Pórto Katsíki, Lefkáda
With its dazzling white sheer cliffs, vivid blue sea and golden sand, this beach is one of the best on the island. It lies in a wide horseshoe-shaped bay and is reached by a series of steps from the parking area, or by boat from nearby Vasilikí (see p61).

2 Lithí Beach, Híos
This huge horseshoe-shaped beach lies just west of Híos Town. It is famous for its natural beauty, its astonishing sunsets and the many fine fish tavernas that vie for attention. ◈ Map K5

3 Navágio Beach, Zákynthos
Also known as Shipwreck Bay because of a freighter that sits partially buried in sand, this white-sand beach lies in a sheltered bay enclosed by soaring cliffs. World famous, it is quiet except when day-trippers descend to take photographs. It is signposted from Volímes village (see p74).

Navágio beach, Zákynthos

4 Yaliskári Beach, Corfu
A small, sandy beach with clusters of rock formations and a pine tree forest that descends almost to the water's edge in places, Yaliskári is one of the most secluded beaches along this coastline. It lies in a bay and is a popular picnic and swimming spot with locals. ◈ Map A5

5 Eliá and Agrári Beaches, Mýkonos
The long Eliá and Agrári beaches merge almost seamlessly, except for a cluster of rocks, to form the island's longest stretch of sand. Both have soft sand but Eliá, a Blue Flag beach, is more organized, with parasols and cafés, while Agrári is quieter and more relaxing. ◈ Map P6

6 Ágios Geórgios Beach, Santoríni
Comprising the Blue Flag award-winning Périssa and neighbouring Perívolos beaches, the long stretch of sand at Ágios Geórgios is touristy, with restaurants, bars tavernas and outlets for water-skiing, diving, snorkelling, sailing and banana-boat riding. It is nonetheless picturesque, with the black sand and clear waters giving it its identity (see p92).

7 Falásarna Beach, Crete
Widely considered to be one of the finest on Crete, this pretty but often windy beach has golden sand and shallow turquoise waters. It lines one of

Falásarna beach, Crete

the bays of the Gramvoússa peninsula and has a small harbour. Nearby are the ruins of the ancient Falásarna city. ◈ *Map D6*

Fínikas Bay, Sýros

A natural harbour sheltered from the northern meltemi winds by a rocky backdrop, which is dotted with white-washed houses, this pretty bay is always buzzing with activity from fishing boats and yachts. It is the island's second port after Ermoúpoli. Its narrow beach is sandy and scattered with tamarisk trees *(see p92)*.

Psilí Ámmos Beach, Pátmos

Meaning "fine sand", the pretty Psilí Ámmos beach lives up to its name with soft, golden sand and secluded dunes. The sea here is shallow and crystal-clear. Tucked cosily in a deep cove, the beach is best visited by boat, although it can be reached by a small road followed by a descent down a rocky path *(see p60)*.

Banana Beach, Skiáthos

One of the beach's two banana-shaped halves is picturesque and sandy. It has umbrellas, sun-loungers, the odd taverna and a few businesses offering watersports. The other half, locally known as Petit Banana, is quiet, secluded and popular with naturists. ◈ *Map M1*

Top 10 Diving Hotspots

1 Chaniá Bay, Crete
Shipwrecks and amphorae are visible in the shallow waters of this bay. ◈ *Map D6*

2 Fiskárdo, Kefalloniá
Dive sites are known for their underwater life here, including damselfish that swim in the canyons. ◈ *Map G2*

3 Kalafátis, Mýkonos
Shoals of barracuda swim amongst shipwrecks off this beach, including a wreck 20 m (66 ft) in the sea. ◈ *Map P6*

4 Ágios Nikólaos, Crete
See ancient remains and study underwater wrecks, caverns and reef off this popular diving spot. ◈ *Map F6*

5 Psalídi, Kos
Psalídi is known for its sheer cliffs, caverns full of sponges and shoals of sea bream. ◈ *Map Y1*

6 Laganás Bay, Zákynthos
This is the breeding ground of the endangered loggerhead turtle *(caretta caretta)* and also a celebrated party resort and diving spot *(see p74)*.

7 Périssa, Santoríni
Underwater rock formations created by the lava from this volcanic island can be seen off Périssa. ◈ *Map V3*

8 Xirókampos, Léros
Ancient artifacts are among the things to see along this stretch of coast, home to the 3rd-century Castle of Lepída. ◈ *Map F4*

9 Paleokastrítsa, Corfu
Caves and marine life draw divers to Liapádes Reef, off Paleokastrítsa. ◈ *Map A5*

10 Vasilikí, Lefkáda
Numerous dive sites can be found off Vasilikí, including those featuring canyons and cave swims. ◈ *Map G1*

Greece has 408 beaches and 10 marinas with a Blue Flag, the award given for coastal eco-sustainability.

Left **Nydrí waterfalls, Lefkáda** Centre **Samariá gorge, Crete** Right **Drogaráti cave, Kefalloniá**

Natural Wonders

1 Islets of the Greek Islands
Thousands of islets dot the sea around the Greek Islands. Some, such as Néa Kaméni off Santoríni, are uninhabited and volcanic, while others, such as the Diapontian islands off Corfu, have rich vegetation, small communities and great beaches.

2 Samariá Gorge, Crete
A stunning creation of nature, the gorge stretches about 16 km (10 miles) from the Omalós plateau to Agía Rouméli to the south. Towering rock walls have been created over millennia by a river, and at a spot called Iron Gates (Sideróportes), they are only 3 m (10 ft) apart. The gorge is a national park (see p97).

3 Blue Caves, Zákynthos
A rock formation of arches and caverns, the Blue Caves are foremost among the natural

Blue Caves, Zákynthos

wonders of Zákynthos. The sea appears bright blue due to the reflection of the sun between the arches, and contrasts sharply with the white cliffs. Take a boat from Cape Skinári lighthouse for the best views (see p74).

4 Korissíon Lagoon, Corfu
This freshwater lagoon is separated from the sea by a narrow stretch of sand dunes and beaches. Enclosed by a forest, it is a natural habitat for wildlife and many bird species, including sandpipers and egrets. Walking beside the lagoon is a magical experience (see p72).

5 Caves of Sámi, Kefalloniá
Melissáni cave and lake is the highlight of an extraordinary network of subterranean waterways and caverns originating at Katavothres, on the other side of the island. It is said to have been the sanctuary of the god Pan and several nymphs, including Melissáni. Nearby is the Drogaráti cave with its famous stalactites and stalagmites (see p70).

6 Extinct Volcano Polyvótis, Níssyros
This extinct volcano is one of the main attractions of Níssyros. It is around 260 m (860 ft) in diameter and 30 m (100 ft) deep, and surrounded by a grey landscape of craters. Steps lead down to its core. Its last eruption is said to have been over 5,000 years ago. ⬡ Map X3

Mýrtos Bay, Kefalloniá

7 **Mýrtos Bay, Kefalloniá**
One of the foremost sights of Kefalloniá, this bay is famous for its dazzling white-pebble beach formed by fragments from the calcite-rich limestone cliffs that surround it, and its vivid turquoise sea. Mýrtos beach has been voted one of the best in the world *(see p70)*.

8 **Nydrí Waterfalls, Lefkáda**
These waterfalls, located in the Dimosári gorge, are the most spectacular of the many falls on the island. Cascades of water fall into pools of crystal-clear water, which are popular with swimmers *(see p69)*.

9 **Caldera, Santoríni**
This water-filled cauldron lies off Santoríni and was created in 1450 BC, when a huge volcanic eruption blasted through the once-circular island, creating its current crescent shape. The Néa Kaméni and Palaia Kaméni islands emerged from the water with subsequent volcanic activity, and continue to be volcanic. *Map U2*

10 **Thérmes Hot Springs, Kos**
These are perhaps the most famous hot springs on the Greek Islands. Thérmes beach is known for its naturally warm pool in the rocks, which is fed by hot springs and is said to have curative powers. *Map Y2*

Top 10 Trees and Fruits

1 **Olives**
Greece is home to the largest variety of olives in the world. The green and black olives found in groves throughout the islands are either eaten or made into oil.

2 **Figs**
The deep purple fig can be seen amongst the large leaves of fig trees in summer.

3 **Vines**
Vines grow wild or in vineyards, with the green and black grapes used to make wine and liquors.

4 **Apples**
Local apples are usually small and sweet, and are used for cooking or served at the end of a meal.

5 **Pomegranates**
Pomegranates, which can be seen in late summer, were mentioned in the *Odyssey* and are used to make grenadine.

6 **Bananas**
The local variety of this fruit is small and grown on the lower, warmer plains of the islands.

7 **Cretan Plane Tree**
Endemic to Crete, the striking plane tree is often found in villages and provides welcome shade.

8 **Carob Tree**
With its dark seed pods used as a chocolate alternative, the carob tree is a key part of the landscape.

9 **Cypress Tree**
Tall and elegant, the cypress tree is from the conifer family and is seen in gardens and in the wild.

10 **Cedar Tree**
Forests of the broad-branched cedar tree can be found at higher altitudes throughout the islands.

Carob seeds were once used to measure the weight of diamonds. The tree's name and "carat" are derived from the Greek, kerátion.

Left **School of Homer, near Stavros, Itháki** Right **Cave of the Apocalypse in Chóra, Pátmos**

Myths and Legends

1 Homer's Odyssey
Believed to date from around the 8th century BC but based on earlier myths, Homer's epic poem *The Odyssey* suggests that Itháki was the home of the ancient hero King Odysseus. In the story, he returns home from the battle at Troy as a great warrior to be reunited with his love, Penelope.

2 Poseidon
As per Greek mythology, Paxí was created by the god of the sea, Poseidon, known as Neptune in Latin. Enraged at having no peace and quiet with his wife Amphitrite, he dealt a blow to Corfu with his three-pronged spear, known as a trident, splitting the island in two. Paxí thus became their place of sanctuary.

3 Sappho
Sappho was a prolific poet from the island of Lésvos who lived from around 620 to 570 BC. One legend claims she was in love with Phaon, an ugly ferryman, whom the goddess Aphrodite transformed into a man of beauty. Phaon then rejected Sappho who, broken hearted, threw herself to her death from the cliffs near Cape Lefkátas, Lefkáda.

Ancient Greek poet, Sappho

4 St John
Often referred to as John of Pátmos, the saint is said to have written the New Testament's *Book of Revelation* after he saw a vision of Christ in the Cave of the Apocalypse in Hóra, Pátmos. The nearby monastery of St John, which was founded in 1088 by the monk Christódoulos Letrínos in his honour, is one of the world's most sacred sites *(see pp12–13)*.

5 Hippocrates
Considered one of the main figures in ancient Greek medicine, Hippocrates was born in around 460 BC on Kos. A teacher of medicine, the physician is credited with rejecting superstitions and pioneering the thinking that diet and environment can cause illness. The Hippocratic Oath is still taken by doctors today.

6 The Giant Polyvotis
Polyvotis was part of an ancient race of fearsome giants, according to Greek mythology. During one of the legendary battles with the gods, Polyvotis infuriated Poseidon and the angry sea god cut off a part of Kos and threw it at the giant. The rock, once called Polyvotis, became known as Níssyros.

7 Minos
The Minoan civilization, which existed from around 2700 to 1450 BC and shaped the history of Crete, was named after Minos,

Minoan mural from Knossos, Crete

the mythical king of the island. He was the son of Zeus, king of the gods, and Europa, and lived at Knossos. Minos features on ancient Greek coins.

8 Helios and Rhode
According to legend, Helios, the sun god, was a handsome Titan who was cult worshipped on an island called Rhode (modern-day Rhodes). The island takes its name from a nymph of the same name with whom Helios had fallen in love.

9 The Lady of Ro
Born in 1890 on the Greek island of Kastellórizo, just off Turkey, Déspina Achladióti was forced to flee to nearby uninhabited Ro during World War II. She became a hero for raising the Greek flag every day, even though Ro was not a Greek island. The flag is still raised today in memory of the Lady of Ro.

10 St Francis of Assisi
A friar of the Roman Catholic Church and founder of the Franciscans, St Francis of Assisi is said to have considered Kefalloniá a spiritual home. In the 13th century he founded the beautiful Moní Theotókou Sisión, near Lourdáta, as a refuge.

Top 10 Ancient Sites

1 Delos
Mythological birthplace of Apollo, this sacred island has been inhabited since around 2500 BC (see pp14–15).

2 Pythagóreio, Sámos
The site of an ancient fortified port and known for its 6th-century BC aqueduct, the Tunnel of Eupalinos (see pp18–19).

3 Phaestos Palace, Crete
Site of a palace dating from 1450 BC, considered to be some of the finest Minoan remains (see pp20–21).

4 Ancient Thíra, Santoríni
Ptolemaic, Hellenistic and Roman remains can be seen at the site of the ancient Dorian city of Thíra (see p90).

5 Ancient Akrotíri, Santoríni
This late-Neolithic complex is well-preserved, as it lay buried after a volcanic eruption in Minoan times (see p90).

6 Paleókastro, Kefalloniá
The fortifications and citadel walls of the ancient city of Paleókastro are well-preserved (see p76).

7 Angelókastro, Corfu
Site of a 13th-century fortress that formed a hilltop acropolis. ◈ Map A5

8 Ancient Erétria, Évvia
Dating from the 6th–5th century BC, this ancient city has yielded important Neolithic and Helladic finds (see p28).

9 Paleóchora, Itháki
Once the capital of Itháki, Paleóchora's medieval ruins include stone houses and churches. ◈ Map H2

10 Ypapantí, Paxí
Legend has it that this cave was a Byzantine church dedicated to the Presentation of Christ in the temple. ◈ Map B2

Left **Icon in the Byzantine Museum, Rhodes** Right **Archaeological Museum, Lefkáda**

🔟 Museums and Galleries

1 Archaeological Museum Pythagóreio, Sámos

This museum's impressive collection includes pottery dating from the 9th to the 2nd centuries BC. A prize exhibit is a marble statue of Aiakes, father of the tyrant Polykrates, who, in the 5th century BC, seized power in the Aegean and Ionian islands. ◎ *Town Hall, Pythagóreio • Map F4 • 22730 62811-3 • Open 9am–4pm Tue–Sun • Adm*

2 Aegean Maritime Museum, Mýkonos

With its collection of nautical instruments, coins and paintings, this museum preserves Aegean maritime history *(see p86)*.

3 Irákleio Archaeological Museum, Crete

This fine museum has Minoan artifacts, including faïence figurines and frescoes, ceramics and jewellery *(see p97)*.

Irákleio Museum, Crete

4 Archaeological Museum, Lefkáda

The collection of artifacts exhibited in this museum date from the early Bronze Age. They were excavated from sites around the island, including Kariotes, outside Lefkáda Town, and Nydrí, on the east coast. ◎ *Ángelou Sikelianoú, Lefkáda Town • Map G1 • 26450 21635 • Open 8am–3pm Tue–Sun • Adm*

5 Antivouniótissa Museum, Corfu

Housed in the Church of Panagía Antivouniótissa, this museum is also known as the Byzantine Museum. It contains Byzantine and post-Byzantine artifacts and ecclesiastical icons dating back five centuries *(see pp8–9)*.

6 Archaeological Museum, Rhodes

Located in the 15th-century Hospital of the Knights, this museum displays a collection of Classical, Hellenistic and Roman sculptures as well as mosaic floors from Rhodes Town and Kárpathos. Rhodian funerary slabs dating from the period of the Knights, with personal coats of arms, are also exhibited *(see pp10–11)*.

Archaeological Museum, Rhodes

Exhibit in the Archaeological Museum, Corfu

7 Archaeological Museum, Corfu

Originally built to house treasures found at the Temple of Artemis on the Mon Repos Estate, this museum now has other exhibits too, including finds from a 13th-century fortress at Kassiópi and the Corfu Town citadel *(see p72)*.

8 Byzantine Museum, Rhodes

The museum has an impressive collection of icons and frescos, including 12th-century examples painted in the Comneni period. Housed in a church near the Mylon Gate that was built as a cathedral under the Knights' rule. ✆ *Apéllou near Mylon Gate, Rhodes Town • Map V4 • 22410 75674 • Currently closed for refurbishment. Exhibits are being temporarily housed in the Palace of the Grand Masters (see p10)*

9 Museum of Solomós, Zákynthos

With its collection of furniture, photographs and personal posses-sions, this museum is dedicated to eminent Zákynthians. These include Dionýsios Solomós, the national poet and author of the Greek national anthem, and the 19th-century writer Andréas Kálvos. ✆ *Plateia Agiou Markou, Zákynthos Town • Map H4 • 26950 42714 • Open 8am–3pm Tue–Sun • Adm*

10 Helmis Natural History Museum, Zákynthos

Exhibits offer an insight into the flora and fauna that make up the island's eco-system. These include rocks, minerals, fossils, shells, corals, fish and birds *(see p74)*.

Top 10 Unusual Museums

1 Phonograph Museum, Lefkáda
This is a private collection of old records and phonographs. ✆ *Map G1 • 26450 21088*

2 Paper Money Museum, Corfu
Banknotes from the German, British, Italian and Greek eras trace Corfu's history. ✆ *Map B5 • 26610 41552*

3 Naval Museum, Zákynthos
Located in Tsilivi, it has exhibits dating from the 1700s to the present day. ✆ *Map H4*

4 Municipal Museum of Modern Greek Art, Rhodes
Greek contemporary art is on display here *(see p10)*.

5 Folk Museum, Mýkonos
A windmill, plus rare textiles and ceramics, show how rural dwellers lived *(see p86)*.

6 Palaeontological Museum, Tílos
Exhibits include fossils of dwarf elephants that became extinct in 4500 BC. ✆ *Map G5*

7 Museum of Contemporary Art, Ándros
Works by Matisse, Picasso and local artists are on display here. ✆ *Map N4 • 22820 22444*

8 Museum of Marble Crafts, Tínos
Exhibits tell the history of Tinos marble and how it is crafted. ✆ *Map N5 • 22830 31290*

9 Kazantzákis Museum, Crete
This is dedicated to the Cretan writer Níkos Kazantzákis. ✆ *Map E6 • 28107 42451*

10 Vamvakáris Museum, Sýros
Musician Márkos Vamvakáris's belongings are displayed here. ✆ *Map N6 • 22813 60914*

Greek Islands' Top 10

Left **Moní Agíou Gerásimou** Centre **Moní Zoödóchou Pigís** Right **Detail, Néa Moní**

♦10 Monasteries and Churches

1 Moní Hozoviótissa, Amorgós

An architectural triumph built into the Prophítis Ilías mountainside, this 11th-century monastery was built for the Virgin Mary, protector of Amorgós island. It contains sacred treasures, including a 15th-century icon of the Virgin. Resident monks host a festival here every 21 November. ✆ *Near Amorgós Town • Map F4*

2 Moní Zoödóchou Pigís, Póros

This 18th-century monastery is called Zoödóchos Pigí (meaning life-giving) because it is built around a curative spring. The white structure, surrounded by pine forest, is an appealing sight. A fine collection of icons and the intricately carved gilded iconostasis separating the nave from the sanctuary are noteworthy. ✆ *Póros Town • Map K3*

3 Néa Moní, Híos

A UNESCO World Heritage Site, this austere monastery was built in the 11th century by Byzantine emperor Constantine IX Monomacho on the site where a miraculous icon of the Virgin Mary was discovered. It is known for its superb mosaics, considered among the finest Macedonian Renaissance art in Greece *(see pp16–17)*.

4 Moní Platytéra, Corfu

Dedicated to the Virgin Mary and to saint Chrysanthos, this 18th–19th-century monastery has post-Byzantine icons by famous local painters Klontzás and Ventoúras. It houses the mausoleum of the first Governor of Greece, Ioannis Kapodistrias, a Corfiot who took office in 1827. ✆ *Corfu Town • Map B5*

5 Moní of the Panagía Odigítria, Lefkáda

Built in the 1400s and noted for its traditional single-aisle architecture, austere exterior and intricate timber roof, this monastery is the island's oldest. It is dedicated to Odigítria, an ancient name for the Virgin Mary depicted in religious icons. ✆ *Lefkáda Town • Map G1*

6 Moní Panagía of Vlachérna, Corfu

A landmark of Corfu, this white monastery stands on an islet in the Chalikópoulos Lagoon off Kanóni. It is reached by a small causeway. The 17th-century building, which has also housed a convent, has interesting architectural features and ecclesiastical icons. ✆ *Kanóni • Map B5*

Moní Panagía of Vlachérna, Corfu

Moní Katharón, Itháki

7 Believed to originate from before the 17th century and built at an altitude of 600 m (1,970 ft), this monastery is one of the oldest and highest in the islands. Remote and beautiful, it was renovated after the earthquake of 1953 and is dedicated to the Virgin Mary. ⊗ *Anogí • Map G2*

Moní Katharón, Itháki

Moní of St John of Lagadá, Zákynthos

8 Frescos and gilded iconostasis, which date back centuries, make the journey to this remote and atmospheric monastery worthwhile. Built in the 16th century and remodelled in the 17th, it had many houses and chapels at one time. Today it is home to just one monk. ⊗ *Katastári • Map H4*

Moní Transfiguration of the Saviour, Zákynthos

9 This Byzantine monastery, dedicated to Ágios Dionýsios, the patron saint of Zákynthos, is an isolated structure on the island of Stamfáni in the Strofádes, a mini archipelago that belongs to the Greek Orthodox Church. ⊗ *Map B4*

Moní Agíou Gerásimou, Kefalloniá

10 A white-walled, red-roofed structure in the Mount Enos foothills, this monastery is dedicated to Gerásimos, Kefalloniá's patron saint. According to legend, Gerásimos lived in nearby caves. His mausoleum is in the monastery. ⊗ *Frangáta • Map G3*

Top 10 Religious Festivals

1 Good Friday
Easter, the most important festival of the year, starts with Epitáfios, a procession depicting the funeral of Christ.

2 Easter Sunday
After midnight on Saturday, worshippers light candles in a church to depict the bringing of holy light and good fortune.

3 Annunciation
Marked by a feast, this festival, held on 25 March, is a celebration of when the angel Gabriel announced that Mary would be the Holy Mother.

4 Epiphany
On 6 January, Epiphany events take place throughout the islands and are marked by the blessing of water.

5 Lenten Monday
Religious services, feasts and carnivals are held in the three weeks prior to Lenten Monday (Katharí Deftéra).

6 Lent
A period of penance to commemorate Jesus fasting before Easter, Lent culminates in Pentecost in June.

7 Pentecost
Sometimes known as the Feast of Weeks, Pentecost marks the descent of the Holy Ghost on the Apostles.

8 Dormition of the Virgin
The most important religious celebration after Easter takes place every 15 August throughout the islands.

9 Traditional Festivals
Taking place throughout the year, these festivals (panegíria) celebrate each island's patron saint.

10 Christmas
Christ's birth is celebrated with services, prayers and the giving of gifts.

Left **Asfendioú village, Kos** Centre **Pélekas, Corfu** Right **Náoussa, Páros**

Picturesque Villages

Pélekas, Corfu
This picturesque village has managed to resist mass tourism. Bougainvillea-covered stone houses sit among olive groves and vineyards, small hotels and traditional tavernas. Sitting on a hill overlooking unspoiled sandy beaches, it is known for its breathtaking sunsets. ◈ *Map A5*

Anogí, Itháki
A traditional village of olive trees and stone walls, Anogí is around 500 m (1,640 ft) above sea level, with great views. One of Itháki's most remote and oldest communities, it has its origins in medieval times. The people observe old customs and speak a distinct dialect. ◈ *Map G2*

Fiskárdo, Kefalloniá
This quintessential picture-postcard village miraculously survived the great earthquake of 1953 and retains many original Venetian buildings. Painted in soft pastel shades, the houses that were once the homes of

merchants line its yacht-filled harbour. Most now host tavernas, restaurants and shops *(see p76)*.

Lagopóda, Zákynthos
One of the mountain villages on Zákynthos, sleepy Lagopóda offers a rare glimpse into how the people of Zákynthos have lived for centuries. It is characterized by its cobbled alleyways, stone houses with vine-covered courtyards and its pretty church. ◈ *Map H4*

Imerovígli, Santoríni
With dazzling white and blue square houses and blue-domed churches descending down the hillside to the bay, Imerovígli is a typical Santoríni village. Facing west, over the flooded caldera, its sunsets are a photographer's dream *(see p90)*.

Kontiás, Límnos
Kontiás is one of the most charming villages on the island. Its architecture reflects Venetian, Byzantine and Ottoman influences. Surrounded by pine forest,

Imerovígli, Santoríni

ontiás, Límnos

has some glorious beaches. Kontiás is the seat of the municipality. ◈ Map E2

Asfendioú Villages, Kos
7 This cluster of villages on the slopes of Mount Dikéos, comprising Ziá (Evangelístria), Ágios Dimítrios, Asómatos and Lagoúdi, is surrounded by forest and springs. The villages retain their old charm with stone houses and Byzantine churches. ◈ Map X2

Pýrgos, Tínos
8 Houses, fountains, churches and public buildings sculpted from white marble give this village a distinct beauty. Marble has been used here for centuries, making it the birthplace of many great sculptors and home of the Tínos School of Fine Arts. ◈ Map N5

Oía, Santoríni
9 A popular holiday spot, Oía is a lovely village of blue-domed churches, white houses and tiny alleyways huddled on the hillside overlooking the volcano. It has many tavernas, gift shops, a maritime museum and the remains of a Venetian fortress (see p90).

Náoussa, Páros
10 Considered one of the prettiest villages in the Cyclades, this small fishing port is characterized by white houses, chapels, a bustling harbour and tiny lanes. Despite development, it has not lost its traditional charm. ◈ Map E4

Top 10 Animals and Birds

1 Loggerhead Turtle
Zákynthos' Laganás Bay (see p74) is one of the key breeding grounds for this endangered turtle.

2 Monk Seal
One of the rarest seals in the world, the monk seal can be seen off the islands, in particular in the Cyclades and northern Sporades.

3 Moorish Gecko
Usually found "sunbathing" on walls in summer, this grey-brown reptile can grow to around 15 cm (6 in) in length.

4 Mílos Viper
This distinctive venomous snake is found mainly on the Mílos and Kímolos islands in the Cyclades.

5 Freyer's Grayling Butterfly
Small and dark brown in colour, the Freyer's Grayling is native to the Mediterranean and seen in July and August.

6 Kri-Kri
A protected species, this wild goat is a native of Crete and found mainly in the Samariá gorge.

7 Dolphin
Look out for bottlenosed, striped and common dolphins when sailing in Ionian and Aegean waters.

8 Sardinian Warbler
This striking native Ionian bird can be identified by its black head and red eye ring.

9 Scops Owl
These small grey owls are hardly visible but their trill can be heard at night.

10 Eleonora's Falcon
Kestrels, eagles and falcons, including Eleonora's falcon, are seen in large numbers around the islands.

Left **Aqualand, Corfu** Centre **Aquarium, Rhodes** Right **Lido Waterpark, Kos**

Children's Attractions

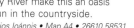

Hydropolis, Corfu

1 Aqualand, Corfu
Water rides, free-fall slides, a giant spa pool and attractions like the Black Hole, the Kamikaze and Crazy River make this an oasis of fun in the countryside.
⊗ Agios Ioánnis • Map A4 • 26610 58531 • Open May–Oct: 10am–6pm daily • Adm • www.aqualand-corfu.com

2 Hydropolis, Corfu
Hydropolis combines a leisure and sports centre with swimming and water-volleyball pools and giant slides. ⊗ Acharávi • Map A4 • 26630 64000 • Open 10:30am–6pm daily • www.gelinavillage.gr

3 Acqua Plus Water Park, Crete
This park has many attractions, including Kamikaze Hydrotube, Acquaslalom, Black Holes and a Crazy River. Its main pool features hydromassage and a children's area. ⊗ Chersónissos • Map E6 • 28970 24950 • May–Oct: 10am–6pm daily (to 6:30pm Jun & Sep, to 7pm Jul & Aug) • Adm • www.acquaplus.gr

4 Luna Fun Park, Zákynthos
A laser arena designed like a war zone with a WWII aeroplane and a climbing tower are a few of the attractions here. Baby-sitting service available. ⊗ Tsiliví • Map H4 • 26950 48035 • Open 10am–late daily • Adm • www.lunafunpark.com

5 Water Park, Santoríni
Family fun is assured here with swimming pools, slides, flumes, a restaurant with dining terrace, gift shop and sunbathing areas. A children's playground features its own pool and a large-scale toy galleon. ⊗ Périssa • Map V3 • 22860 83311 • Open 10am–7pm daily • Adm • www.santoriniwaterpark.gr

6 Glass Bottom Boat, Kefalloniá
This boat heads out to Mounda Bay, where a submarine wreck, the Perseus, can be seen. Dolphins often swim alongside. ⊗ Skála • Map H3 • Open from 9am daily • Adm

Acqua Plus Water Park, Crete

Cretaquarium, Crete

7 Cretaquarium, Crete
There are around 2,500 species of marine life to see at this state-of-the-art aquarium, with viewing tanks, multimedia presentations and observation points. ◈ *Gournés Naval Base, Irákleio • Map E6 • 28103 37788 • Open May–Sep: 9:30am–9pm daily; Oct–Apr: 9:30am–5pm daily • Adm • www.cretaquarium.gr*

8 Aquarium, Rhodes
A centre for marine research and a hospital for injured marine life, this fascinating aquarium is also a tourist attraction. Dolphins, sharks, seals, sea turtles, fish and crabs can be seen in the tanks. ◈ *Kos Street, Rhodes Town • Map V4 • 22410 27308 • Open Apr–Oct: 9am–8:30pm daily; Nov–Mar: 9am–4:30pm daily • Adm*

9 Bowl'm Over, Zákynthos
This bowling centre in central Tsiliví offers four bowling lanes, a pool, foosball and air-hockey tables and a special children's play area. It has bars for refreshments. ◈ *Tsiliví • Map H4 • 26950 25142 • Open 11am–late daily • Adm • Special packages available • www.bowlmover.gr*

10 Lido Waterpark, Kos
One of the Greek Islands' largest waterparks, this complex offers swimming pools for adults and kids, a large wave pool, giant spa, slides and flumes. ◈ *Mastichári • Map X2 • 22420 59241 • Open 10am–6:30pm daily • Adm • www.koswaterpark.com*

Top 10 Films Shot in the Greek Islands

1 Mamma Mia, Skiáthos
A 2008 film starring Meryl Streep and Pierce Brosnan, based on the music of ABBA.

2 Captain Corelli's Mandolin, Kefaloniá
Nicolas Cage and Penelope Cruz were in this 2001 film set during the Italian occupation.

3 Zorba the Greek, Crete
Based on the book by Cretan writer Nikos Kazantzákis, this 1964 film starred Anthony Quinn.

4 Tomb Raider: The Cradle of Life, Santoríni
A 2001 film starring Angelina Jolie as Lara Croft, this film was shot on Santoríni.

5 For Your Eyes Only, Corfu
The casino scene of this 1981 film starring Roger Moore as 007 was shot in the Achílleion Palace, Corfu *(see p72)*.

6 Shirley Valentine, Mýkonos
This 1989 film starred Pauline Collins as a bored housewife on holiday in Greece.

7 Bourne Identity, Mýkonos
The concluding scenes of this 2002 film starring Matt Damon were shot here.

8 Guns of Navarone, Rhodes
Gregory Peck and David Niven were the big names in this 1961 film about German-occupied Greece.

9 Boy on a Dolphin, Ýdra
Starring Sophia Loren as sponge-diver Phaedra, this 1957 film made Ýdra famous.

10 Big Blue, Amorgós
Released in 1988, this English-language version of the French classic *Le Grand Bleu* starred actor Jean Reno.

Left **Windsurfing in the Ionian Sea** Right **Horses for riding, Corfu**

TOP 10 Outdoor Activities

1 Sailing

The Greek Islands boast some of the best sailing waters in the world, as well as marinas and anchorages. Although tidal variation is minimal and the climate is mild, winds can vary between the island groups and present a challenge for even the most experienced sailor. For example, in the Ionians, the *maïstro* wind tends to be gentler than the Aegean Sea's meltemi, which can reach gale force.

Climbing Mt Ida, Crete

2 Fishing

The islands are known for their fishing harbours. While most of these are industry-driven to provide fish and seafood for restaurants, others offer organized pleasure trips for holiday makers. Among the harbours where boats leave for trips are Égina in the Argo-Saronics, Pátmos in the

Dodecanese and Fiskárdo in Kefalloniá.

3 Walking

The islands offer fabulous countryside to explore on foot, with some areas, such as Crete's Samariá gorge *(see p97)*, having designated hiking trails. These pass by valleys and rivers, villages, vineyards and olive groves, plus the odd taverna for refreshment. Always carry bottled water and a phone.

4 Cycling

Bicycles, mountain bikes and mopeds can be hired at moderate cost in most resorts, including those on Santoríni and Mýkonos in the Cyclades, Corfu or Crete. Enjoy leisurely family outings along plains and coastal roads. For endurance cyclists, the rugged terrain of many of the islands can be a challenge.

Cycling in Menetés, Kárpathos

Snorkelling off Corfu

5 Watersports

Snorkelling and dive sites can be found on almost every island, with qualified companies offering tuition and outings for beginners, as well as challenging deep dives. Surface watersports like windsurfing, which is popular in Náxos because of the strong winds, along with water-skiing and kayaking, are available. Families can also enjoy the thrill of banana rides and pedalos.

6 Paragliding

Major resorts such as Kos and Rhodes in the Dodecanese, Mýkonos and Páros in the Cyclades, Nydrí on Lefkáda and Sidári on Corfu offer visitors the chance to enjoy the thrill of paragliding. The charges are usually for about an hour.

7 Golf

Although there are only a handful of international-standard courses in the Greek islands, golf is a very popular sport on the islands. Among the best courses are the 18-hole ones at Ropa Valley on Corfu, Afandou Golf Course on Rhodes and the Crete Golf Club at Chersónissos (Hersonissos), Crete. The sport is promoted by the Hellenic Golf Federation. • www.hgf.gr

8 Tennis

Most of the larger hotels and resorts have flood-lit courts, and the all-weather municipality courts are generally open for visitors' use. Tennis has been played in Greece for centuries; in fact, it was a feature of the celebrations marking the first modern Olympic Games in Athens in 1896. The regulating body is the Hellenic Tennis Federation. • 21075 63170
• www.efoa.org.gr

9 Horse Riding

Privately owned riding centres are dotted around the islands, including the Náxos Horse Riding Club on Náxos and the Trailriders Horse Riding Club on Corfu. Taking a trek through olive groves, farmland, woodland, mountains or along the beach in the early morning or late evening, when the sun is at its lowest and coolest, is a magical experience. • *Naxos Horse Riding Club: www.naxoshorseriding.com; Trailriders Club: www.trailriderscorfu.com*

Waterslide at Lido Waterpark, Kos

10 Adrenaline Activities

All the islands' main holiday resorts offer adrenaline sports for those who love the idea of jumping off a bridge on the end of bungee cord, kayaking down a mountain river, parachuting from a plane, canoeing, depth diving or taking a kamikaze water ride at a theme park.

Left **Kléftiko** Centre **Keftédes** Right **Greek market**

🔟 Greek Dishes

1 Mezédes

An assortment of small dishes, usually starting with salad, dips and pitta bread, *mezédes* are a great way to sample many local dishes in one meal. Typical main dishes include octopus, shrimp and *keftédes*, *souvláki* and *kléftiko* for the meat option. Most restaurants also offer vegetarian *mezédes*.

Typical **mezédes**

2 Saganáki

This dish, often eaten for lunch, consists of cheese cooked in a frying pan *(saganáki)* and served with bread. The ingredients added to the pan can vary, but usually include seafood, onions or just lemon juice. The dish is often flambéed at the table.

3 Pastitsáda

A speciality on Corfu but served throughout the islands, *pastitsáda* is a dish of chicken, or occasionally beef, cooked in the oven with tomato, peppers, onion and cinnamon. It is generally served with pasta. Variations include substituting the meat with seafood such as lobster, or using tofu.

4 Kléftiko

Kléftiko, meaning stolen meat, is a dish of lamb or goat that is cooked slowly over coals in a special oven, sometimes for around 8 hours. Traditionally the meat would be sealed in paper with herbs to keep it moist and flavoursome, but nowadays foil is more commonly used.

5 Sofríto

Although most popular on Corfu, where it originated, this dish is now increasingly seen elsewhere on the islands. It is made using a delicious recipe featuring veal cooked slowly in a creamy white wine, garlic and herb sauce, traditionally topped with herbs and served with rice and salad.

6 Souvláki

Souvláki is a dish of diced pork on skewers, chargrilled and served with lemon and herbs, accompanied by salad and fried potatoes or in a pitta sandwich. It is also a popular fast-food option, served in *souvlatzídiko* outlets in pitta bread with salad and dressing. Chicken, fish and vegetables are modern variations.

Souvláki

Moussakás

7 Moussakás

A delicious dish made of aubergine sautéed in olive oil, sliced tomatoes and potato layered with minced meat – usually lamb – and topped with a béchamel sauce. Lots of garlic, herbs, spices and onion, plus a dash of wine, give it its flavour. Generally served with a salad.

8 Glyká Koutalioú

These confectionaries can be eaten as a snack or to complete a meal. Cherries, pineapple pieces, melons and even peppers, aubergines, almonds and walnuts are candied until they are soft and syrupy. *Glyká koutalioú*, literally "spoon sweets", have been made in the villages for decades and are often served with ice cream.

9 Loukoumádes

A sweet snack, often served at street festivals, *loukoumádes* are small dough balls deep-fried and sprinkled with sugar. Restaurants also dip the balls in honey or sugar syrup, sprinkle with cinnamon and serve with ice cream.

10 Keftédes

These tasty meatballs, made of minced meat – usually beef – with breadcrumbs, garlic and herbs, are fried in olive oil and sometimes served with a tomato sauce. It is a popular dish in the islands, especially on Crete.

Top 10 Mezé Dishes

1 Taramosaláta
A dip made from the roe of mullet or cod, and also often served as a starter with bread.

2 Tahíni
Made with pureed sesame seeds, this *mezé* or appetiser dip has a distinctive flavour.

3 Tzatzíki
A light dip always served cold, *tzatzíki* is made with strained yoghurt, garlic and cucumber.

4 Dolmádes
Vine leaves stuffed with currants, rice and pine nuts, *dolmádes* is a popular *mezé* dish.

5 Skordaliá
A dip or sauce of the Ionians, *skordaliá* is made of mashed potato, garlic and lemon.

6 Loukánika
Pork sausage flavoured with fennel and orange, and usually served sliced, as a *mezé* dish.

7 Olives with Garlic
Black and green olives are always served as a part of *mezédes*; garlic is often added, giving them bite.

8 Melitzanosaláta
Aubergines are cooked and pureed with tomatoes, garlic and lemon to create this tasty dip.

9 Revithosaláta
Sometimes known as hummus, *revithosaláta* is a Greek dip made with chickpeas, garlic and coriander.

10 Choriátiki Saláta (Greek Salad)
An appetizing blend of tomatoes, cucumber, peppers and olives, topped with feta cheese and basil.

Left **Religious icons** Centre **Colourful souvenirs** Right **Wooden honey dippers**

Arts and Crafts

1 Lace and Embroidery

Lace and embroidered cushions, tablecloths and bread baskets are still hand-made in many villages. Karyá in central Lefkáda is famous for its needlecraft, known as *karsanía,* and has a small museum dedicated to the craft. Tourist areas may have similar items, but these are often mass-produced.

2 Leatherware

Craftsmen can be seen in small workshops making leather sandals or the traditional knee-high boots. Both are made by hand as they have been for centuries. Hand-crafted leather purses, handbags and belts are also popular souvenirs.

3 Rugs

The art of making a genuine sheep- or goat-wool rug, known as a *flokáti*, has a long tradition in the Greek Islands. It dates from the 5th century, when mountain shepherds wore them for warmth. More recently they covered the stone floors of village homes. Nowadays, most rugs are made by machine.

4 Jewellery

Gold and silver are a good purchase in the islands and main towns offer a wide choice of modern and traditional designs. Often the pieces echo ancient Greek styles. In Crete,

Gold jewellery

for example, many items are styled on Minoan jewellery. Rustic handmade pieces may be found in the villages.

5 Copperware

Nowadays, copper-ware tends to be used for decorative purposes only, but there was a time when local communities relied on the metal to make everyday household pots and pans. The traditional pot with a handle used to make Greek coffee, a *bríki*, is still in daily use.

6 Carved Wooden Spoons

Almost always made from olive wood, these beautiful spoons are products of a craft that has been handed down through generations. The wood is crafted into the shape of a spoon and its handle can be ornate or simply a figure. They are usually for display purposes and can be found in most gift shops.

Woollen rugs

Preceding pages **Elafoníssi beach, Crete**

Painted ceramics

7 Ceramics
Individual islands have their own style of painting ceramics. Egina is known for its more flowery designs, while Mýkonos artisans often paint traditional Greek figures. Villages are the best place to see authentic items. Rural ceramics tend to be unglazed rather than the colourful glazed items in gift shops.

8 Icons
Religious icons depicting the Virgin and Child, and saints and angels, have been created for centuries, many originating on Crete. St Luke is credited with being the first iconographer and his icons are considered sacred in the Greek Orthodox Church. Visit churches to see genuine icons, as those on display in gift shops will be mass-produced.

9 Beads
Known as *komboloi* (worry beads), these strings of beads can be found in gift shops, markets and jewellers throughout the islands. Greeks thread them through their fingers for relaxation. Some strings are coloured and worn as a fashion accessory.

10 Wall Hangings
Weaving thick cloth and mounting it on a top frame for hanging on a wall is an old craft still practised today. Locals will have several of these hangings in their home as decoration. Gift shops sell them as souvenirs.

Top 10 Popular Souvenirs

1 Olive Oil
Bottles of oil produced from the olives grown on the islands can be found in gift shops and supermarkets.

2 Honey
Honey, sometimes flavoured with thyme, is produced and used in traditional cakes and desserts.

3 Herbs and Spices
Grown in quantity throughout the islands, herbs and spices can make good souvenirs.

4 Leather Sandals
Leather sandals made in a village workshop are useful, as well as being reminders of the holiday.

5 Plaques
Sculpted in wood, stone and resin, plaques are usually ornate and depict scenes of rural life.

6 Baklava Pastries
Made of *fýllo* pastry layers with nuts and drenched in honey, baklava makes a great gift.

7 Jewellery
Strings of coloured worry beads and items of gold or silver are popular souvenirs.

8 Ornate Pottery
Pottery jugs, bowls, candle holders and plates painted in traditional designs are ideal to take back home.

9 Glyká Koutalioú Confectionery
Candied pieces of fruit, nuts and sometimes vegetables, these sweets, though full of calories, are mouthwatering.

10 Embroidered Linen
Often trimmed with lace, these cushions and tablecloths are beautiful and elegant reminders of a holiday in the Greek Islands.

Exploring a street market, known as a laïkí agorá, *is a great way to find a souvenir.*

Left **Folklore festival** Centre **Carnival mask** Right **Celebration of a patron saint's day**

Festivals and Events

Festivals for Patron Saints
Ágios Nikodímos Day on Náxos and the Litany of Ágios Spyrídon in Corfu are just two of the many festivals that take place around the Greek Islands through the year, commemorating each island's patron saint. Festivals usually involve parades, music, dance, fireworks and feasts.

Hippocrátia Festival, Kos
The annual Hippocrátia Festival's highlight is a recital of the Hippocratic Oath. Kos, Hippocrates' birthplace, celebrates with educational displays for children, folkloric exhibitions, music programmes and theatrical shows. The festival runs for several weeks from July to September.

Cultural Festivals
The islands are known for their festivals of art, literature, history and theatre. These include the Festival of the Aegean, held in Sýros each July, which involves opera and performances of Shakespeare. In May, Rhodes hosts its Medieval Rose Festival, while in August, Lefkáda hosts its Festival of Art and Literature.

Folklore Festivals
It is the tradition for every village in Greece to host a folklore festival *(panegýri)* at least once a year, usually during the summer. It is a time when people meet up with friends, feast together and dance.

Musicians play traditional songs, while dance troupes perform folkloric dances.

Religious Festivals
After Easter and Christmas, the most celebrated religious day is the Dormition of the Virgin, or Feast of Assumption, on 15 August. It is believed that on this day the Virgin, Mary the Theotókos, ascended to heaven. Families celebrate with prayer, a feast and traditional dancing and music.

Ochi Day
A public holiday on 28 October commemorates the day in 1940 when the Greek Prime Minister, Ioánnis Metaxás, rejected Mussolini's ultimatum to allow Axis forces to occupy parts of Greece. Metaxás said *"ochi"*, meaning "no". It marked the start of Greece's involvement in WWII.

Ochi Day

Easter festivities

7 International Festivals
Among the many festivals held on the islands are the Winter Festival in Kos, which boasts international music and dance performers, the Argostóli International Choral Festival in Kefalloniá (August), the International Puppet Festival in Ýdra (July) and the International Music Festival in Santoríni (September).

8 Name Days
Most children born in Greece are given the name of a saint. On that saint's feast day everyone with the same name celebrates. For example, 7 January is the name day for Ioánnis (John). In Chaniá on Crete, many males with this name will visit the Church of Ágios Ioánnis and then have a party. Name days are more important than birthdays.

9 Town Carnivals
February is the carnival month on the Greek Islands, and every town puts on events lasting about a week, usually culminating in a procession of floats. Most people, especially children, wear fancy dress.

10 Food and Wine Festivals
A successful food harvest or wine year is celebrated in style. On Kos, for example, there is a Fish Festival and a Honey Festival in August, while Crete has a Chestnut Festival in October. All islands host a wine festival with live music, usually in September.

Top 10 Drinks

1 Retsína
A powerful wine flavoured with pine resin, *retsína* is the traditional white wine of Greece. It is quite often served chilled.

2 Oúzo
Oúzo is a strong, aniseed-flavoured spirit which can be enjoyed neat or mixed with water.

3 Greek Coffee
Brewed in a copper pot known as a *bríki*, thick and strong Greek coffee is made by boiling finely ground coffee and sugar together.

4 Metaxa
Metaxa is a famous brand of strong, cask-matured wine. It is dark brown in colour and tastes rather like brandy.

5 Tsípouro
Distilled from the residue of grapes as well as olives, *tsípouro* is a popular after-dinner liqueur.

6 Cocktails
Served mainly in beach bars, cocktails are almost always colourful and highly decorated.

7 Kumquat Liqueur
A popular speciality on Corfu, this is a sweet liqueur, flavoured with the citrus fruit kumquat.

8 Mythos Beer
This light lager is probably the best-known of all the Greek beers.

9 Frappé
A great way to enjoy coffee when the weather is hot, a frappé is a frothy, iced version.

10 Soft Drinks
Major international soft drinks are sold in the Greek Islands, and there are some good local brands too.

Left **Papagalos Restaurant, Santoríni** Right **Ristorante Italiano Veneto, Crete**

Restaurants

1 Papagalos Restaurant, Santoríni

Traditional Greek coffee

One of the best on the island and among the 50 best Greek restaurants, Papagalos has a refreshing approach to cuisine. Its Greek menu uses only the freshest seafood and organic produce direct from the farmer. Lamb chops with crispy vine leaves and *tzatzíki*, and the baby spinach and haloumi salad are house specialities. Fine wines, martinis and espresso complete the experience. The restaurant also offers takeaway meals and wines *(see p91)*.

2 Taverna Karbouris, Corfu

One of Corfu's oldest north-coast tavernas, Karbouris has become a local landmark. Traditional Greek cuisine, such as *kléftiko*, is served at this family-run establishment. You can sit near the pool or inside in the attractive dining room *(see p73)*.

3 Tassia, Kefalloniá

Run by cookbook author Tassía Dendrínou, who still does much of the cooking herself, this restaurant is housed in a delightful Venetian building overlooking Fiskárdo's harbour. The menu features dishes from Tassía's own books, including traditional Kefallonian meat pie and lobster spaghetti. The extensive wine list has international and local vintages *(see p77)*.

4 Sirines Restaurant, Itháki

Located in Ithaki Yacht Club, Sirines (Sirens) Restaurant is known both for its menu and the collection of shipping memorabilia that adorns the walls. Run by Marína Fotopoúlou, who specializes in Ithakian cuisine, it offers delicious dishes such as langoustine prawns in a mustard and lemon sauce and vegetarian *moussakás*. Organically grown vegetables are used. *Ithaki Yacht Club • Map H2 • 26740 33001 • €€€€*

Taverna Karbouris, Corfu

5 Mesogeios Restaurant, Kárpathos

Located on the waterfront, this lively restaurant is known for its good selection of local dishes and its friendly staff. Diners sit at tables and chairs painted the colour of the sea, and can select from a menu that includes stuffed clams, squid or arti-chokes, goat *stifádo* (stew) and *makarónia*, a delicious local pasta. Right next to Mesogeios is its twin restaurant, Didyma, an integrated grill house *(see p113)*.

6 Adonis Fish Tavern, Égina

This is one of the many traditional-style fish tavernas that line Pérdika's bustling harbour-side. Its delicious menu offers starters such as Greek salad and dips, followed by dishes that include octopus cooked with tomatoes and herbs, prawns with *oúzo*, lobster and pasta, and sea bream with onions. Wine is mainly local *(see p147)*.

7 Alexis4Seasons, Rhodes

Housed in a period mansion with a roof garden and lounge bar, this award-winning restaurant has a gourmet-style menu with Mediterranean and Greek influences. The emphasis is on seafood and the vegetables come from its own garden. Specialities include smoked salmon, scallops in white vodka sauce and prawn risotto. A fine wine list, immaculate staff and elegant surroundings complete the dining experience *(see p111)*.

8 Ristorante Italiano Veneto, Crete

This super Italian-themed restaurant is housed in a restored 15th-century stone mansion. Gnocchi, noodles and fusilli pasta, tempting home-made sauces and pizzas fresh from the wood oven are on the menu, along with classic Italian à la carte dishes and desserts. It has a collection of vintage Italian wines *(see p101)*.

9 Sea Satin Market, Mýkonos

This waterfront restaurant, located below the famous windmills offering views of Little Venice's neighbourhood, is one of the trendiest in town. Diners can select their fish from the day's catch at the ice counter, see it cooked on charcoal grills and then enjoy the exquisite flavour, or select a starter and platter from the menu *(see p87)*.

Sea Satin Market, Mýkonos

10 La Maison de Catherine, Mýkonos

This classy restaurant is known for its artfully presented tables, à la carte menu of Greek dishes with a Gallic twist and its fine wine list. Classical music playing in the background enhances the experience. Be sure to try the prawns in a delicious tomato and *oúzo* sauce. Elegant touches like crisp linen make this a memorable place *(see p87)*.

Left **Agrári beach, Mýkonos** Right **Elafoníssi beach, Crete**

🔟 Secluded Beaches

1 Kouloura Beach, Corfu

Set in a tiny cove surrounded by cypress trees, this sandy, horseshoe-shaped beach has escaped development and offers a peaceful place to relax. Its plentiful trees provide ample shade. The beach looks out over the picturesque fishing harbour of Kouloura village, where a handful of small tavernas serve refreshments.
🚫 Near Kalámi • Map B5

Kouloura beach, Corfu

2 Psilí Ámmos Beach, Pátmos

Located in a scenic cove, Psilí Ámmos, meaning "fine sand", has golden dunes dotted with tamarisk trees, which provide welcome shade. Access to the beach is on foot along a small track or by fishing boat from Skála, which means it is rarely crowded. A small taverna at the North end serves local cuisine 🚫 *Southwest coast near Diakófti • Map F4*

3 Ágia Marína Beach, Spétses

Spétses has some of the best beaches in the Argo-Saronics, with Ágia Marína beach being one of the most popular. For seclusion, head off around the headland, between some rocks, to a tiny bay of fine golden sand and pebbles lapped by the sea. Excavations here have unearthed Early Bronze Age remains. 🚫 Near Dápia • Map D4

4 Ftenágia Beach, Chálki

The quintessential secluded beach, Ftenágia is nestled in a small cove along a hiking route from Emporió village, which is its only access. It is popular with yacht owners, who often anchor offshore and swim in its safe waters. The beach is a mix of sand and pebbles, and has a small taverna.
🚫 Near Emporió • Map G5

Psilí Ámmos beach, Pátmos

Pórto Katsíki beach, Lefkáda

5 Pórto Katsíki Beach, Lefkáda

Reached by descending a series of steps, or by boat from the resorts of Nydrí and Vassilikí, this beach attracts visitors because of its reputation as the island's most beautiful spot. It is horseshoe shaped, with fine golden sand, striking white cliffs topped by lush vegetation and some interesting rock formations. ⊗ *Southwest near Vasilikí • Map G1*

6 Agrári Beach, Mýkonos

Sand dunes set amongst green shrubs characterize this secluded beach, which is popular with nature lovers. It is enclosed in a bay by a hillside of forest and rock formations, and can be reached by a sharply descending, narrow footpath or by caïque. It has a small taverna. Nearby is the busier Eliá beach. ⊗ *South coast • Map P6*

7 Pahiá Ámmos Beach, Tínos

Pahiá Ámmos beach is a world away from the crowds: the only noise you will hear is the sound of the sea. It is surrounded by rugged terrain, with a small road providing access. Set in a natural bay, the beach is made up of a series of sand dunes. ⊗ *Near Ágios Ioánnis • Map P5*

8 Megálo Limonári Beach, Meganíssi

This long stretch of beach, shielded by trees, is reachable only on foot or bike along a track from Katoméri village. As a result, only those keen on seclusion are likely to make the journey. However, it is worth the effort as the beach is sandy and the crystal-clear water is ideal for swimming. ⊗ *East coast near Katoméri • Map H1*

9 Adrína Beach, Skópelos

Reached from Pánormos by walking through a forest of scented pine trees, or by boat, this beach is often deserted. It is a mix of pebbles and sand, with lots of tiny coves to explore. Opposite is Dasiá island, which, according to legend, is named after a female pirate who drowned off its shore. ⊗ *Near Pánormos • Map M1*

10 Elafoníssi Beach, Crete

With its white sand that has a pinkish tint due to fragments of coral, and its great expanse of shallow turquoise sea, this beach is one of the most idyllic spots on Crete. It is located on Elafoníssi islet and can be reached by crossing the reef on foot or by boat. ⊗ *Elafoníssi islet, off Palaiochóra • Map D6*

Left **Viveur Wine Bar, Rhodes** Centre *Oúzo* bottles Right **Pikiona Cocktail Bar, Kefalloniá**

Top 10 Nightlife Spots

1 Central Café Bar, Corfu
Central has become known for its live music nights, when local bands play anything from rock to R&B, and as a popular venue for cocktails. Screens show live sporting events of the day, and a range of café-style snacks are on offer. ◎ *Acharávi • Map A4 • 26630 63204*

2 Rescue Club, Zákynthos
This is the biggest club on Zákynthos, and also on the Ionian islands, with a capacity for 2,000 revellers. There are three huge rooms and six bars, which host world-famous DJs and some unusual theme nights. These include a paint party and "Back to School" disco. ◎ *Laganas Main Road, Laganas • Map H4 • 26950 51612*

3 Colorado Club, Rhodes
Live bands and frequent concerts by Greek singers make this a great venue. There are

Colorado Club, Rhodes

three different rooms, with three different styles – a live stage, a dance club and a room with R&B music. Things usually get going after 11pm and run on until 6am. ◎ *Orfanidou 57, Rhodes Town • Map V4 • 22410 75102*

4 Pikiona Cocktail Bar, Kefalloniá
With its colourful decor and lounge areas overlooking its swimming pool and gardens, Pikiona is a place to relax by day. By night it becomes a pulsating bar where music plays, cocktails are mixed, Mediterranean dishes are served and visitors can be seen in animated conversation. ◎ *Skála • Map H3 • 26710 83410*

5 Medusa Nightclub, Crete
A mix of subtle lighting, loud music and glamorous stage dancers gives this adult night-spot a glowing reputation. Quiet corners are provided for relaxing over drinks and conversation. A full range of cocktails, wines, spirits and beers are available, along with a menu of light meals. ◎ *Moussoúron Street, Chaniá • Map D6 • 28210 28648*

6 Viveur Wine Bar, Rhodes
More a club than a wine bar, Viveur is known for live music, cocktails, fine wines by the glass and dancing. Depending on the day's event, the music can range from classical to R&B, pop, indie and Greek rock. Snacks are also

Koo Club, Santoríni

available. ⊛ *Corner of Platánou and Evripídou streets, Rhodes Old Town* • *Map V4* • *69372 28252*

7 Delon Club, Kos

Run by a friendly Greek family, this popular bar has customers returning year after year for the first-rate beer, good times and reasonable prices. Sports fans are catered for with big-screen TVs, one of which is usually given over to UK soaps. The English breakfasts come highly rated. ⊛ *Lampi* • *Map Y1* • *22420 22824*

8 Palazzo Cocktail Bar, Corfu

This bar serves breakfast, coffee and international meals by day, then transforms into one of Sidári's liveliest evening venues. The resident DJ plays music ranging from indie to hip-hop, and on occasion is accompanied by live music. Like many venues in Sidári, it unashamedly caters for tourists, with darts and a pool table. There is a kids' play area too. ⊛ *Sidári* • *Map A4* • *26630 95946*

9 Koo Club, Santoríni

This nightspot, one of the few on the island, has a dramatic location on the edge of the caldera. Unwind by dancing in the massive main room, with an arched roof ceiling adorned with chandeliers and mirror balls. Alternatively, you can relax with drinks and conversation on one of the three outside terraces, each with its own bar. The music is a mix of techno and radio summertime hits. Koo is one of the earliest-established clubs in town ⊛ *Firá* • *Map U2* • *22860 22025*

10 Skandinavian Bar, Mýkonos

Open since 1978, this bar is a long-established fixture on the club scene and is always very popular. Famous DJs, good music and a variety of groovy cocktails make for a memorable night. The dancefloor is upstairs, but there's also a great patio outside which is perfect for cooling off. ⊛ *Mýkonos Town* • *Map P6* • *22890 22669*

Skandinavian Bar, Mýkonos

Left **Blue Lagoon Resort, Kos** Right **Esperos Village Resort, Rhodes**

Beach Resorts

1 Mediterranean Beach Resort, Zákynthos

A luxurious resort comprising eight buildings designed to echo a traditional Ionian village, the Mediterranean Beach has 113 rooms, maisonettes and suites. The accommodation is situated in gardens around a swimming pool and overlooks the bay. On-site amenities include a gym, restaurant, bars and a children's area.
Seafront, Laganás bay • Map H4 • 26950 55230 • €€€ • www.medbeach.gr

2 Negroponte Resort, Évvia

Built in stone and painted with Mediterranean colours to blend with its surroundings, this five-star resort offers 100 top quality guestrooms with amenities such as Internet access. There is a restaurant, children's playground and activity programme, plus swimming pools and tennis courts.
Erétria • Map D3 • 22290 61935 • €€€€ • www.negroponteresort.gr

3 Blue Lagoon Resort, Kos

A theatre, hair studio, crêpe stand and teenagers' dance bar are some of the features of this family resort with 600 guestrooms. It also has swimming pools, sun terraces, restaurants, as well as a spa and children's centre. *Kos Town • Map Y1 • 22420 54560 • €€€€ • www.bluelagoonresort.gr*

4 Archipelagos Resort, Páros

A compact beach resort characterized by its Cycladic-style square white buildings, the Archipelagos has a modern feel. Its guestrooms are decorated in white with splashes of vibrant colour. The poolside terraces, Greek à la carte restaurant and fitness suite are also elegant.
Agía Iríni • Map E4 • 22840 24176 • €€€€ • www.archipelagosresort.com

5 Santoríni Kastelli Resort

This deluxe resort reflects Aegean Cycladic architecture. It has elegantly decorated lounge

Santoríni Kastelli Resort

[]

AKS Annabelle Village, Crete

and conference areas, bars and restaurants, along with swimming pools and tennis courts. Its spa has a steam room and provides massage and aromatherapy. ◈ *Kamári • Map V3 • 22860 31530 • €€€€ • www.kastelliresort.com*

6 AKS Annabelle Village, Crete

One of Crete's foremost family beach resorts, the five-star AKS Annabelle offers bungalow-style suites with sea and garden views. It overlooks a Blue Flag beach. Services for children include play areas, paddle pools, the Cinderella Club, a special buffet menu and babysitting services. ◈ *Seafront, Chersónissos • Map E6 • 28970 23561 • €€€€€ • www.akshotels.com*

7 Esperos Village Resort, Rhodes

This luxurious resort offers pleasing features like guestrooms with a personal bar area. There are tennis courts, a fitness suite and watersports, plus a piano bar and à la carte restaurant specializing in Mediterranean dishes. Adults only. ◈ *Seafront, Faliráki • Map V4 • 22410 84100 • €€€ • www.esperia-hotels.gr*

8 Candia Maris Resort & Spa, Crete

The 285 rooms and suites of this beachside resort are all beautifully appointed and offer Internet access. Its spacious seawater spa has many thalassotherapy treatments. The three restaurants serve buffet and à la carte dining. ◈ *Andréa Papandréou Street 72, Irákleio • Map E6 • 28103 77000 • €€€€€ • www.candiamaris.gr*

9 Lemnos Village Resort, Límnos

Among the facilities at this sprawling five-star resort are tennis courts, watersports and swimming pools, along with a choice of restaurants. Children have their own pool and play area. Offering 134 stylish rooms and suites, this resort lies next to the beach. ◈ *Platý beach, Mýrina • Map E1 • 22540 23500 • €€€€ • www.lemnosvillagehotel.com*

10 Paradise Beach Resort and Camping, Mýkonos

Popular with visitors who like to party, this beachside resort and camp site has facilities like canoeing, water- and jet-skiing by day and dancing by night. The site also offers apartments and cabins and has a restaurant and Internet café on site. ◈ *Map P6 • 22890 22852 • €€ • www.paradise-greece.com*

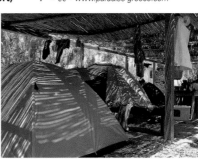

Paradise Beach Resort and Camping, Mýkonos

AROUND THE GREEK ISLANDS

GREEK ISLANDS' TOP 10

Left **Caves of Sami, Kefalloniá** Centre **Vríka beach, Andípaxi** Right **Windmill, Kefalloniá**

The Ionians

THE GREENEST AND MOST FERTILE *of all the island groups, the Ionian islands sit in turquoise waters off the western coast of Greece. They consist of six main islands: Kefalloniá, the largest, followed by Corfu, Paxí, Zákynthos, Itháki and Lefkáda. There are also many smaller inhabited islands, including Andípaxi and Meganíssi, as well as clusters of tiny islets such as the Strofádes. The islands have been populated by ancient Greeks, Romans, Byzantines, Venetians, French and British, all of whom have left their legacy in traditions and architecture. They offer a fabulous combination of mountain and forest landscapes, beaches, bustling towns, idyllic villages and ancient sites.*

Boats moored off Piso Aetós, Itháki

🔟 Sights

1 Corfu Old Town, Corfu
2 Paxí
3 Lefkáda
4 Nydrí Waterfalls, Lefkáda
5 Kefalloniá
6 Mýrtos Bay, Kefalloniá
7 Caves of Sámi, Kefalloniá
8 Itháki
9 Zákynthos
10 Andípaxi

Preceding pages **Fishing boats, Kárpathos**

1 Corfu Old Town, Corfu

At the heart of the capital and port of Corfu, the Old Town is a mixture of imposing fortresses, cobbled streets, elegant squares and bustling harbour. It is the largest medieval city in Greece. It is an easy distance between the main sights, which include the fortresses, the Old Fort, the French-inspired Listón and the Palace of St Michael and St George. To its south is the Mon Repos Estate (see p72), site of the ancient city of Palaeópolis.

2 Paxí

To the south of Corfu is Paxí, a pretty island covered in olive groves. Its busy capital, Gáios, sits in a harbour lined with tavernas from where you can relax and watch yachts sail by. In the bay are two islets, the fortified Ágios Nikólaos and Panagía, which provide a natural breakwater. Paxí has a rugged coastline interspersed with small coves and fishing villages like Longós and Lákka. Magaziá is famous for its sunsets. ✎ Map B2

3 Lefkáda

The small, mountainous island of Lefkáda is covered with forests of pine and cypress trees. Its capital is Lefkáda Town,

Brightly coloured buildings, Lefkáda Town

which is connected to the mainland by two bridges. Its buildings were reconstructed after a devastating earthquake in 1948 using brightly coloured metals. Vasilikí and Nydrí, along with the Pórto Katsíki beach (see p61), are popular tourist spots, while offshore lie the Meganíssi, Madourí and Spárti islands (see p80). ✎ Map G1

4 Nydrí Waterfalls, Lefkáda

Lefkáda has a rare beauty where nature has created some spectacular gorges with sheer rock faces and amazing waterfalls. The Nydrí Waterfalls, which lie to one end of the Dimosári gorge near Perigiáli and Nydrí, are the most impressive. Underground caverns of water help fuel the cascades, which plunge at an astonishing rate to crystal-clear pools. The waterfalls are a wondrous sight and visitors can take a refreshing dip in the pools. ✎ Map G1

A rooftop view of Corfu Old Town

Kýthira is officially the seventh main island of the Ionians, and lies off the Peloponnese in southern Greece.

Limestone cliffs, Mýrtos Bay

5 Kefalloniá

The largest Ionian island, Kefalloniá is green and mountainous. It is known for its vineyards, subterranean waterways, caves and indented coastline. Its Mount Énos (Aínos) is over 1,600 m (5,200 ft) high and carpeted with black fir trees and old olive trees. Kefalloniá's main towns and villages include Sámi, the capital Argostóli, Fiskárdo, Skála and Lixoúri *(see p76)*. ◎ *Map G2*

6 Mýrtos Bay, Kefalloniá

Mýrtos Bay is considered the most photographed bay on the island. Its waters are brilliant turquoise, created by a beach of white pebbles that glisten in the sunlight. The steeply shelving seabed gives a graduated richness to the colour. It lies between Mt Kalón Oréon and Mt Agía Dynatí, famous in Greek mythology as the rock thrown by Cronus, leader of the Titans. ◎ *Near Divaráta • Map G2*

7 Caves of Sámi, Kefalloniá

Sámi has an extraordinary network of subterranean waterways and caves. The huge Drogaráti cave, believed to be more than a million years old, has hundreds of stalactites and stalagmites, formed over thousands of years. With superb acoustics, the creatively lit cave is often used for cultural and musical events. Nearby is the equally famous Melissáni cave, said to have been the sanctuary of the god Pan. Its lake is deep blue, highlighted by the sun shining through a hole in the cave's roof. Other minor caves nearby are Angaláki, Zerváti, Ágii Theódori and Agía Eleoúsa. ◎ *Map G3 • Drogaráti and Melissáni caves: open 8am–8pm daily; adm*

8 Itháki

Itháki is famous for being mentioned in the works of Homer, and is thought to be the home of the mythological King Odysseus. It has a contrasting landscape with mountains and cliffs to the west and dense forest and pebble coves to the east. Its Heptanesian capital, Vathý, has buildings of traditional architecture, which look out over one of the world's largest

---

Gerald Durrell

When Durrell moved with his family to Corfu as a boy in 1935, he became fascinated by the island's flora and fauna. The start of a life-long love of animals, Durrell's Corfiot years were later recounted in his *Corfu Trilogy – My Family and Other Animals* (1956), *Birds, Beasts, and Relatives* (1969) and *The Garden of the Gods* (1978).

Frikes harbour, Itháki

arbours. Other attractions include Píso Aetós, believed to be the site of Odysseus's palace, and the pretty Fríkes harbour. ◈ Map H2

9 Zákynthos

Zákynthos is a gem of an island with high mountains clothed in cypress trees and some stunning beaches, the most famous of which are Navágio (see p74) and Laganás Bay in the south. Its bustling capital, Zákynthos Town, was rebuilt to its original Venetian look and layout after being destroyed in the 1953 earthquake. Places to visit include the beautiful Blue Caves (see p36), where the sea has eroded the rocks into caverns. ◈ Map G4

Venetian-style arcade, Zákynthos Town

10 Andípaxi

Lying to Paxí's south is the small satellite island of Andípaxi, with a population of less than 50 permanent inhabitants. It is a haven of clear turquoise waters and golden beaches, including Vríka beach, nestled in a sheltered cove, and nearby Voutoúmi beach. It is possible to take a walk along the coastal path that links the two. Andípaxi, which can be reached by boat from Gáios on Paxí, is covered with vineyards, which provide the grapes used to make its local wine. ◈ Map B2

Island Hopping Around the Ionians

Morning

The Ionian islands are scattered over a large area and not given to island hopping in the same way as the other Greek island groups. However, it is still possible to get from one island to another relatively easily. Kefalloniá, Zákynthos and Corfu, for example, all have airports offering domestic flights, while yacht charter companies offer boat hire. Ferries also ply between most of the islands.

One of the most popular ferry routes is a day-trip to **Paxí** from Corfu. Start your day at the New Port in **Corfu Town** and look for the signs indicating where you can catch the Flying Dolphin hydrofoil. There are daily departures in summer, but the first departure time varies depending on the day of the week. On board you can relax before disembarking at **Gáios** New Port on Paxí. The journey time is about an hour. In Gáios you can hire a car or taxi to take you around the island. Head to the fishing village of **Longós** for a delicious lunch at one of the waterfront tavernas.

Afternoon

After lunch take the road signposted to **Lákka**. Be sure to explore the town before driving south past the communities of Magaziá and Oziás, then back to Gáios. Take time to explore the harbourside. Enjoy a meal, and then hop on your hydrofoil, which departs at around 7pm, for the return journey.

Left **Pediment, Archaeological Museum** Centre **Achílleion Palace** Right **Mon Repos Estate**

Sights: Corfu

1. Archaeological Museum
The 590 BC Gorgon Medusa, a frieze from the Artemis Temple, is the star exhibit here. ◎ Vrailá Arméni Street, Corfu Town • Map B5 • 26610 30680 • Closed for renovation until summer 2015 • Adm

2. Mon Repos Estate
This grand estate was built in the 1820s by the second High Commissioner of the Ionians, Sir Frederick Adam. ◎ Corfu Town • Map B5 • 26610 41369 • Open summer: 8am–4pm daily (to 3pm daily in winter) • Adm

3. Achílleion Palace
Empress Elisabeth of Austria, known as Sissi, created this Neo-Classical palace in the 1890s. Statues of Greek gods adorn the house and gardens. ◎ Gastoúri, Corfu Town • Map B5 • 26610 56245 • Open 8am–7pm Mon & Tue, 8am–2:30pm Sat & Sun • Adm

4. Mount Pantokrátor
At 900 m (3,000 ft), Corfu's highest mountain offers great views. Its tiny villages are set among olive groves and pine forests. ◎ Map B4

5. Korissíon Lagoon
This 5 km- (3 mile-) long freshwater lagoon is home to many species of wildlife. ◎ Map B6

6. Gardiki Castle
The ruins of this bastion, built by a 13th-century duke, Michail Angelos Komninós II, are well-preserved. ◎ Map B6

7. Lefkimmi Town
The tall houses and tiny streets in this attractive riverside town, famous for its excellent wine, are good examples of local architecture. ◎ Map B6

8. Kassiópi
A popular tourist village, Kassiópi offers a wide choice of harbourside tavernas. Important artifacts excavated at its Angevin castle ruins are displayed in the Archaeological Museum. ◎ Map B4

9. Sidári
Pre-Neolithic remains found here reveal Sidári's long history. It is now a tourist hotspot famous for its rock formations, which have created a channel known as the Canal d'Amour. ◎ Map A4

10. Benítses
Benítses is one of the liveliest tourist resorts on the island, with tavernas, children's play areas, watersports and a buzzing nightlife. ◎ Map B5

Special tickets to the Archaeological Museum allow entry to the nearby Old Fortress and Antivouniótissa Museum (see pp8–9).

Left **Taverna Karbouris** Right **La Famiglia**

10 Places to Eat: Corfu

1 Agnes Restaurant
This attractive restaurant is known for its authentic Corfiot dishes prepared by Agnes, the owner, using organic ingredients. The menu includes *moussakás* and squid served with herbs. ◈ *Pélekas • Map A5 • 26610 94997 • €€€€*

2 Taverna Karbouris
Classic Greek dishes like *pastitsáda* (beef in tomato) and *kléftiko* (lamb with herbs) are served in this traditional stone taverna in a village setting. Eat inside or alfresco on the terrace. ◈ *Ágios Spyrídon, Teríthia • Map B4 • 26630 98032 • Closed Mon–Fri in winter • €€€*

3 Vergina
Classic Greek music played on a bouzouki, dancing and Corfiot dishes are the order of the day at this taverna, housed in what was once a village bakery. ◈ *Gouviá • Map B5 • 26610 90093 • €€*

4 Panorama Restaurant
Perched on a cliff overlooking the beach, this is the place to dine on local dishes while watching the sun set over the waters below. ◈ *Agios Georgios Bay, Afionas • Map A5 • 26630 51846 • €€€€*

5 Taverna Sebastian
This taverna serves its own Corfiot recipes with a modern twist and accompanied by good house wine. Try the prawn *saganáki*. ◈ *Ágios Górdios, Sinarádes • Map B5 • 26610 53256 • €€€*

6 Lemon Garden Restaurant
Surrounded by citrus trees that give it its name, this restaurant serves char-grilled meat and fish dishes flavoured with herbs from the garden, and wine and cocktails. ◈ *Acharávi • Map A4 • 26663 64446 • €€€*

7 Bistro Boileau
Artfully presented Corfiot dishes are served on the terrace at this stylish bistro. Special diets are also catered for. ◈ *Kontókali • Map B5 • 26610 90069 • €€*

8 Trilogia Restaurant
An imaginative menu of appetizers, pasta, meat and seafood dishes, fine wines and a great location overlooking the sea combine to give this place an edge. It offers a children's menu too. ◈ *Kassiópi • Map B4 • 26630 81589 • €€€€*

9 EY Lounge Café
This fashionable bistro-café has an earth-themed decor and serves creatively presented light meals and desserts with wine. ◈ *32 Kapodistríou, Plateía Spianáda, Corfu Town • Map B5 • 26610 80670 • €€€€*

10 La Famiglia
Decorated to resemble a traditional Italian trattoria and serving authentic dishes and wines from Italy, La Famiglia is one of the best restaurants in the town centre. ◈ *Maniarízi Antioti 16, Corfu Town • Map B5 • 26610 30270 • €€€€*

> Try a *mezé* which comprises lots of small Greek dishes – it is a great way to try local cuisine.

Left **Laganás Bay turtle viewing** Centre **Ágios Dionýsios church** Right **Blue Caves**

Sights: Zákynthos

Zákynthos Town
The island's capital and port, Zákynthos Town, is characterized by Neo-Classical architecture, elegant squares and a bustling harbourside. Sights include the Ágios Dionýsios church. ✆ *Map H4*

Helmis Natural History Museum
More than 1,500 exhibits showcase the island's flora and fauna. Educational and enchanting, it is fun for children too. ✆ *Agia Marina • Map H4 • 26950 65040 • Open summer: 9am–6pm, winter: 9am–2pm daily • Adm*

Blue Caves
These caves have amazing sculpted rock formations and caverns, surrounded by a sapphire blue sea. Take a boat out for the best view. ✆ *Cape Skinári • Map H3*

Kerí
One of the few villages to escape destruction in the 1953 earthquake, Kerí retains original stone houses. Surrounded by vineyards, it produces some of the island's best wine. ✆ *Map H4*

Laganás Bay
This is a breeding ground for the endangered loggerhead turtle. These creatures come ashore to lay their eggs on the protected Laganás beach. ✆ *Map H4*

Volímes
This mountain village is best known for its traditional textiles and its Venetian Baroque church,

Agía Paraskeví, which has the finest gilded iconostasis screens on the island. ✆ *Map G4*

Navágio Beach
This stunning beach is often called Shipwreck Bay because of a freighter that sits partially buried in the sand in this sheltered cove. ✆ *Near Volímes • Map G4*

Anafonítria
Zákynthos' patron saint, St Dionýsios, was a monk at the 14th-century monastery of Panagía Anafonítria, located in this sleepy mountain village. ✆ *Near Volímes • Map G4*

Melinádo
This small, traditional village is best known for the temple of Artemis, where remains, such as coins and ceramics, were discovered. ✆ *Map H4*

Maherádo
Visit the 14th-century Agía Mávra church here, with its frescoes and well-preserved icons, one of which is believed to be miraculous. ✆ *Map H4*

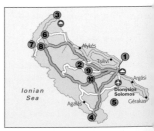

It is easy to find your way around Zákynthos Town, because most of its roads run parallel with the esplanade, the Strata Marina.

Price Categories

For a three-course meal for one with half a bottle of wine (or equivalent meal), taxes and extra charges.

€	under €20
€€	€20–€30
€€€	€30–€40
€€€€	€40–€50
€€€€€	over €50

Left **Buon Amici**

🔟 Places to Eat: Zákynthos

1 Zakanthi Restaurant

Known for its home-made dips, such as *tzatzíki* made from local yoghurt, cucumber and garlic, and its classic dishes, this restaurant offers the option to dine in its garden. ⊗ *Kalamáki • Map H4 • 26950 43586 • €€*

2 Mouria Restaurant

With great views of the Gulf of Laganás, this long-established restaurant serves Greek and international dishes accompanied by local wines. It is a great place to chill out with friends. ⊗ *Laganás beach • Map H4 • 26950 51113 • €€€*

3 Flocas Café

If you fancy mingling with locals while enjoying an informal meal of crêpes and pancakes, both sweet and savoury, or a Greek evening meal, then this is the place to go to. ⊗ *Argási • Map H4 • 26950 24848 • €€*

4 Buon Amici

Popular with visitors and locals, this Italian eatery serves pasta, pizza straight from the oven, seafood dishes, delicious home-made sauces and wine. ⊗ *Kalamáki • Map H4 • 26950 22915 • €€€*

5 Dennis Taverna

A family-run taverna with nostalgic village memorabilia, this taverna is known for its delicious meat and fish dishes served char-grilled with herbs, salad and home-made olive bread. ⊗ *Lithákia • Map H4 • 26950 51387 • €€*

6 Lofos Restaurant

With panoramic views from its hilltop location, Lofos serves authentic Greek dishes using local produce. Dine on the terrace if the weather is good. ⊗ *Méso Gerakári • Map H4 • 26950 62643 • €€*

7 Peppermint

This restaurant grows its own produce in an organic garden. The menu includes special fish dishes and traditional Greek plates. ⊗ *1st Argasi, Zákynthos • Map H4 • 26950 22675 • €€€*

8 La Bella Napoli

This restaurant celebrates all things Italian, from its pasta and pizza dishes, desserts and regional Italian wine to its decor. Soft music completes the dining experience. ⊗ *Laganás • Map H4 • 69794 02819 • €€€€*

9 Spitiko Taverna

Char-grilled meat and fish, and classic Zákynthian dishes such as *pastitsáda* (tender beef served in a spicy sauce), are served with flair at this taverna. ⊗ *Plateía Agíou Pávlou, Zákynthos Town • Map H4 • 26950 41519 • €€€*

10 Romios

Serving Italian pizza with a choice of toppings, home-made pasta, Mexican nachos and Greek *mezédes*, this lively, family-orientated restaurant in the centre of Tsiliví caters for almost every taste. ⊗ *Tsiliví • Map H4 • 26950 22600 • €€€*

Left **Argostóli harbourside** Right **Mýrtos Bay**

Sights: Kefalloniá

1 Mýrtos Bay
Widely considered one of the most beautiful bays in the world, Mýrtos Bay boasts exquisite turquoise sea and dazzling white sand. ◈ *Near Divaráta • Map G2*

2 Sámi
With its traditional houses and lively harbour full of tavernas, Sámi is popular with visitors. It is famous for Melissáni lake and Drogaráti cave. ◈ *Map G2*

3 Argostóli
Kefalloniá's capital was almost entirely destroyed in the 1953 earthquake. It was rebuilt partly in its original Venetian style, and life here revolves around its main square, Plateía Valliánou. ◈ *Map G3*

4 Lixoúri
The island's second-largest community, Lixoúri is an elegant town on the coast of the Pallíki peninsula. It has been a popular tourist spot since the 19th century. ◈ *Map G3*

5 Paleókastro
This is one of the oldest sites on the island. Excavations here have revealed the remains of a fortress, coins, pottery and 1600 BC Mycenaean tombs. ◈ *Map G3*

6 Lake Ávythos
According to folklore, Lake Ávythos is bottomless. It is a habitat for diverse flora and fauna. ◈ *Near Agios Nikólaos • Map H3*

7 Skála
The remains of Old Skála, which was destroyed in the 1953 earthquake, and a Roman villa with well-preserved mosaics are worth seeing in this attractive beach-side resort. ◈ *Map H3*

8 Ássos
One of the island's prettiest coastal villages, Ássos has traditional architecture and sandy beaches. A small isthmus joins it to a Venetian castle's remains atop an islet. ◈ *Map G2*

9 Lourdáta
Overlooking the bay, this picturesque fishing harbour, lined by tavernas, has clear water and a long sandy beach. Nearby are the remains of a small 13th-century monastery. ◈ *Map G3*

10 Fiskárdo
Pastel-coloured Venetian buildings that survived the 1953 earthquake and cypress trees characterize Fiskárdo. It is known for its fish restaurants. ◈ *Map G2*

Price Categories

For a three-course meal for one with half a bottle of wine (or equivalent meal), taxes and extra charges.

€	under €20
€€	€20–€30
€€€	€30–€40
€€€€	€40–€50
€€€€€	over €50

Left **Platanos, Ássos** Right **Patsouras, Argostóli**

🔟 Places to Eat: Kefalloniá

1 Tassia

Overlooking the bay, this elegant restaurant serves Greek meat, fish and vegetarian dishes, many taken from the cookbooks written by its owner, Tassía Dendrínou. The wine served here is international. ❧ *Harbourside Fiskárdo • Map G2 • 26740 41205 • €€€€*

2 Siroco

Located in the centre of the village of Skála, Siroco serves a wide selection of fresh local dishes. ❧ *Main St, Skála • Map H3 • 26710 83613 • €€€*

3 To Perasma

Overlooking the harbour, this friendly taverna is run by two brothers. The extensive menu offers delicious regional cuisine and includes plenty of dishes made with locally caught fish. ❧ *Sea Front, Agia Efimia • Map G2 • 26740 61990 • €€€*

4 Aquarius Restaurant

Salkitier, a dish of pork in a spicy mustard sauce, and *stifádo* cooked with veal are just two of the recipes you might find on the menu at this stylish restaurant. ❧ *Skála • Map H3 • 26710 83612 • €€€€*

5 Pikiona Restaurant

Serving breakfast and lunch around its swimming pool, the Pikiona transforms into a cocktail bar and fine dining restaurant by night. The menu is Greek and Mediterranean. ❧ *Skála • Map H3 • 26710 83410 • €€€€*

6 Patsouras

This traditional taverna, with a terrace surrounded by bougainvillea, is popular for lunch and evening dining. On the menu are classic Kefallonián dishes, such as pork *krasáto*, flavoured with wine. ❧ *Adóni Tritsi Street, Argostóli • Map G3 • 26710 22779 • €€€*

7 Platanos

Taking its name from the massive plane *(plátanos)* tree outside, this restaurant specializes in fresh fish. There are meat and vegetarian options too. ❧ *Ássos • Map G2 • 26740 51381 • €€*

8 Alexis

The bright pink and blue property that houses Alexis is easy to find on the harbourside. The menu includes meals based on classic Kefallonián cuisine and local wines. ❧ *Main Square, Fiskárdo • Map G2 • 26740 41212 • €€€€*

9 Tzivras

Known for its authentic country dishes, such as *moussakás (see p51)* and meat pie, Tzivras has offered a taste of rural Kefalloniá for over 75 years. ❧ *Vasíli Vandórou 1, Argostóli • Map G3 • 26710 24259 • €€*

10 Casa Grec

The menu here offers a mix of Mediterranean styles, such as Greek, French and Italian, often combining them in one dish. Try the prawns. ❧ *Stavrou Metaxa 12, Argostóli • Map G3 • 26710 24091 • €€€€*

Left **Café Bar Muses, Kefalloniá** Right **Harbour Bar, Corfu**

Bars and Cafés

1 Harbour Bar, Corfu
Open since 1980, the Harbour Bar is a landmark on the waterfront. It is a great place to relax over coffee or evening cocktails while watching the bustling harbour. ® *Kassiópi harbour* • *Map B4* • *26630 81227*

2 La Grotta, Corfu
Housed in an underground cave off the beach, the lively La Grotta offers different genres of music, ranging from jazz to hip-hop, plus an array of cocktails. ® *Paleokastrítsa* • *Map A5* • *26630 41006*

3 Genesis Taverna and Café Bar, Paxí
Renowned for its doughnuts, this café also serves a wide range of drinks, snacks and ice creams, and has beautiful views across Gäios Harbour. ® *Gäios* • *Map B2* • *26620 32495*

4 Tavern Nefeli, Kefalloniá
Aromas from its wood oven tend to tempt passers-by to stop at the Tavern Nefeli. This family-run eatery serves Mediterranean-style breakfasts, snacks and light meals on its terrace. ® *Lássi* • *Map G3* • *26710 25203*

5 Café Bar Muses, Kefalloniá
A lively café-bar, Muses has a menu of light snacks and exotic-looking cocktails, a lounge with screens showing live sports and a garden terrace with a children's play area. ® *Lourdáta* • *Map G3* • *26710 31175*

6 Parathinalos, Itháki
The chic decor, imaginative light-food menu and fabulous wine list of this attractive café are French-inspired. It is open all day for lunch and dinner. ® *Vathý* • *Map H2* • *26740 33567*

7 The Mill Bar, Zákynthos
Built on the site of a Greek watermill, this venue has been a favourite with locals and tourists for years. There are two bars and a rooftop lounge with pool access for customers. Friday night is Greek night. ® *Alikanas* • *Map H4* • *26950 83073*

8 Saratseno Café Bar, Zákynthos
This lively café-bar has three widescreen TVs, Greek-themed evenings and bingo and table games nights. ® *Tsiliví* • *Map H4* • *26950 45738*

9 155 Cocktail Bar, Lefkáda
Its chic decor, central location, 60-plus cocktails and non-alcoholic "mocktails", and jazz tunes playing in the background, make 155 Cocktail Bar a fashionable place to relax. ® *Vasilikí* • *Map G1* • *26450 337658*

10 Café Liotrivi, Lefkáda
The charming Café Liotrivi is housed in an old harbourside olive-oil press building. Items used to crush the olives can still be seen. The café has a menu of cool drinks and light snacks. ® *Sývota harbour* • *Map G1* • *26450 31870*

Delfini, Lefkáda

Restaurants: Paxí, Lefkáda, Itháki

Taka Taka, Paxí
Opened in 1970, this restaurant has a faithful clientele and is known for its delicious chargrilled fish dishes served with herbs and lemon. Dine inside or on its vine-covered terrace.
🔊 *Gáios • Map B2 • 26620 32329 • €€€*

Nassos, Paxí
Great for lunch or evening dining, Nassos is known for its local fish dishes, such as swordfish, sea bream, octopus and squid, served in tangy sauces. Wines are from local vineyards.
🔊 *Longós harbour • Map B2 • 26620 31604 • €€€€€*

Taverna Vassilis, Paxí
This traditional eatery has an extensive menu of classic Greek dishes. Try the *moussakás* made with local ingredients or something different, like octopus in red wine. 🔊 *Main Square, Gáios • Map B2 • 26620 31587 • €€€€*

Tom's Seaside Restaurant, Lefkáda
Artfully presented lobster, along with *souvláki (see p50)*, *kalamári* (squid) and *pastítsio* (pasta dish), plus special coffees, are served at this popular restaurant set in its own harbourside gardens.
🔊 *Nydrí • Map G1 • 26450 92928 • €€€*

Delfini, Lefkáda
You can dine alfresco at this trendy seafront taverna. The house speciality is its range of char-grilled fish from the

harbour's fishermen and wines from the local vineyards. 🔊 *Vasilikí harbour • Map G1 • 26450 92335 • €€€€*

Fryni Sto Molo, Lefkáda
Fryni Sto Molo is known for its *mezédes*, a traditional way of eating where small portions of local dishes are brought to your table at intervals. Beer is served cold from the cask. 🔊 *Golémi, Lefkáda Town • Map G1 • 26450 24879 • €€*

Limni Taverna, Lefkáda
Serving dishes such as its signature *kléftiko* (lamb cooked with herbs in a Greek oven), the Limni Taverna stands in its own gardens of olive trees and shrubs.
🔊 *Lygiá • Map H1 • 26450 72013 • €€*

Kantouni, Itháki
This charming waterfront restaurant serves *moussakás*, *souvláki* and *stifádo (see pp50–51)*, based on old family recipes. 🔊 *Vathý harbour • Map H2 • 26740 32918 • €€*

Taverna Kalkanis, Itháki
This family-run taverna is one of the longest established in Vathý and serves traditional Greek dishes handed down through the generations.
🔊 *Vathý • Map H2 • 26740 33233 • €€€*

Paliocaravo, Itháki
Serving classic Greek dishes and fresh fish, plus local wines, this family-run eatery is one of the oldest in Vathý. 🔊 *Vathý harbour • Map H2 • 26740 32573 • €€€€*

Left **Spilia beach, Meganíssi island** Right **Lazaréto islet, in Vathý harbour**

℃10 Islands and Islets

1 Ereíkoussa Island
Characterized by its cypress trees, great beaches and the small town of Pórto where most of its inhabitants live, Ereíkoussa is one of the Diapontian islands and can be reached by boat from Sidári. ◈ Corfu • Map A1

2 Samothráki Island
The smallest Diapontian island, Samothráki is known for its quiet pace of life. Tiny communities can be found in Benátika and around the port of Plákes. ◈ Corfu • Map A1

3 Othonoí Island
Othonoí is where Odysseus met Nausika, according to Greek mythology. Offering a peaceful way of life, it is the largest Diapontian island, located between Samothráki and Ereíkoussa. ◈ Corfu • Map A1

4 Meganíssi Island
Rural Meganíssi is the largest island off Lefkáda. It has quiet beaches and just three villages, including attractive Katoméri and the capital Vathý, which has a harbour lined with yacht moorings. ◈ Lefkáda • Map H1

5 Madourí Island
Located in the bay off Nydrí, Madourí is a heavily forested island. Its sheltered coastline makes it a popular spot to sail around. The Greek poet Aristotélis Valaorítis (1824–1879) once lived here. ◈ Lefkáda • Map H1

6 Spárti Island
Spárti is covered with dense forest. Boats on day trips often drop anchor in the shallow water and sheltered coves of its slightly indented coastline. ◈ Lefkáda • Map H1

7 Diá Island
Sometimes known as Theionísi, Diá island is the source of many legends. The most popular of these is that it was home to a temple dedicated to the Greek god Zeus. ◈ Off Argostóli, Kefalloniá • Map G3

8 Skorpídi Islet
A small islet off the private Skorpiós island, Skorpídi is known for its wildlife and wide variety of birds. You can take a boat from Nydrí and anchor up for a lovely day out. ◈ Lefkáda • Map H1

9 Lazaréto Islet
The serene little islet of Lazaréto brings a smile to your face as you pass it by in the harbour of Vathý. It has a pretty whitewashed chapel, set among dense trees. ◈ Itháki • Map H2

10 Strofádes Islands
Part of the Zákynthos National Sea Park, the Strofádes islands of Arpiá and Stamfáni, plus a few smaller islets, are uninhabited except for the wildlife and a lone monk who is said to live there. ◈ Near Zákynthos • Map B4

 Ereíkoussa, Samothráki and Othonoí make up the Diapontian islands, situated off the northwest coast of Corfu.

Left **Pórto Katsíki beach, Lefkáda** Right **Laganás beach, Zákynthos**

TOP 10 Best Beaches

1 Paleokastrítsa Beach, Corfu

A favourite of Sir Frederick Adam *(see p72)*, this sandy beach is quiet, with just a handful of nearby tavernas. Offshore lies the Liapádes reef, a popular diving and snorkelling spot.
◎ *Paleokastrítsa • Map A5*

2 Myrtiótissa Beach, Corfu

Sheer cliffs and golden sand characterize this horseshoe-shaped beach, which has been described as Europe's most beautiful. It is favoured by naturists because of its seclusion. ◎ *West coast • Map A5*

3 Káthisma Beach, Lefkáda

There are interesting caves and rocks for snorkellers to explore around this west coast beach. For those who like to take it easy, the sand is soft and the waters cool. ◎ *Kalamítsi • Map G1*

4 Pórto Katsíki Beach, Lefkáda

With its horseshoe-shaped bay of golden sand and high cliffs, forested backdrop and curious offshore rock formations, this is among the most picturesque beaches on Lefkáda *(see p61)*.

5 Laganás Beach, Zákynthos

This beach is particularly sandy, making it popular not only with visitors, but also with the endangered loggerhead turtles, the *caretta caretta*, which lay their eggs here. ◎ *Map H4*

6 Megálo Limonári Beach, Meganíssi

Surrounded by forest and with beautiful soft sand, this isolated beach is tucked in a small bay on Meganíssi island. To find it, look out for signposts from Katoméri village *(see p61)*.

7 Gidáki Beach, Itháki

With a hiking track as its only access, Gidáki beach is unknown to most visitors and is therefore a great place to relax. Its bay, however, attracts some boats from Vathý during summer. ◎ *Near Vathý • Map H2*

8 Arkoudáki Beach, Paxí

This secluded sandy beach can only be reached by boat and is therefore quiet. It is a favourite spot with people coming ashore from their yachts anchored in the bay. ◎ *Near Lákka • Map A2*

9 Navágio Beach, Zákynthos

World famous, this white sandy beach is protected by soaring cliffs on both sides. Also known as Shipwreck Bay, which refers to the freighter that sits partially buried in the sand, the beach is accessible only by boat *(see p74)*.

10 Emblísi Beach, Kefalloniá

Located in a deep bay surrounded by cypress trees and olive groves, this secluded sand and pebble beach is one of the finest here. Its waters are shallow and safe. ◎ *Fiskárdo • Map G2*

Left **Tínos harbour** Centre **Fresco in a museum, Santoríni** Right **Georges bay beach, Náxos**

The Cyclades

WITH QUAINT BLUE AND WHITE HOUSES, *windmills and domed churches set against a backdrop of alluring beaches and crystal-clear water, the Cyclades are among the most stunning Greek islands. The villages are often perched on stark mountainsides, while the sea is full of yachts and fishing boats. Located between mainland Greece and the Dodecanese islands, they number 140, of which 24 are inhabited. Some, such as volcanic Santoríni, the party island of Mýkonos and the group's largest, Náxos, are cosmopolitan holiday destinations, while Ándros, Tínos, Sýros and Mílos are more traditional.*

Left **Windmills, Mýkonos** Right **Columns, Delos**

Statue of *Hermes*, Ándros'
Archaeological Museum

🔟 Sights

1. Delos
2. Ándros
3. Tínos
4. Ermoúpoli, Sýros
5. Páros and Andíparos
6. Mýkonos
7. Náxos
8. Milos and Kímolos
9. Santoríni
10. Íos

The name of the island group derives from the word kýklos (circle), because the islands surround the holy island of Delos.

1 Delos

An open-air museum, the uninhabited island of Delos is a UNESCO site in its entirety. It has fabulous archaeological remains dating mostly from Hellenistic times, among them a sanctuary, the Sacred Harbour and a huge amphitheatre. The birthplace of Apollo and Artemis, ancient Delos was a major place of worship. The Ionians arrived in 1000 BC, bringing with them the idea of cult worship, followed by the Naxians, the Polykrates and the Athenians. Great wealth preceded abandonment in favour of Athens, but it remains one of Greece's foremost historic sites *(see pp14–15)*.

2 Ándros

Ándros is the northernmost island in the Cyclades. Life on this largely mountainous island revolves around the capital, Ándros Town, also known as Hóra, which boasts elegant Neo-Classical mansions in its pedestrianized centre, and a fascinating Archaeological Museum. The island's main settlements include Korthí, the inland medieval village of Mesariá, and Gávrio, while ancient Paleópolis lies near the west coast. The harbour wall that once protected it can still be seen just offshore. ◆ *Map M4 • Archaeological Museum, Plateía Kaiiri, Andros Town: 22820 22820; • Open Tue–Sat (Fri & Sat in winter); adm*

A street in Ermoúpoli, Sýros

3 Tínos

This holy island is famous for the church of the Panagía Evangelístria and its miraculous icon of the Virgin Mary, which attracts pilgrims throughout the year. Tínos is an unspoiled, fertile island and one of the most picturesque in the Cyclades. Its landscape is dotted with appealing villages, windmills, hundreds of chapels, and magnificent dovecotes. Its inhabitants are known for their creative skills – marble sculptures and folk art can be seen everywhere. ◆ *Map N5*

4 Ermoúpoli, Sýros

Known as the "Queen of the Aegean", the city of Ermoúpoli on Sýros is the administrative and commercial capital of the Cyclades. In the 19th century it was Greece's leading port and had a thriving shipbuilding industry, which made the island very wealthy. The capital is built in the style of an amphitheatre around one of several harbours that line the coastline of Sýros. The island is mountainous, interspersed with fertile plains and villages, and cosmopolitan, offering fine beaches and various amenities. ◆ *Map N6*

The tree-lined beach at Mpatsi bay, Ándros

Páros and Andíparos

5 Páros is a popular European holiday destination and, as such, offers a huge choice when it comes to tavernas, restaurants and nightspots, especially in the main towns of Paroikía, the capital, and Náoussa. Inland are tiny mountain villages, with the former capital of the island, Léfkes – a charming hamlet of medieval houses and alleyways – being the highest. Nearby Andíparos, with its elegant cafés, centres on its Venetian Kástro and is popular for day trips from Páros. Frequent ferries link the two islands. ◈ *Map E4*

Mýkonos

6 Mýkonos is known for its marvellous beaches. Picturesque Psaroú and Eliá are two of the most popular, while Paradise and Super Paradise are livelier and popular with nudists. A round-the-clock party island, Mýkonos revolves around its eponymous capital town, an agreeable place of alleyways and stone houses, many now housing restaurants and bars. Do visit Alefkándra, known as Little Venice, and the town's outstanding museums. Inland, the landscape is sprinkled with windmills and villages full of traditional charm. ◈ *Map P6*

Náxos

7 The centre of the Cycladic civilization during the Early Bronze Age (3000–2000 BC), Náxos has a phenomenal history. It was one of the first islands to use natural marble, a feature of the ancient artifacts found at its archaeological sites and the material used for its landmark Portára gateway, said to be the entrance to a 5th-century-BC Temple of Apollo.

7th-century amphora, Mýkonos

Náxos is the largest of the Cyclades, with its bustling capital the most populated. It is an island of citrus groves, beaches and sea caves. ◈ *Map Q4*

Mílos and Kímolos

8 Mílos is famous for being where the *Venus de Milo* statue, now in the Louvre in Paris, was discovered. It is a volcanic island of extraordinary horizontal white rock formations that have created an almost lunar landscape. Wealthy under the Minoans and Mycenaeans, and colonized by the Athe-nians in the 4th century BC, Mílos is an island of rural villages and beaches today. Its main town is Pláka, believed to be built

Náxos town and harbour

White church, Santoríni

on the acropolis of Mílos. About an hour away by boat lies serene Kímolos, home to the endangered monk seal (see p45). ◈ Map D5

9 Santoríni

Crescent-shaped Santoríni owes its formation to a massive volcanic eruption that destroyed part of this once-circular island in 1450 BC. The resulting underwater crater has been associated with the legend of the lost city of Atlantis. Santoríni remains at the centre of the South Aegean Volcanic Arc. Inhabited since Minoan times and named by the Venetians in the 13th century, this stunning island of dazzling white villages, museums, black-sand beaches, thermal springs and luxuriant vineyards is a quintessential Greek island. ◈ Map T1

10 Íos

In antiquity Íos was famous being the burial place of the ancient Greek poet Homer, and each year a festival, the Omíra, is held in his honour. This mountainous island is speckled with hundreds of chapels and tiny villages, and its capital, Hóra, is an enchanting conglomeration of white houses, blue-domed churches and courtyards. There is also a continually growing number of tavernas and bars here. The island boasts some of the best beaches in the Cyclades, and has long established itself as a young people's party island. ◈ Map E5

Day Trip from Mýkonos to Delos

Morning

After a hearty breakfast at your accommodation, head down to the quayside at **Mýkonos Town** and look out for the departure points marked for **Delos** (see pp14–15). There are ferries and many smaller boats to choose from. Timings vary according to the season and the weather conditions, so be sure to check in advance to ensure you arrive in good time. Take refreshments with you as there is a limited choice on the boats and on Delos. Most of the boats leave at around 10am for the 30-minute crossing. The sea can get a bit rough so be prepared. Once aboard, enjoy the sea breeze and your first glimpse of Delos ahead. On disembarking, head for the Maritime Quarter and see the Sacred Harbour, the Theatre Quarter, with its remains of mosaic-rich houses, the Sacred Lake, with its iconic terrace of lion statues, and the Sanctuaries of Apollo and Dionysos. There is a small restaurant in the Sanctuary of Apollo for a quick bite before you head back to Mýkonos.

Afternoon

Boats tend to leave Delos at 12:30pm, 1:30pm and 3pm, but again be sure to check as timings can vary. If you aim for the 3pm crossing it will give you plenty of time to see the extensive archaeological site on Delos and absorb its atmosphere. Once back on Mýkonos, enjoy a leisurely afternoon siesta before a delicious meal at a taverna on the harbourside.

Around the Greek Islands – The Cyclades

Left **Aegean Maritime Museum** Centre **Mýkonos harbour** Right **Monastery, Paleokástro**

🔟 Sights: Mýkonos

1 Alefkándra

With colourful 16th- and 17th-century pirates' houses built on the water's edge, Alefkándra, also called Venetía or Little Venice, is the artists' quarter of Mýkonos Town. A landmark is the Panagía Pigadiótissa cathedral. ✎ *Mýkonos Town • Map P6*

2 Archaeological Museum

Housed in a beautiful Neo-Classical building, this museum has a fine collection of jewellery and funerary statues. ✎ *Harbourside, Mýkonos Town • Map P6 • 22890 22325 • Open 8am–3pm Tue–Sun • Adm*

3 Aegean Maritime Museum

Recording the maritime activity from Minoan times to the present day, this museum displays nautical instruments and model ships. ✎ *Tría Pigádia, Mýkonos Town • Map P6 • 21081 25547 • Open summer: 10:30am–1pm & 6:30pm–9pm, winter: 8:30am–3pm daily • Adm*

4 Panagía Paraportianí

This unconventional 15th-century church, with four chapels and a fifth one built on top, is located on a medieval fortress's gate. ✎ *Kástro, Mýkonos Town • Map P6*

5 Léna's House

This 19th-century mansion was the home of local resident Léna Skivánou. Now a museum, the building has been beautifully restored. ✎ *Tría Pigádia, Mýkonos Town • Map P6 • 22890 22591 • Open Apr–Oct: 6:30–9:30pm Mon–Sat*

6 Folk Museum, Mýkonos

This museum displays rare traditional textiles, ceramics, historical photographs and furnishings. ✎ *Kástro, Mýkonos Town • Map P6 • 22890 22591 • Open Apr–Oct: 4:30–8:30pm Mon–Sat (closed Sun)*

7 The Harbour

Home to the island's official pelican mascot, Petros Peter, the harbour contains many cafés and tavernas. It is dotted with white reed-roofed 16th-century windmills, once key to the grain industry. ✎ *Mýkonos Town • Map P6*

8 Áno Méra

This village, the island's largest after Mýkonos Town, offers a glimpse into the island's past. Stone houses covered with bougainvillea line its alleyways and the monastery of Panagía Tourlianí dominates the skyline. ✎ *Central Mýkonos • Map P6*

9 Moní Panagía Tourlianí

Founded in the 16th century and restored in 1767, this superb monastery is dedicated to the island's protectress. Its white exterior, red-domed roof and a sculpted marble tower, the work of Tíniot craftsmen, have made it a landmark. ✎ *Central Mýkonos • Map P6 • 22890 71249 • Open by arrangement*

10 Paleokástro

Believed to be the site of an ancient city, Paleokástro lies on a hill in the island's most verdant area. ✎ *Central Mýkonos • Map P6*

➲ *Mýkonos is known for its cheeses, including the spicy cream cheese, kopanistí piperáti.*

Price Categories

For a three-course	
meal for one with half	€ under €20
a bottle of wine (or	€€ €20–€30
equivalent meal), taxes	€€€ €30–€40
and extra charges.	€€€€ €40–€50
	€€€€€ over €50

Left **Sea Satin Market, Mýkonos Town** Right **La Maison de Catherine, Mýkonos Town**

Places to Eat and Drink: Mýkonos

1 Tasos Restaurant
A favourite with locals, this restaurant offers fine fish and seafood dishes – octopus cooked on charcoal is a speciality. The terrace overlooks the bay, and local wines are served. ◈ *Parága beach • Map P6 • 22890 23002 • €€€€*

2 Sea Satin Market
This trendy eatery along the shore from Little Venice comes alive after sunset as the lights go on and fresh fish is cooked on charcoal grills. ◈ *Alefkándra, Mýkonos Town • Map P6 • 22890 24676 • €€€€*

3 Kiku
This restaurant's Japanese menu provides a delicious alternative to local cuisine. Fresh fish is cooked to authentic oriental recipes. ◈ *Harbourside, Mýkonos Town • Map P6 • 22890 20100 • €€€€*

4 La Cucina di Daniele
With its colourful décor and lively atmosphere, this restaurant is a great place to enjoy home-made pasta dishes from different Italian regions. The Italian owner makes wine suggestions based on the day's menu. ◈ *Áno Méra • Map P6 • 22890 71513 • €€€€*

5 Avra Restaurant
This attractive restaurant offers intimate indoor and out-side dining. A tasty salad and appetizer menu is complemen-ted by mains plus an à la carte selection. ◈ *Kalogéra Street, Mýkonos Town • Map P6 • 22890 22298 • €€€*

6 Fokos Taverna
With a menu featuring aubergine salad, mussels in wine and delicious desserts, Fokos is located in a traditional house. Drinks include fine wines, special-ity coffees and *oúzo*. ◈ *Fókos beach • Map P6 • 69458 28561 • €€*

7 La Familia
Open from breakfast until late, this restaurant fuses the cuisines of Greece and Italy on its imaginative menu. ◈ *Goumenio, Mýkonos Town • Map P6 • 22890 78638 • €€€*

8 Spilia
Enjoy fresh fish at this elegant beachside taverna. Diners choose the main ingredient of their meal from a water pool replenished by the sea. The menu has Italian flair, with lovely pasta dishes and wines. ◈ *Seafront, Kalafáti • Map P6 • 22890 71205 • €€€*

9 La Maison de Catherine
Famed for its à la carte menu, this fashionable restaurant offers classic Greek dishes with a French twist. The wines are great too. ◈ *Nikíou 1, Ag. Gerasimou, Mýkonos Town • Map P6 • 22890 22169 • €€€€€*

10 Raya Restaurant
This stylish lounge bar and restaurant serves breakfasts of fresh juices and feta omelettes as well as lunches, dinners, cock-tails and coffees. ◈ *Gialós waterfront • Map P6 • 22890 28223 • €€€€*

Athiri, Assyrtiko and Aidani are three of the many wines from the vineyards of Mýkonos.

Left **Apeíranthos village** Right **Church, Glinádo village**

Sights: Náxos

1 Náxos Town
Dominated by the Protára gateway, Náxos Town is a heady mix of history and modernity. Its Venetian castle and the church of Panagía Myrtidiótissa are well worth a visit. ◈ *Map Q4*

2 Mount Zeus
Also known as Mount Zía or Zía Óros, this is the Cyclades' highest mountain at more than 1,000 m (3,300 ft). Well known for its hiking trails. ◈ *Map R6*

3 Chalkí
The former capital of Náxos, Chalkí is full of Neo-Classical buildings. It is surrounded by olive groves and its 9th-century church has notable frescoes and well-preserved towers. ◈ *Map R5*

4 Apeíranthos
White marble houses dot the hillside of this pretty village. Sights of interest include one of the island's oldest churches, the Panagía Apeíranthos, and four small museums. ◈ *Map R5*

5 Glinádo
A charming village of white-washed stone houses with blue painted doors and tiny courtyards full of bougainvillea, Glinádo has been preserved as a traditional Náxiot community. ◈ *Map Q5*

6 Apóllon
The fishing village of Apóllon, or Apóllonas, is the site of an ancient marble quarry. Its entrance has a huge 6th-century-BC marble statue, Kouros. Tavernas line its sandy beach, popular with swimmers. ◈ *Map S4*

7 Komiakí
Komiakí, or Koronída, is one of the island's highest villages and is known for traditional crafts, especially lace. ◈ *Map R4*

8 Melanés Valley
Full of olive and citrus trees, this valley has many pretty villages including Kourounchóri, Fleríó and Melanés. ◈ *Map R5*

9 Áno Sagrí
Windmills and Byzantine churches dot the lush plateau around Áno Sagrí. Its chapel of Ágios Ioánnis Gyroulás is said to be built over the 530 BC Temple of Demeter. Located nearby is the Tower of Somarípa. ◈ *Map R5*

10 Tragéa Valley
The Panagía Drosianí church is one of this valley's most memorable sights. Tragéa has one of the Cyclades' largest olive industries. ◈ *Map R5*

Left **Scirocco Restaurant, Náxos Town** Right **Kavouri Restaurant, Agios Geórgios**

Places to Eat and Drink: Náxos

Price Categories

For a three-course meal for one with half a bottle of wine (or equivalent meal), taxes and extra charges.

€ under €20
€€ €20–€30
€€€ €30–€40
€€€€ €40–€50
€€€€€ over €50

1 Scirocco Restaurant
Lemonáto, a dish of lamb in lemon, and Katerina's chicken, cooked with mustard and orange, feature on the menu of this popular eatery. It is open from breakfast to dinner. ◊ *Náxos Town* • *Map Q4* • *22850 25931* • *€€€*

2 Kavouri Restaurant
A landmark since 1955, this restaurant has traditional Greek decor and is near the beach. It serves classic dishes and tasty fresh fish. ◊ *Agios Geórgios beach* • *Map Q5* • *22850 23729* • *€€*

3 Apolafsis Grill Room
Shrimp balls and veal stroganoff are among the 100 or so dishes on this attractive waterside restaurant's menu. A large wine list and live entertainment add to the experience. ◊ *Náxos Town* • *Map Q4* • *22850 75483* • *€€*

4 Cavo d'Oro
With its green and white decor and great sea views, this lively pizzeria serves pizzas fresh from the oven, pasta and some Greek classics. Its wine list has been selected to complement the dishes. ◊ *Agios Prokópios beach* • *Map Q5* • *22850 41877* • *€€€*

5 Platia Taverna
Breakfast to evening, Náxiot and Greek meals are served at this taverna. Be sure to try the *mezédes* and the taverna's own wine. ◊ *Plateía Protódika, Náxos Town* • *Map Q4* • *22850 23575* • *€€*

6 Yialos Restaurant
Located near St George beach, this taverna and beach bar serves cool drinks, snacks and delicious meals of meat and fish straight off the charcoal grill. ◊ *Agios Geórgios beach, Náxos Town* • *Map Q4* • *22850 25102* • *€€€*

7 The Old Inn
With its summer terrace and cosy lounge for winter complete with a roaring fire, this inn captures a German house's atmosphere. Appetizers are followed by large helpings of German cuisine and beer. ◊ *Náxos Town* • *Map Q4* • *22850 26093* • *€€€*

8 Picasso Mexican Bistro
Quesadillas filled with meat and beans plus tacos, fajitas and burritos, are served with salads and frozen Margaritas at this town centre "tex mex". ◊ *Náxos Town* • *Map Q4* • *22850 41188* • *€€€*

9 Kontos Restaurant
Apart from growing its own fruit and vegetables, this lovely open-air restaurant also rears its own animals to produce the freshest of Náxiot dishes. ◊ *Mikrí Vígla* • *Map Q5* • *22850 75278* • *€€*

10 Faros Restaurant
With its stone walls, reed ceiling, grill oven and sea views, Faros is a very Greek taverna. Produce comes from its own garden and fish is from the daily catch. ◊ *Alíko beach, near Glinádo* • *Map Q6* • *22850 75244* • *€€*

Left **Archaeological Museum** Centre **Picturesque Oía** Left **A view of Firá**

☝10 Sights: Santoríni

1 Firá
The island's capital, Firá, also called Thíra, has beautiful Venetian buildings that survived the 1956 earthquake. It has a range of tavernas. ◈ *Map U2*

2 Museum of Prehistoric Thíra
Fascinating exhibits here include fossilized olive leaves and clay pots, plates, tools and other artifacts from ancient Thíra. ◈ *Firá • Map U2 • 22860 23217 • Open 8:30am–3pm Tue–Sun • Adm*

3 Archeological Museum
Sculptures and inscriptions from Archaic to Roman times and vases and clay figurines from Geometric to Hellenistic eras tell the story of Santoríni's past. ◈ *Firá • Map U2 • 22860 22217 • Open 8:30am–5pm Tue–Sun • Adm*

4 Ancient Thíra
The site of the ancient Dorian city of Thíra can be found laid out on terraces at the end of the Mésa Vounó peninsula. ◈ *Mésa Vounó peninsula • Map V3*

5 Ancient Akrotíri
This late Neolithic-era city is among Greece's most important. Buried by volcanic lava in the late Minoan period, it is well preserved. ◈ *Akrotíri • Map U3 • 22860 81366 • Open 10am–5pm daily*

6 Imerovígli
This quiet, traditional village provides visitors with a rare glimpse into everyday life. It has stone houses and chapels and great views of the flooded caldera. ◈ *Map U2*

7 Pýrgos
A hilltop village of white and blue houses built around a Venetian castle, Pýrgos' landmark is the Monastery of Prophítis Ilías. ◈ *Map U2*

8 Oía
Much photographed due to its pretty blue and white houses, Oía is also famous for its sunsets. Near the port is a small maritime museum. ◈ *Map U1*

9 Kaméni Islets
These two uninhabited islets, Néa Kaméni and Palaia Kaméni, appeared in the sea after a volcanic eruption in 1450 BC. They were formed from lava and ash – and are still volcanic. ◈ *Map U2*

10 Thirassía Island
Separated from Santoríni by volcanic activity, Thirassía is a rocky island dotted with small hamlets, such as Manolás, and a few tavernas. ◈ *Map T2*

Price Categories

For a three-course meal for one with half a bottle of wine (or equivalent meal), taxes and extra charges.	
€	under €20
€€	€20–€30
€€€	€30–€40
€€€€	€40–€50
€€€€€	over €50

Archipelagos Restaurant, Firá

10 Places to Eat and Drink: Santoríni

1 Mario No 1 Restaurant
Baked aubergine and seafood pasta dishes are among the delicacies on the menu at this chic, long-established taverna located right beside the beach. ◈ Agía Paraskeví, Monólithos • Map V2 • 22860 32000 • €€€

2 Ambrosia Restaurant
Ambrosia is known for its elegant furnishings, a candle-lit terrace that looks out over the volcano and its à la carte Mediterranean menu and wine list. Booking is advisable. ◈ Oía • Map U1 • 22860 71413 • €€€€

3 Blue Note Restaurant
Tucked away in an old stone building, this restaurant opens on to a terrace overlooking the bay. The menu mainly offers fish dishes, with lobster being a speciality. ◈ Imerovígli • Map U2 • 22860 23771 • €€€

4 Archipelagos Restaurant
Housed in one of the oldest captains' houses from the 19th century, with local artists' works adorning its walls, this charming restaurant has a Mediterranean food and wine menu. ◈ Firá • Map U2 • 22860 24509 • €€€€

5 Lithos Restaurant
This popular restaurant is housed in a period building on the harbourside. A Mediterranean menu features fish platters, grills and local wines. ◈ Firá • Map U2 • 22860 24421 • €€€

6 Mama Thira Taverna
Mama Thira's dining hall has nostalgic items adorning its walls and a terrace overlooking the bay. The Mediterranean cuisine and wine is served with exceptional flair. ◈ Harbourside, Firostefáni, Akrotíri • Map U3 • 22860 22189 • €€€

7 Restaurant Poseidon
An attractive eatery, the Poseidon serves seafood, such as squid and lobster, and traditional Greek dishes cooked to age-old recipes, accompanied by local wines. ◈ Kamári beach, Kamári • Map V3 • 22860 32462 • €€€

8 Papagalos Restaurant
A gourmet-style menu and slick decor set Papagalos apart. The chef creates dazzling "New Greek" dishes with seafood and fresh organic produce. ◈ Oía • Map U1 • 22860 71469 • €€€€

9 Nikolas Restaurant
One of the best restaurants in Firá, this family eatery serves wholesome Greek cuisine. Fish cooked with local herbs, kléftiko and moussakás are menu classics. ◈ Erithroú Stavroú, Firá • Map U2 • 22860 24550 • €€

10 1800 Restaurant
Housed in a restored 19th-century mansion overlooking the bay, this award-winning, elegant restaurant serves Mediterranean cuisine and Greek wine. ◈ Oía • Map U1 • 22860 71485 • €€€€€

Among the local dishes of Santoríni are white aubergine served with herbs, and keftédes (meat balls) made with tomato.

Left **House, Andíparos** Centre **Super Paradise beach, Mýkonos** Right **Agrári beach, Mýkonos**

Islands, Bays and Beaches

1 Kímolos Island, Mílos
Taking its name from *kimólia*, meaning chalk, which is mined here, this volcanic island is home to a few small communities and good tavernas. Beaches and caves make it a popular day-trip destination. ◈ *Map E4*

2 Síkinos Island, Íos
This rugged island, with deep bays and pretty beaches, is known for squid-fishing, sweet wine and delicious, aromatic thyme honey. Hóra, its main town, has lovely cobbled streets. ◈ *Map E5*

3 Andíparos Island, Páros
This unspoiled island has beautiful beaches and bays. Its tavernas are welcoming, cafés chic and a range of activities, from diving to kayaking, are on offer. ◈ *Map E4*

4 Agrári Beach, Mýkonos
This attractive sandy beach, enclosed by rocks, is an ideal setting in which to relax. Its azure water is safe and there is a taverna and bar. ◈ *South coast • Map P6*

5 Ágios Geórgios Beach, Santoríni
A lively black-sand beach, Ágios Geórgios has tavernas and bars galore, plus parasols and sun-beds to rent, as well as scuba diving and windsurfing. ◈ *Southeast coast • Map V3*

6 Golden Beach, Ándros
One of the best beaches on Ándros, this long stretch of sand lies next to Batsí resort. It has shallow water and all amenities for visitors. ◈ *Batsi • Map M4*

7 Pahiá Ámmos Beach, Tínos
Set in a natural bay of deep water, this beach is made up of seemingly endless sand dunes. Surrounded by a rugged landscape, it is isolated and peaceful *(see p61)*.

8 Fínikas Bay, Sýros
Picturesque and bustling with fishing boats and yachts, this sheltered bay has a long sandy beach. Its barren backdrop is dotted with pine trees and white houses, many of which house fish tavernas. ◈ *Southwest coast • Map M6*

9 Super Paradise Beach, Mýkonos
This long stretch of beach, which boasts crystal-clear water and many tavernas, is famous for its party atmosphere. It is especially popular with nudist and gay holiday-makers. ◈ *South coast • Map P6*

10 Agathopés Beach, Sýros
Protected by the Ministry of Environment as a natural habitat for birds and flowers, including wild lilies, this sandy beach has an offshore islet and safe swimming water. ◈ *Near Poseidonía • Map M6*

Price Categories

For a three-course meal for one with half a bottle of wine (or equivalent meal), taxes and extra charges.

€	under €20
€€	€20–€30
€€€	€30–€40
€€€€	€40–€50
€€€€€	over €50

Left **Palada Taverna, Tínos** Right **Levantis Restaurant, Páros**

Restaurants

Metaxy Mas, Tínos
With its stone courtyard, elegant decor and crisp linens, this charming restaurant has a fine wine cellar, complemented by international and Greek dishes. ⊙ *Paláda • Map N5* • *22830 25945 • €€€€*

Takis Restaurant, Sérifos
Located on the tree-lined waterfront, Takis serves Greek dishes such as *kléftiko* and *souvláki (see pp50–51)* from an extensive menu. Wines focus on vintages from the islands. ⊙ *Livádi • Map E4 • 22810 51159 • €€€*

Lilies Restaurant, Sýros
This landmark restaurant is known for *mezédes*-style dining, with a selection of Greek meat, fish and vegetable dishes. Desserts are home-made and the wine is local. ⊙ *Áno Sýros, Ermoúpoli • Map N6 • 22810 88087 • €€€*

Delfini Restaurant, Sífnos
Overlooking the picturesque port and bay, this quintessential blue and white taverna has an innovative Mediterranean meat, vegetable and fish menu.
⊙ *Kamáres • Map E4 • 22840 33740 • €€*

Kritikos, Folégandros
This traditional taverna is more than 30 years old. It is known for its spinach, pumpkin and cheese pies along with meat and fish dishes, desserts and local wine. ⊙ *Piátsa Square, Hóra • Map E5 • 22860 41219 • €€€*

Lord Byron, Íos
Mediterranean cuisine, fine wines and jazz music give the Lord Byron a sophisticated edge. The menu features Íos lamb with honey, seafood and pasta, plus home-made desserts. ⊙ *Hóra • Map E5 • 22860 92125 • €€€*

Restaurant Platia, Kýthnos
This attractive taverna serves traditional Cycladic cuisine. Meats are cooked on charcoal to age-old recipes. Sweets and cheese are home-made. ⊙ *Kanála • Map E4 • 22810 32843 • €€*

Aragosta Restaurant, Mílos
This elegant restaurant, housed in a Neo-Classical mansion, offers an extensive Greek and international menu. Grills are a speciality, along with *tyropitákia* (cheese pies) and local seafood. ⊙ *Adámas • Map D5 • 22870 22292 • €€€€*

Levantis Restaurant, Páros
Delicious Mediterranean and Asian dishes are on offer at this little restaurant in the old town. Try its rabbit in yogurt with olives and aubergine. ⊙ *Pároikia • Map E4 • 22840 23613 • €€€*

Palada Taverna, Tínos
The popular Palada, decorated to resemble a taverna, serves a good selection of meat dishes cooked with herbs, along with vegetarian options and local wine. ⊙ *Old Palada, Tínos Town • Map N5 • 22830 23516 • €€*

Left **Palace of Knossos** Centre **Irákleio harbour** Right **Exhibit in Irákleio Archaeological Museum**

Crete

CRETE HAS ALWAYS BEEN *an island that captures the imagination, with some of the world's finest ancient sites, including the palaces of Phaesto and Knossos. The birthplace of Europe's oldest civilization, the enigmatic Minoan culture that flourished over 4,000 years ago, Crete was also ruled by the Romans, Byzantines and Venetians. Cretan resistance against occupation by the Ottoman Turks (1669–1898) and the Germans in World War II is legendary. The largest of the Greek Islands and the fifth-largest in the Mediterranean, mountainous Crete has a distinct culture and its own dialect. Its capital city is the cosmopolitan Irákleio, also known as Heraklion. Chaniá and Réthymno are its other two major towns, while the Samariá gorge is its top natural attraction.*

Traditional Cretan gateway

🔟 Sights

1. Phaestos Palace
2. Palace of Knossos
3. Samariá Gorge
4. Irákleio
5. Irákleio Archaeological Museum
6. Chaniá
7. Réthymno
8. Górtys
9. Royal Villa at Agia Triada
10. Palace of Malia

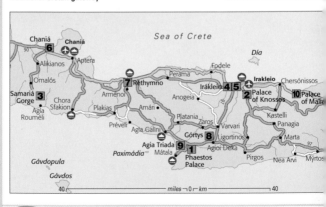

Preceding pages **Santoríni**

Phaestos Palace

One of the great city-state palaces of the Minoan period, this fabulous structure lay hidden for over 3,000 years before being discovered by Italian archaeologist Frederico Halbherr in the late 19th century. The well-preserved sights include the grand staircase and the central courtyard *(see pp20–21)*.

Palace of Knossos

Knossos was the capital of Minoan Crete and its palace was an architectural marvel. The original palace, dating from about 1900 BC, was destroyed by an earthquake but was quickly rebuilt. The remains were discovered and restored by Sir Arthur Evans in 1878 *(see pp22–3)*.

Samariá Gorge

Created over millennia by a river running between two mountains, the dramatic Samariá gorge is one of the longest and deepest canyons in Europe. Visitors can walk from the village of Omalós, along the 16 km- (10 mile-) long gorge to the coastal village of Agía Rouméli. Along the way are towering rock faces, springs and chapels, such as Ágios Nikólaos. The area became a national park in 1962, primarily to protect the rare kri-kri goat *(see p45)* and its natural habitat. 🕲 *44 km (27 miles) south of Chaniá • Map D6 • 28210 67179 • Open May–Oct: 8am–4pm daily (weather permitting) • Adm*

Irákleio

With a mixture of elegant Venetian mansions, busy streets, a harbour full of fishing boats and squares full of chic restaurants, tavernas

Magnificent Samariá gorge

and designer fashion shops, Irákleio is a traditional Greek city with a distinctly modern twist. It is Crete's capital city and its administrative, commercial and cultural hub. At its heart is the pedestrianized Plateía Eleftheríou Venizélou, with the restored 13th-century church of Ágios Márkos. Must-see sights include the Archaeological Museum, which boasts an impressive collection of Minoan art. 🕲 *Map E6*

Irákleio Archaeological Museum

This magnificent museum houses the island's finest collection of Minoan treasures. Among its exhibits are the famous Phaestos Disc found at the Phaestos Palace *(see p21)*. Other exhibits on display are the Snake Goddess figurine and the Bull's Head Rhyton from the Palace of Knossos *(see p22)*. A huge renovation project finished in 2014 added state-of-the-art interactive exhibits, plus many archaeological treasures on display for the first time. 🕲 *Map E6 • 28102 79086 • Open summer: 8am –8pm daily, winter: noon–5pm Mon, 8am–3pm Tue–Sun • Adm*

Vase, Irákleio Archaeological Museum

Left **Stepped path, Chaniá** Right **Ruins at Górtys**

Chaniá

A sprawling fortified city in the foothills of the Lefká Óri mountains, Chaniá was the city-state of Kydonia in ancient times. Along with Phaestos and Knossos, it was one of the most powerful cities during the Minoan period. Decline was followed by renewed importance under the Venetians. Chaniá was the capital of Crete until 1971. Today, life in the city revolves around its scenic harbour and the historic Spiántza Quarter, with its Venetian houses lining cobbled streets, modern restaurants and art galleries. ◎ Map D6

Traditional weaving, Réthymno museum

Réthymno

With a well-preserved Venetian fortress, picturesque harbour famous for its 13th-century lighthouse, and fish tavernas, Réthymno is a refined holiday destination. One of its elegant Venetian mansions now houses the small Historical and Folk Art Museum. Along with Irákleio, Réthymno is home to the Crete University and a school of philosophy. Once the Greco-Roman city of Rithymna, it was important enough to mint its own coins. The town's crest is based on one of these old coins. ◎ Map E6 • Historical and Folk Art Museum: Vernadou; 28310 23398; open 10am–2:30pm Mon–Sat; adm

Górtys

Thought to have been inhabited since Neolithic times, Górtys, or Gortyn, became the powerful capital of Crete, ahead of Phaestos, after the Roman invasion of 65 BC. Its power lasted until AD 7, when invading Arabs destroyed the city. The remains of its citadel and agora (market place), the *praetorium* (governor's house), temples and a cemetery can be visited. A three-aisled basilica, Ágios Títos, dominates the entrance. The *odeion* (small theatre) ruins are famous for their inscriptions. ◎ Ágii Déka, Irákleio • Map E6 • 28920 3114 • Open 8am–6pm daily • Adm

Royal Villa at Agia Triada

Built during the Neopalatial period of the 16th century BC, this Minoan villa was one of the

Górtys Law Code

Inscribed on the north round wall of Górtys Odeion, the Law Code was on public display and related to all domestic matters, from marriage to the division of property. The script, known as boustrophedon, has alternate lines written from right to left, then left to right. It uses symbols of the Doric Cretan dialect, dating from around 500 BC.

Crete is divided into four administrative provinces: Chaniá, Réthymno, Irákleio and Lasíthi.

first palaces to be constructed in much smaller proportions than those of Phaestos and Knossos, which was the fashion of the day. Believed to be a summer residence, it consisted of two wings built to form an L-shape, with courtyards, staircases and workshops. Excavations revealed artifacts, including clay seals and tablets with Minoan script. Other finds include a black stone vase depicting Neopalatial art *(see p25)* and a carved boxer rhyton jug, which suggest this was a palace of great wealth. ✆ *3 km (2 miles) west of Phaestos, Irákleio • Map E6 • 28920 91564 • Open summer: 8am–8pm daily, winter: daily 8:30am–3pm (noon–5pm Mon) • Adm • Combined ticket for Villa and Phaestos Palace (see p20)*

Ruins, Palace of Malia

10 Palace of Malia

A little inland from the bustle of one of Crete's most popular holiday hotspots are the archaeological remains of Malia, one of the island's most prosperous Minoan cities. The palace, noted for its layout, was constructed around a courtyard with a central altar. It has raised paths, known as processional ways, leading to its west entrance. Inside there is a labyrinth of crypts that were probably used for cult worship. Important treasures unearthed here include the famous *kernos*, believed to be a vessel used for sacrifices. ✆ *Malia, Irákleio • Map E6 • 28970 31597 • Open 8:30am–3pm Tue–Sun • Adm*

A Hike Along the Samariá Gorge

🕐 Have a hearty breakfast, pack plenty of snacks, a water bottle (which can be replenished in the gorge), sun cream and plasters before heading off on this approximately 6-hour trip. Wear light clothing but take a jumper as it can be cold at higher altitudes, and always wear a hat. You will need sturdy walking shoes.

Fully prepared, head for the village of **Omalós**. The best option, if you plan to hike the length of the gorge, is to go by bus because you'll be tired going home, but if you intend hiking just a short distance and returning to Omalós, there is a car park. Opening times can vary according to the weather, so be sure to check. Aim to arrive early.

From Omalós, make your way across the plateau before taking a sharp descent down the snaking path known as Xylóskalo. It is around 2 km (1 mile) long. Follow the signposted route, which will take you past chapels like the tiny **Ágios Nikólaos** and **Óssia Maria**, which has some fine 14th-century frescoes. You will pass the deserted village of **Samariá** and a landmark spot known as Sideróportes, where the path considerably narrows between towering mountainsides. Heading down the gorge, you will pass by the old village of **Agía Rouméli**, before reaching the new Agía Rouméli on the coast, about 6 hours after you started. Take a ferry to **Chóra Sfakíon**, where there are buses.

Left **Mátala** Centre **Harbour, Kastélli** Right **Amári valley**

Best of the Rest

1 Ágios Nikólaos
Overlooking the picturesque Mirabéllou bay, Ágios Nikólaos has grown from a small Venetian fishing village to a cosmopolitan holiday resort. In Hellenistic times it was a city known as Lato. ◈ *Northeast coast • Map F6*

2 Siteía
This coastal village is surrounded by vineyards and is known for its quality Cretan wines. See its restored Venetian fort, now a cultural venue, its historic harbour and Victorian mansions. ◈ *Northeast coast • Map F6*

3 Kastélli Kissámou
Often just called Kastélli, this quiet town with a handful of tavernas is a great base for exploring the unspoiled Gramvoússa peninsula. Nearby is the superb beach and ancient site of Falásarna. ◈ *West coast • Map D6*

4 Amári Valley
Dotted with cherry orchards, traditional villages and chapels with outstanding frescoes, the Amári valley is a mountainous area of natural beauty. It is dominated by Mt Ídi at 2,456 m (8,080 ft). ◈ *Central Crete • Map E6*

5 Mátala
Mátala is a bustling holiday resort with a fabulous history. It is said to be where St Paul landed on Crete and where Menelaos, the husband of Helen of Troy, was shipwrecked. ◈ *South coast • Map E6*

6 Paleochóra
Paleochóra's landmark is the remains of a Venetian castle destroyed by pirates. The village stands on a headland that divides the beach in two. The resort is popular with windsurfers. ◈ *West coast • Map D6*

7 Préveli
The site of two monasteries, the 18th-century Moní Préveli and the earlier Moní Agíou Ioánnou, Préveli is a small village reached via the Kourtaliótiko gorge. A steep path leads to its idyllic beach. ◈ *South coast • Map E6*

8 Zákros
Located on the slopes of Mt Deléna, Zákros is an unassuming coastal village. It gained prominence in 1961 when the remains of a Minoan palace with priceless artifacts were discovered. ◈ *East coast • Map F6*

9 Eloúnda
With its sandy beaches and coves, Eloúnda is a busy holiday destination. Site of the ancient city-state Olous, it was fortified under Venetian rule. An isthmus links it to the Spinalónga peninsula. ◈ *Northeast coast • Map F6*

10 Spinalónga
This heavily fortified islet and one-time leper colony makes a dramatic sight from the ferries crossing from Eloúnda. It's been home to Olouites, Venetians and Ottomans. ◈ *Northeast coast • Map F6*

Price Categories

For a three-course meal for one with half a bottle of wine (or equivalent meal), taxes and extra charges.

€	under €20
€€	€20–€30
€€€	€30–€40
€€€€	€40–€50
€€€€€	over €50

Left **Pacifae Restaurant, Ágios Nikólaos** Right **To Pigadi Restaurant, Réthymno**

🔟 Restaurants

1 Ristorante Italiano Veneto
Some of the finest pizzas, pasta, desserts and wines from Italy are served at this restaurant housed in a renovated 15th-century Venetian building. 🕔 *Zampelíou Street 8, Chaniá • Map D6 • 28210 93527 • €€€*

2 To Pigadi Restaurant
Tucked inside a 16th-century building at the foot of a fortress, this eatery specializes in Cretan dishes. Dine inside or in the courtyard. 🕔 *Xanthoudidou Street 31, Réthymno • Map E6 • 20310 27522 • €€*

3 Remezzo Restaurant
On the water's edge, this landmark restaurant serves great *souvláki*, juices and cocktails. 🕔 *El. Venizélou Square 16A, Old Port, Chaniá • Map D6 • 28210 52001 • €€*

4 Dionysos
This long-established taverna overlooking the lake is a favourite with locals. Serving breakfast through to evening meals, it specializes in meat and seafood, influenced by Cretan and French cooking. 🕔 *Ágios Nikólaos lake, Ágios Nikólaos • Map F6 • 28410 25060 • €€*

5 Belvedere Restaurant
With great sea views, this restaurant serves Cretan food, *stifádo* (stew) being its signature dish. An extensive wine list and Greek musicians complete the experience here. 🕔 *Ano Platanias, Chaniá • Map D6 • 28210 60003 • €€*

6 Marilena Restaurant
Enjoy flambéed dishes, fresh fish and seafood or try Greek *mezédes* in this attractive taverna-style restaurant's garden. In the winter dine inside by the fire. Entertainment includes dancers in traditional dress. 🕔 *Harbourside, Eloúnda • Map F6 • 28410 41322 • €€€*

7 Portes
Nestling under the city walls, Portes serves adventurous Greek cuisine, which sets it apart from its neighbours. Expect dishes such as pork fillets stuffed with chestnuts. 🕔 *Portou 48, Chaniá • Map D6 • 28210 76261 • €€€€*

8 Pacifae Restaurant
Mediterranean dishes with an emphasis on Greek cuisine are prepared by the chefs at this waterside eatery. International and Cretan wines are served. 🕔 *Ágios Nikólaos lake, Ágios Nikólaos • Map F6 • 28410 24466 • €€*

9 Erganos Tavern
Designed to resemble a Cretan village house, this restaurant serves local classic dishes such as *sarikópittes* (cheese pies). 🕔 *Georgiádi 5, Irákleio • Map E6 • 28102 85629 • €€*

10 Loukloulos
With elegant Neo-Classical surroundings, white linen and soft music, this is one of the foremost places to dine in Irákleio. The menu is Mediterranean. 🕔 *Koraí 5, Irákleio • Map E6 • 28102 24435 • €€€€€*

Left **Figaro Art and Music Café** Right **Klik Scandinavian Bar**

TOP 10 Bars and Cafés

1 Cosmos Piano Bar
A stylish venue overlooking the bay, this piano bar serves upmarket wines, cognacs and malts from a selection of around 300, along with gourmet delicacies. ◊ *Páno Plataniás, Chaniá • Map D6 • 28210 68558*

2 Maleme Tavern Snack Bar
Pancakes and coffee are served for breakfast and light Cretan dishes, such as cheese pies and salad, through the day at this bar near the beach. Enjoy a cocktail in the evening. ◊ *Maleme, Chaniá • Map D6 • 28210 62049*

3 Diamonds Night Club
This private club, a short distance from the centre of town, fits the bill for a more adult way to spend an evening, with a mix of low lighting, sultry music and exotic dancers. ◊ *Káto Stalós, Chaniá • Map D6 • 28210 84995*

4 Kinimatografos Music Café
Open round the clock, this harbourside café transforms into a lively evening venue with cocktails and dancing. ◊ *Old Venetian Port, Chaniá • Map D6 • 28210 99293*

5 Klik Scandinavian Bar
Every night is a party at the Klik for the young and trendy who dance to R&B, indie, hip-hop and rock. Cocktails, shots and snacks are served. ◊ *Old Venetian Port, Chaniá • Map D6 • 69459 32971*

6 Rock Café
Enjoy drinks and cocktails to the sounds of R&B, rock and pop music at this dance venue. With light snacks and a house DJ, it is a great place to spend an evening. ◊ *Ioánni Peticháki Street 1, Réthymno • Map E6 • 28310 54325*

7 Figaro Art and Music Café
Full of atmosphere, this super café has art on the walls, two courtyards with ivy-covered archways, fig trees, and a menu of tasty snacks, speciality coffees and fine wines. ◊ *Vernádou 21–23, Réthymno • Map E6 • 28310 29431*

8 Fagotto Jazz Bar
Housed in a restored Venetian building, this bar is informal and a good place to meet friends. Its menu is chic and jazz is usually performed here live. ◊ *Ángelou 6, Chaniá • Map D6 • 28210 71877*

9 Dwyer's Irish Pub
This live music bar is located on a lovely beachfront terrace overlooking the bay. There's food and drinks all day, and live music every night. ◊ *Beach Rd, Stalis • Map E6 • 28970 33724*

10 Rose Café Beach Bar
More than a beach bar, this venue offers a volleyball court, playground, swimming pools, watersports, sunbeds and an extensive choice of drinks and light meals. ◊ *Adelianós Kámbos, Réthymno • Map E6 • 28310 72776*

ft **Inside Christie** Right **Shopping street in central Rethymno**

10 Places to Shop

1 Ikaros
Set in a beautiful hilltop lIage, high above Plakias ay, Ikaros has stylish, unique wellery, fashioned by silver-nith Yannis. Pieces can also be nade to the client's own designs r specifications. ॐ *Sellia • Map E6* 28320 31271

2 Gold Bees
With a range of gold and Iver bracelets, necklaces and ngs in both modern and tradi-onal Greek designs, Gold Bees s known for its competitive rices. ॐ *Adelianós Kámbos, Réthymno Map E6 • 28310 72876*

3 Christie
Names such as Gucci, Prada nd Dolce & Gabbana fill the helves of men's and women's vatches at this shop. Contem-orary jewellery ranges feature old, silver and gems. ॐ *Arkadíou treet, Réthymno • Map E6 • 28310 0405*

4 Savoidakis Sweet Shop
Artfully presented chocolate nd *glyká koutalioú* (candied fruit) onfectionary are among the isplays at this shop. ॐ *Geronimáki 6, Irákleio • Map E6 • 28102 28531*

5 Kreta Gold
This jewellery store pecializes in local handmade old and silver necklaces, racelets and charms, along with eligious icons. ॐ *Chálidon Street 7–71, Chaniá • Map D6 • 28210 42623*

6 Stamatakis Andreas
One of several branches in Chaniá, this bakery serves delicious handmade sweet and savoury pastries, cakes and chocolates. Do try its honey-drenched baklava or mini cheese pies. ॐ *Selínou 128, Chaniá • Map D6 • 28210 95926*

7 Mystis Book Store
Both Greek and international books, many in bilingual editions, along with local music and maps of Crete are available here. Mystis has a store in Irákleio too. ॐ *Chálidon Street 89, Chaniá • Map D6 • 28210 92512*

8 Creta Ceramics
The age-old craft of creating *píthoi*-style clay pots, vases and bowls is demonstrated at this delightful village workshop and shop. ॐ *Thrápsano Pediádos, Irákleio • Map E6 • 28910 41717*

9 Idols Art
This workshop and shop specializes in recreated figurines from Crete's Bronze Age. These handmade items make ideal gifts or souvenirs. ॐ *Kato Archanes, Irákleio • Map E6 • 2810 373131*

10 Cicada Gallery
With an eclectic range of stone sculptures, plaques and unique jewellery, this is a great place to buy contemporary and traditional Greek gifts of quality. ॐ *Ágios Nikólaos Road, Eloúnda • Map F6 • 28410 41684*

⟹ *Shops often close in the afternoon, so call ahead to check.*

Left **Váï beach** Centre **Falásarna beach** Right **Gramvoússa peninsula**

🔟 Best Beaches

1 Falásarna Beach
One of the cleanest beaches on Crete, this long stretch of golden sand is lapped by turquoise sea. It is known for its magical sunsets. Nearby tavernas provide refreshment. ◎ *West coast • Map D6*

2 Gramvoússa Peninsula
Along with Falásarna, there are many isolated and peaceful beaches and sandy coves dotting the coast of this unspoiled peninsula. Most are only accessible only by boat. ◎ *West coast • Map D6*

3 Váï Beach
With its wild date-palm grove, perhaps Europe's largest, and its golden sand dunes, Váï beach is among the island's most beautiful. ◎ *East coast • Map F6*

4 Amníssos Beach
The main beach of Irákleio is a stretch of golden sand with lots of charm. It is famous for having been the port of Knossos, and archaeological remains have been discovered here. ◎ *Map E6*

5 Siteía Beach
Awarded a Blue Flag for cleanliness, this sandy beach lines a deep, horseshoe-shaped bay and is near the picturesque Siteía village. It is popular for windsurfing. ◎ *North coast • Map F6*

6 Sísi's Beaches
Sísi village has two beaches, one a secluded stretch of sand in the small Avláki bay and the other just off the harbour near tavernas and bars. ◎ *East coast • Map F6*

7 Préveli Beach
The Kourtaliótis river meets the sea at Préveli, where the green river, blue sea, date palms and "Greek bamboo" (calamus reeds) create a tropical oasis feel. ◎ *South coast • Map E6*

8 Stavros Beach
Tucked in a sandy cove, this unspoiled beach is best known as one of the locations for the film *Zorba the Greek*. There are only a few small tavernas. ◎ *North coast • Map D6*

9 Réthymno Beach
Although usually crowded because its main section is in Réthymno city, this beach is nonetheless beautiful. It is about 20 km (13 miles) long and dotted with palm trees and tavernas. ◎ *North coast • Map E6*

10 Mýrtos Beach
Surrounded by citrus groves and banana plantations, the secluded beach of Mýrtos is an idyllic spot on the island. It is sandy, with a few pebbles. ◎ *South coast • Map F6*

Mýrtos beach

eft **Gávdos island** Right **Elafoníssi islet**

10 Islands and Islets

Gávdos Island
This cedar- and pine-covered island has the distinction of being Greece's southernmost boundary. It has quaint villages and beaches. According to Homer's *The Odyssey*, the nymph Calypso lived here. Ⓢ *Off Sfakiá • Map D6*

Día Island
This island is a nature reserve for the rare Cretan goat, the kri-kri *(see p45)*. It boasts excellent waters for swimming and snorkelling, coves to explore and a church to visit. Ⓢ *Off Irákleio • Map E6*

Dragonáda Island
Remains of ancient habitation and early Christian tombstones have been found on this island in the Dionysádes archipelago. Now uninhabited, it is covered with vegetation. Ⓢ *Off Siteía • Map F6*

Koufoníssi Island
Characterized by its desert landscape of fine sand dotted with tamarisk trees, this deserted island has archaeological remains, now being excavated, that suggest it was inhabited in ancient times. Ⓢ *Off Goúdouras • Map F6*

Chryssí Island
An island of volcanic rock and sand dunes, Chryssí is uninhabited. However, it has a well-preserved 700-year-old church, Agios Nikólaos, an ancient port and remains from the Minoan period to explore.
Ⓢ *Off Ierápetra • Map E6*

Paximádia Island
Comprising two small rocky islets, Paximádia island was once named the Islets of Dionýsoi, after Dionysos, the god of wine. Today, they are a popular boat-trip destination from Mátala. Ⓢ *Off Mátala • Map E6*

Elafoníssi Islet
Reached by crossing a reef, this scenic islet is covered with trees and has beaches made up of tiny coral fragments, which give them a pinkish hue. It is surrounded by shallow aquamarine water. Ⓢ *Off Paleochóra • Map D6*

Spinalónga Island
An imposing Venetian fortification dominates this lush island, making it a popular day-trip spot. Ferry boats dock at its picturesque quayside, allowing visitors to explore the island.
Ⓢ *Off Ágios Nikólaos • Map F6*

Gramvoússa Island
This small island off the Gramvoússa peninsula is a haven for wildlife. In Venetian times it was a key defense location. The former stronghold now attracts day-trippers in summer. Ⓢ *Off Kastélli Kissámou • Map D6*

Psíra Island
This barren island traces its history back to Minoan times, when it was inhabited and lay off what is believed to have been a harbour lined with merchants' homes. Ⓢ *Off Ágios Nikólaos • Map F6*

Left **City wall, Rhodes Old Town** Centre **Monastery of St John, Pátmos** Right **Rhodes village**

The Dodecanese

SCATTERED ALONG THE COAST OF TURKEY, *the Dodecanese is the most southerly group of Greek islands, its hot climate, pretty whitewashed villages and fine beaches attracting many visitors. The largest islands are Rhodes, Kárpathos and Kos, all of which are popular holiday spots. Many smaller islands and islets make up the rest of the group. The history of the Dodecanese spans millennia, from the Dorians, who settled here in ancient times, through the Knights Hospitallers, the Ottomans and the Italians – all of whom left an indelible mark on the look and culture of the islands.*

Waterfront façade, Sými

Remains of a hill-top castle, Léros

10 Sights

1. Rhodes Old Town
2. Monastery of St John, Pátmos
3. Kos
4. Léros
5. Kálymnos
6. Astypálea
7. Sými
8. Chálki
9. Kárpathos
10. Nissyros

1 Rhodes Old Town

The Palace of the Grand Masters and the Street of the Knights are two of the fabulous sights to see in this city, which dates largely from the time of the Knights Hospitallers. Bounded by imposing city walls, it also has Ottoman mosques and a Jewish Quarter. The city offers a choice of restaurants, churches and museums, such as the Municipal Museum of Modern Greek Art *(see pp10–11)*.

Exhibit, Palace of the Grand Masters

2 Monastery of St John, Pátmos

Known as the Jerusalem of the Aegean, Pátmos is renowned as the place where St John wrote the biblical *Book of Revelation* (or Apocalypse) in AD 95. At its heart is the UNESCO World Heritage Site, Hóra: a collection of Byzantine monasteries and chapels, including the Monastery of St John. Nearby is a small church, Agía Ánna, and the Cave of the Apocalypse, the spot where St John is said to have written the work *(see pp12–13)*.

3 Kos

The home of Hippocrates, the father of medicine, Kos is the third-largest island in the group. It dates from Neolithic times and was a founding member of the Dorian Hexapolis *(see p32)* in 700 BC. Life today revolves around its capital, Kos Town, which is dominated by the 15th-century Castle of the Knights. Boulevards lined with cafés and chic restaurants sit beside ancient ruins. A marina full of yachts and a vibrant nightlife characterize the modern town, created after an earth-quake destroyed the old town in 1933. ◉ *Map X2*

4 Léros

With its pretty valleys and slow pace of life, Léros is a great place to unwind. It tends to attract writers, musicians and artists, who have helped create its identity as a cultural centre. Its capital, Agía Marína, ascends from the harbourside through alleyways of Neo-Classical buildings and tiny white cottages to a hilltop dominated by the remains of a Knights' castle. Lakkí, the island's main port, is one of the largest natural harbours in the Mediterranean. ◉ *Map F4*

5 Kálymnos

Several remains of ancient settlements testify to Kálymnos's long history. Be sure to visit its Archaeological Museum, where locally found Neolithic, Minoan and Mycenaean figurines are on display. Its capital is Póthia, a picturesque town where brightly coloured houses of local spongefishers line the deep harbour in amphitheatre-fashion. A church dedicated to Christ the Saviour, notable for its beautiful frescoes and iconostasis, is Póthia's principal landmark. Except for two valleys with tiny villages, the rest of the isle is mountainous.
◉ *Map F4 • Archaeological Museum, Kálymnos: 22430 23113 • Open Mar–Nov: 8:30am–3pm Tue–Sun • Adm*

Restored columns, Kos

Pastel-coloured houses overlooking Sými's harbour

6 Astypálea

The small island of Astypálea, which means "old city", was ruled by a Venetian family for several hundred years. They gave it the style it retains to this day. Its capital, Hóra, has many white houses with brightly painted windows and doors that dot the landscape as it rises towards a fortified castle. Astypálea's villages include the growing resort of Maltezána, while its coastline has coves that are popular with yacht owners. Important finds from the island's prehistoric period are housed in the Archaeological Museum. ◈ *Map F5 • Archaeological Museum • 22430 61500 • Open summer: 8am–8pm Tue–Sat, 9am–3pm Sun & Mon*

7 Sými

A popular destination for holidays and day trips from Rhodes, Sými is a mountainous

Church of Agios Nikólaos, Chálki

island with villages, beaches and bustling harbours. The streets of its capital, Sými Town, and its main port of Gäios are lined with stately mansions from the 19th century, when the island had a thriving boat-building industry. Said to be the birthplace of the ancient Greek goddesses the Three Graces *(see box)*, and taking its name from Syme, Poseidon's wife, Sými has a history spanning millennia. Its museum has some important artifacts. ◈ *Map G5 • Archaeological Museum • 22460 71114 • Open 8.30am–3pm daily • Adm*

8 Chálki

Chálki is a small island that revolves around its only community, the 200 or so inhabitants of Emborió. It is reached by boat from Rhodes. Emborió boasts the highest bell tower in the Dodecanese, on the golden-stone Ágios Nikólaos church. In

---

The Three Graces

In Greek and Roman mythology, the Three Graces were ancient goddesses. Also known as the Charites, they were believed to be the daughters of Zeus, the god of thunder, and his wife Eurynome. The youngest, Aglaea, was the goddess of beauty and Hephaestus' wife. Her sisters, Euphrosyne and Thalia, were the goddesses of joy and good cheer.

the past, Chálki had flourishing copper-ore mining and sponge-fishing industries but it now relies only on tourism. Visitors can enjoy its rural feel, its beaches, such as Ftenágia and Trachiá, and the deserted Chorió village, with its Knights' castle. ◈ *Map G5*

9 Kárpathos

The group's second-largest island, Kárpathos is characterized by its indented coastline, sandy beaches and high mountains. The highest is Kalí Límni, at 1,214 m (3,983 ft). The capital, Pigádia, also known as Kárpathos Town, is cosmopolitan, with a mix of hotels and restaurants. The island boasts bustling resorts, such as Ammopí and Lefkós. Thriving traditional rural villages, such as Menetés, where artifacts have been discovered from the Middle Ages, and Óthos, famous for its traditional Kárpathian houses, are definitely worth a visit. ◈ *Map X5*

Traditional windmill, Kárpathos

10 Níssyros

A volcanic island, Níssyros is known for the unique species of flora and fauna that grow in its mineral-rich soil. It is possible to visit the 260 m- (853 ft-) wide crater of the extinct volcano at Polyvótis, in the isle's centre. Villages and towns, including Mandráki, the pretty capital and port, lie in the lower coastal plains. According to mythology, Níssyros and Kos were once one island *(see p38)*. ◈ *Map F5*

Day Trip from Rhodes to Chálki

🕐 Although the Dodecanese islands are strung out and the only way to see all of them is to sail or take ferries over several days, it is possible to take a day trip from one island to another. A popular route is from **Rhodes Town** *(see p107)* to **Emborió** on **Chálki**. Boats also leave from **Skála Kameírou** *(see p110)* on Rhodes to Chálki.

Morning

🔹 After a good breakfast, head for **Mandráki harbour** in Rhodes New Town. You will need to get there early as most boats and hydrofoils to Chálki leave at about 9am. It is a good idea to check the timings a day before at a travel agency. Hop on board for the 2-hour sail that takes you along the coastline, past the islet of **Alímnia** to the gorgeous harbour of **Emborió**.

🔹 Refreshments are usually available on board. Upon disembarking, take time to walk along the harbourside and enjoy a delicious lunch at one of the tavernas that line the harbour.

Afternoon

Take a taxi to see the imposing crusader castle that sits high above the harbour. It is worth the trip and the view across towards Rhodes is rewarding in itself. You can also visit the island's churches and monasteries, such as the **Moní Agíou Ioánnou Prodrómou**, which has breathtaking icons. Refresh yourself at Ftenagia Restaurant near **Ftenágia beach** *(see p60)*, before making your way back to the harbour for the return crossing.

Tílos is said to have been where dwarf elephants lived in prehistoric times, the remains of which have been found in caves.

Left **Archaeological site, Kámeiros** Centre **Petaloúdes valley** Right **Hotel at Profítis Ilías**

ⓘ⓪ Sights: Rhodes

1 Asklipeió
Home to some fine 17th-century frescoes, the Dormition of the Virgin church has put this pretty village on the map. Ⓢ *Inland from Líndos • Map U5*

2 Ancient Ialyssos
This mountainside city was part of Rhodes' ancient city-state and retained its importance during Byzantine, Knights and Ottoman times. It is the site of Moní Filerímou. Ⓢ *Near Triánda • Map V4*

3 Líndos Acropolis
The ancient acropolis and a 3rd-century BC temple dedicated to the goddess Athena are the main remains of a great Doric city-state formed by Líndos, Ialyssos and Kámeiros. Ⓢ *Líndos • Map U5*

4 Ancient Kámeiros
This fascinating site from the 5th century BC is one of the finest examples of Doric city plan-ning. See remnants of a temple, dwellings and public baths.
Ⓢ *Kámeiros, near Kalavárda • Map U4*

5 Petaloúdes
Known as the Valley of Butterflies, this area has numer-ous trees that secrete a vanilla-scented gum, used for incense. It attracts thousands of butterflies and moths. Ⓢ *Petaloúdes • Map U4*

6 Monólithos
This quiet village is famous for a 15th-century fortress built on a sheer rock by Grand Master d'Aubusson of the Knights Hospitallers. It has a lovely beach Foúrnoi. Ⓢ *Near Foúrnoi • Map T5*

7 Profítis Ilías
The densely forested Profíti Ilías mountain was a natural par under Italian rule. It is famous fo its nature trails and walks today. Ⓢ *Inland from Kalavárda • Map U5*

8 Moní Filerímou
A place of worship for over 2,000 years, the Moní Filerímou is famous for the Our Lady of Filérimos complex of four chapels. Ⓢ *Near Triánda • Map V4*

9 Skála Kameírou
This once major ancient city port has one of the most impressive castle ruins on the island – the 16th-century Castle of Kritinía. Ⓢ *Map T5*

10 Émbona
Characterized by endless vineyards, Émbona is a delightfu traditional mountain village.
Ⓢ *Inland from Skála Kameírou • Map U5*

Price Categories

For a three-course meal for one with half a bottle of wine (or equivalent meal), taxes and extra charges.

€	under €20
€€	€20–€30
€€€	€30–€40
€€€€	€40–€50
€€€€€	over €50

Romeo, Rhodes

🔟 Places to Eat: Rhodes

1 Mavrikos
Famous for its gourmet Greek cuisine, the award-winning Mavrikos is one of the longest established restaurants in Líndos. ◈ Plateía Kentrikí, Líndos • Map U5 • 22440 31232 • €€€€

2 I Kouzina Tis Mamas
A lively restaurant serving pizza fresh from the griddle and pasta with delicious home-made sauces, this Italian-themed eatery is in the heart of the pretty seaside Gennádo village. ◈ Gennádo • Map U6 • 22440 43547 • €€

3 Alexis4Seasons
The acclaimed Alexis is housed in a historic building and serves fabulous fish and classic Greek dishes with flair. A roof garden offers panoramic views. ◈ Aristotélous Street 33, Rhodes Old Town • Map V4 • 22410 70522 • €€€€€

4 Belmo Palace Restaurant
Tucked inside a medieval building, this super blue and white taverna serves traditional dishes. Informal and friendly, it is a great place to relax. ◈ Octovríou Street 28, Rhodes Town • Map V4 • 22410 25251 • €€€

5 Tamam
This small and quaint taverna serves traditional Greek food, all cooked by Maria, the owner's daughter. The house wines are good quality and value for money. ◈ Leontos Georgiou 1, Rhodes Town • Map V4 • 22410 73522 • €€€

6 Romeo
An array of Greek dishes will tempt the palate at this taverna, located in an early 16th-century house. ◈ Corner Menekléous and Sokrátous Street, Rhodes Old Town • Map V4 • 22410 25186 • €€€

7 Epta Piges Taverna
Epta Piges, meaning Seven Springs, is an alfresco taverna nestled under huge pine and plane trees. The menu is classic Greek, with speciality home-made moussakás. ◈ Archángelos • Map U5 • 22410 56417 • €€

8 Restaurant Wonder
This elegant restaurant, set in a mansion, serves international cuisine with a Swedish and Asian twist. It has a good selection of coffees and pre-dinner drinks. ◈ El Venizelou Street 16–18, Rhodes Town • Map V4 • 22410 39805 • €€€€€

9 Kalypso Roof Garden Restaurant
With Líndian ceramics and nautical memorabilia adorning its walls, this delightful restaurant in a 17th-century waterfront house serves great fish. ◈ Líndos • Map U4 • 22440 32135 • €€€

10 Philosophia Beach Taverna
Overlooking a beach, this taverna offers the chance to dine alfresco on home-made Greek dishes prepared using organic produce from its own gardens. Known for its delicious desserts. ◈ Péfkoi • Map U4 • 22440 48044 • €€€€

Left **Menetés village** Right **Lefkós bay and beach**

Sights: Kárpathos

1 Pigádia (Kárpathos Town)
Tavernas line the harbour-side of this modern capital, which has grown from an ordinary port town into a centre of finance and commerce. The adjacent Vróndis bay has a lovely beach.
◈ Map Y6

2 Menetés
This charming village's main street is lined with pastel-coloured Neo-Classical houses and interspersed by tiny alleyways of steep steps. ◈ Map X6

3 Arkása
Arkása is a bustling resort, but it is also the site of the ancient city of Arkesia. You can see ruins of the 4th-century church of Agía Anastasía, where important archaeological finds were discovered. ◈ Map X6

4 Apéri
A village of elegant white-washed mansions and squares that sit amphitheatre-fashion in the foothills of Mt Kalí Límni, Apéri was the capital of Kárpathos until 1892. ◈ Map X5

5 Óthos
A pretty village of traditional Karpathian houses, Óthos is the island's highest community at 450 m (1,500 ft). It is known for its red wine and festivals. ◈ Map X5

6 Diafáni
A picturesque village that revolves around its intermittently busy harbour, Diafáni is popular with day-trippers. It offers sandy beaches and family tavernas.
◈ Map Y4

7 Ólympos
With its working windmills, painted stone houses and locals in traditional dress speaking a Dorian dialect, Ólympos is like a living museum. ◈ Map X4

8 Ammopí
The Ammopí resort is best known for its beaches, which are among the best on the island. Mikrí Ammopí occupies a crescent of golden sand. Megáli Ammopí and Votsalákia are also fine. ◈ Map Y6

9 Lefkós
This pretty village, a top holiday spot, boasts a series of white sandy bays nestled in deep coves, crystal-clear water and a backdrop of pine trees.
◈ Map X5

10 Surrounding Islands
To the north is Saría, said to be the site of the ancient Níssyros city, while to the south is unspoiled Kássos. Other islets include Platý, Armathiá, Kouríka and Mákra.

Kárpathos was once known as Porfýris, after the red dye made locally.

POTALI BAY
PIZZA RESTAURANT CAFE

Price Categories

For a three-course meal for one with half a bottle of wine (or equivalent meal), taxes and extra charges.	
€	under €20
€€	€20–€30
€€€	€30–€40
€€€€	€40–€50
€€€€€	over €50

Left **Manolis Taverna, Menetés** Right **Potali Bay Restaurant**

⁝₁₀ Places to Eat: Kárpathos

1 To Helliniko Taverna
Along with seafood and grills fresh from the charcoal, this small, attractive eatery specializes in salads. Try the Venus salad, served with the local *haloúmi* cheese. You can dine inside or alfresco. ◎ *Pigádia • Map Y6 • 22450 23932 • €€*

2 Dolphin Taverna
Overlooking Finíki beach and the working fishing harbour, this taverna serves authentic Karpathian delicacies. The *mezédes* and fish cooked with local herbs and cheese are particularly good. ◎ *Finíki • Map X6 • 22450 61060 • €€*

3 Mesogeios Restaurant
Diners sit at bright blue tables to enjoy exquisite local dishes like *makarónia* (Karpathian pasta) and stuffed clams at this lively waterfront restaurant. ◎ *Pigádia • Map Y6 • 22450 23274 • €€€*

4 Glaros Restaurant
An alfresco restaurant that overlooks the beach, the Glaros specializes in Karpathian and Greek dishes such as stuffed calamari. It has a special children's menu and delicious desserts. ◎ *Ágios Nikólaos beach, Arkása • Map X6 • 22450 61015 • €€*

5 Potali Bay Restaurant
Fish is high on the menu at this super restaurant right on the beach. Choose from octopus, shrimps and lobster, plus grills and pizzas, all served with added extras like pumpkin cakes. ◎ *Potáli bay • Map Xb • 22450 71221 • €€*

6 I Anna
Located right by the harbour, this popular restaurant is known for its fresh fish dishes, including sardines and octopus. ◎ *Pigádia • Map Y6 • 22450 22820 • €€€*

7 Manolis Taverna
Housed in one of Menetés' traditional little houses, this taverna has a menu of wholesome dishes, such as *souvláki* and chicken char-grilled with herbs. ◎ *Menetés • Map X6 • 22450 81103 • €€€*

8 La Gorgona
Greek and Italian cuisine combine effortlessly at this blue and white-coloured eatery. Drinks include authentic Italian coffees and a home-made Limoncello (lemon liqueur). ◎ *Diafáni • Map Y4 • 22450 51509 • €€*

9 Milos Tavern
This taverna has been built around a working windmill with a brick oven as its centrepiece. The menu features local dishes, such as savoury *píttes* (pies), prepared using organic produce. ◎ *Ólympos • Map X4 • 22450 51333 • €€*

10 Orea Karpathos
This attractive eatery serves *mezédes* with lots of local dishes plus a selection of fish and grills. ◎ *Pigádia • Map Y6 • 22450 22501 • €€*

➤ *With a network of more than 18 hiking paths, Kárpathos is popular with hikers.*

Left **Kéfalos island** Centre **Mastichári beach** Right **Pedalos on Tigáki beach**

Sights: Kos

1 Kos Town
The 16th-century Castle of the Knights and remains such as the 3rd-century BC agora, dominate the capital city. Restaurants along palm-lined avenues give it a cosmopolitan feel. ◈ *Map Y1*

2 Asklepieíon
Once a centre of healing, Asklepieíon is one of Greece's most important historic sites. See remains of the 3rd-century Temple of Apollo, Hippocrates' garden and Roman baths. ◈ *Map Y1*

3 Ziá
Preserved as a model village, Ziá has a Byzantine church and stone houses lining cobbled pathways. It is one of the Asfendioú Villages *(see p45)*. ◈ *Map X2*

4 Paleó Pýli
Spectacularly perched on a clifftop, with its walls built into the rock, this abandoned fortified town is famous for its Byzantine churches. ◈ *Map X2*

5 Kardámena
One of Greece's liveliest resorts, Kardamena, a former fishing village, offers watersports, boat trips, nightclubs, bars and tavernas. ◈ *Map X2*

6 Mastichári
Boasting some of the best beaches on the west coast, this pretty fishing harbour is popular with locals. Its tavernas serve fabulous fish. ◈ *Map X2*

7 Andimácheia
Known for its windmills and traditional houses, this village is dominated by the 14th-century Castle of Andimácheia built by the Knights Hospitallers as a prison. ◈ *Map X2*

8 Kéfalos
An elevated village of whitewashed houses and cobbled pathways descending to the beach, Kéfalos is home to the ruined Castle of the Knights. ◈ *Map W2*

9 Kamári
With its volcanic backdrop and soft, sandy beach, known as Paradise beach, this village is a popular holiday spot. Resorts and restaurants line its waterfront. ◈ *Map W2*

10 Tigáki
Popular with ornithologists, Tigáki is known for its abundance of wetland bird species, which flock to its salt lakes. The village also has sandy beaches and shallow waters, making it safe for children. ◈ *Map X1*

Hippocrates is believed to have been the first holistic healer and a descendant of the god Asklepios.

Price Categories

For a three-course meal for one with half a bottle of wine (or equivalent meal), taxes and extra charges.

€	under €20
€€	€20–€30
€€€	€30–€40
€€€€	€40–€50
€€€€€	over €50

staurant Museum, Kos Town

10 Places to Eat and Drink: Kos

O Makis Taverna
Specializing in Greek dishes, uch as *souvláki* served straight om the grill with parsley and mon, this super little taverna ear the harbour is an informal ace to dine. ◈ *Mastichári • Map X2 22420 59061 • €€€*

Avanti Restaurant
This cheerful waterfront afé-pizzeria has an extensive alian-themed menu featuring avoury home-made crêpes and zzas cooked in its wood-fired ven. ◈ *Vasileíou Georgíou, Kos Town Map Y1 • 22420 20040 • €€€*

Platanos
This large restaurant is right ext to the Castle of the Knights nd the plane tree here is said have been planted by ippocrates. The menu is Greek nd French. ◈ *Plateía Platanoú, Kos wn • Map Y1 • 22420 28991 • €€€€*

Kalymnos Restaurant
The family-run Kalymnos is a etty taverna minutes from Kos wn's main beach. It specializes home cooking, with Greek cipes handed down through e generations. ◈ *Kos Town • Map 1 • 22420 48540 • €€€*

Restaurant Museum
Located near the rchaeological Museum, this ttractive eatery serves inter-ational fare, often straight from e coals, great seafood and egetarian dishes, home-made

desserts and local wines. Dine inside or alfresco. ◈ *Ríga Feréou Street 2, Kos Town • Map Y1 • 22420 20999 • €€€*

Ristorante Otto e Mezzo
Dine on dishes inspired by the regions of Italy. Terraces overlook the old town and the gardens. ◈ *Apéllou Street 21, Kos Town • Map Y1 • 22420 20069 • €€€*

Tam Tam Taverna
With its rustic straw parasols, huge palm trees and children's play areas, this informal beach bar and taverna is fun. Enjoy grills and cocktails by the ocean. ◈ *Mastichári • Map X2 • 69444 37027 • €€*

Lofaki Restaurant
One of Kos's premier eateries, Lofaki serves artfully presented Greek dishes with local and international wines. ◈ *Agios Nektarios, Kos • Map Y1 • 22420 21982 • €€€*

Sagittarius Restaurant
This elegant restaurant and cocktail lounge has a menu that spans Italian, Indian and Greek dishes. Open from breakfast to dinner, it is close to the beach. ◈ *Tigáki • Map X1 • 22420 68113 • €€€€*

Restaurant Jumbo Style
Housed under the canopy of the covered market, this popular grill house is informal by day and lively by evening. *Mezédes* are a speciality. ◈ *Plateía Agías Paraskevís, Kos Town • Map Y1 • 22420 24780 • €€*

> A mezédes *selection features 20 or more small portions of Greek dishes and is a great way to sample different specialities.*

Left **Arginónta beach, Kálymnos** Right **Psérimos islet**

TOP 10 Beaches and Islets

1 Psilí Ámmos Beach, Pátmos

A long stretch of golden sand, dotted with trees and sand-wiched between turquoise sea and a mountainous back-drop, this is the best beach on the island of Pátmos. Accessibility is difficult, so it is rarely crowded (see p60).

2 Arginónta Beach, Kálymnos

A forested hillside descends almost to the water's edge here, gently giving way to the sand and pebble Arginónta beach. Tavernas are located in a village nearby. ◈ *West coast near Masoúri • Map F4*

3 Katsadiás Beach, Lipsí

A series of sandy coves lead to the beautifully wide sand and shingle Katsadiás beach. It is a popular anchorage for yachts due to its seclusion, shelter and shallow water. ◈ *Katsadiás • Map F4*

4 Tría Marmária Beach, Astypálea

These three beaches are known by a single name. Each is horseshoe-shaped and secluded, enclosed by a rugged landscape and deep bays of azure water. ◈ *Astypálea Town • Map F6*

5 Ágios Antónis Beach, Tílos

High and rugged mountains plunge to meet this sandy beach and its crystal-clear blue bay. The view is dramatic. ◈ *Ágios Antónis village • Map G5*

6 Póntamos Beach, Chálki

Chálki has several beautiful beaches, including Ftenágia and Dýo Yialí, but Póntamos is the only one you do not need a boat to reach. Golden sand and shallow water make this beach ideal for children. ◈ *Emborió • Map G5*

7 Psérimos Islet

This tiny islet has one of the best beaches in the Dodecanese. It is long, with soft sand and shallow waters, and is popular with day trippers. ◈ *Map F4*

8 Faliráki Beach, Rhodes

More famous for the nightlife that lines the waterfront, this beach is exceptionally beautiful. About 4 km (2.5 miles) long, it has golden sands and safe swimming waters. Located near-by is the quieter Kathará beach. ◈ *East coast • Map V4*

9 Finíki Beach, Kárpathos

Lying within a horseshoe-shaped bay and set among hills dotted with the whitewashed, red-roofed houses of Finíki village, this sandy beach is one of the prettiest on the island. ◈ *Finíki village • Map X6*

10 Thérmes Beach, Kos

With its natural hot springs and an underground spa, Thérmes beach is popular with locals as well as visitors. Accessibility is good, and car parking facilities and tavernas plentiful. ◈ *East coast • Map Y2*

Price Categories

For a three-course meal for one with half a bottle of wine (or equivalent meal), taxes and extra charges	
€	under €20
€€	€20–€30
€€€	€30–€40
€€€€	€40–€50
€€€€€	over €50

ft **Benetos Restaurant, Pátmos** Right **Restaurant Drosia, Kálymnos**

🔟 Restaurants

1 Australia Restaurant, Astypálea
iis harbour restaurant with a ne-covered terrace serves fresh sh and local home-made dishes e *moussakás*. Open from breakst until dinner. 🟦 *Limáni, Péra Gialós Map F5 • 22430 61275 • €€€€*

2 Restaurant Drosia, Kálymnos
hoose your fish before it is ooked at this fabulous beach verna, which serves delicious shes. Open for breakfast, lunch d beverages. 🟦 *Melitsachás beach Map F4 • 22430 48745 • €€*

3 Ftenagia Restaurant, Chálki
oused in a rustic building, this egant restaurant has a Greek enu. Roasted octopus, Chálki rimp and *mezédes*, along with cal wine and beers, tempt the stebuds. 🟦 *Ftenágia beach Map G5 • 22460 45384 • €€€*

4 Kalypso, Lipsí
This lively restaurant has a rrace overlooking the harbour. n the menu are grilled classics ccompanied by local wines. *Harbourside, Lipsí Town • Map F4 22470 41242 • Closed Oct–Mar • €€*

5 Taverna Paradisos, Léros
In an idyllic location right on e beach, this family-run taverna rves delicious food cooked to uthentic home-made recipes. ne service is excellent. 🟦 *Vromoli- os • Map F4 • 22470 24632 • €€*

6 Kelari Pitsaria, Pátmos
Located on the harbourside, this is one of Skála's trendiest pizzerias. Its extensive menu includes pizzas with creative toppings, fresh from the oven, plus imaginative salads. 🟦 *Harbourside, Skála • Map F4 • 22470 32610 • €€*

7 Mylopetra, Sými
Known for its global wines and Mediterranean-inspired gourmet dishes, this elegant restaurant, housed in a restored mansion, is worth a visit. Dine inside or in its courtyard. 🟦 *Sými Town • Map G5 • 22460 72333 • €€€€€*

8 Zorbas, Léros
This landmark restaurant, located next to a pretty beach, serves Lerian dishes, such as its own take on *moussakás* with local herbs. 🟦 *Panteli beach, Pantelí • Map F4 • 22470 22027 • €€€*

9 Armenon, Tílos
A wide selection of dishes made with fresh, local ingredients is on offer at this taverna, which has unrivalled views across Livadia Bay. They produce their own olive oil and honey. 🟦 *Livadia • Map G5 • 22460 44134 • €€€€*

🔟 Benetos Restaurant, Pátmos
Dine on fish, served with herbs and lemon, on the terrace of this super, traditional restaurant over-looking the sea. 🟦 *Sapsíla, near Skála • Map F4 • 224/0 33089 • €€€*

Left **View of Sámos** Centre **Red-roofed mansions, Vathý Town** Right **Pythagóreio ruins, Sámos**

The Northeast Aegean Islands

A COLLAGE OF ANCIENT RUINS, *fabulous beaches, quaint villages and lush countryside, this archipelago is one of the least touched by modern-day tourism.* The group comprises the larger islands of Límnos, with its elegant capital, Mýrina, Lésvos, famous for its olives, Híos, which is both beautiful and vibrant, Sámos, known for its potent Muscat wine, and quiet, unspoiled Ikaría. The group also includes Thássos, inhabited since the Stone Age and with a tourism-oriented present, and undeveloped Samothráki, both up near the Macedonian coast. The islands share a landscape of rugged mountains, indented coastlines and glorious beaches. Tiny islets dot the surrounding waters, including Foúrni, Ágios Efstrátios, Psará and the wildlife haven of Andípsara.

Moored boats, Lésvos

🔟 Sights

1. Néa Moní, Híos
2. Vathý, Sámos
3. Pythagóreio and Heraion, Sámos
4. Thássos
5. Foúrni
6. Lésvos
7. Límnos
8. Ikaria
9. Psará and Andípsara
10. Samothráki

1 Néa Moní, Híos

Pride of the Northeast Aegean Islands, this once wealthy 11th-century monastery is considered one of the finest examples of Macedonian Renaissance art and architecture in the world *(see pp16–17).*

2 Vathý, Sámos

The capital of Sámos, Vathý is an attractive town that hugs the base of the island's deepest bay. Its narrow, cobbled lanes are lined with red-roofed Neo-Classical mansions, while the

Detail, Néa Moní monastery, Híos

more modern area is a shoppers' delight. Beyond are lush mountains with valleys of vineyards. Also known as Sámos Town, Vathý and its surrounding villages are famous for their golden, sweet Muscat wine. Its Archaeological Museum has a rich collection of artifacts, including the famous 580 BC *koúros* (male nude statue). Ⓢ *Map F4 • Archaeological Museum of Sámos: Kapetán Gymnasiárchou Katevéni, Vathý; 22730 27469; open 8:30am–5pm Tue–Sun; adm*

3 Pythagóreio and Heraion, Sámos

The town of Pythagóreio is a popular tourist spot but beyond the tavernas lining its harbour, visitors will find vestiges of a centuries-old civilization. Nearby is the Sanctuary of Heraion, said to be where Hera, the goddess of fertility, was cult worshipped *(see pp18–19).*

Plinth from Polykrates temple, Heraion

4 Thássos

This almost circular island has remains from the Bronze Age that suggest it had strong links with the Cyclades. In the 7th century BC, settlers from Páros colonized parts of Thássos and, with its natural gold and marble resources, the island has known a history of wealth and power. Today, this pine-covered island of white beaches, ancient ruins and a coastline of deep bays is a popular package holiday destination. Its inland villages offer a glimpse of the past. Ⓢ *Map E1*

5 Foúrni

While almost every family on Foúrni owns a fishing boat, few own a car, which probably explains why activity centres around its bustling harbourside. It is here where most Foúrni residents live and work, and where visitors can find small tavernas and some excellent shops. An island of cliffs, long stretches of sandy beach and deep bays that once made it a pirates' paradise, this is a popular day-trip destination from the nearby islands of Sámos, Pátmos and Ikaría. Ⓢ *Map F4*

Mytlíni harbourfront, Lésvos

Sanctuary of the Great Gods, Samothráki

This sanctuary dates from Pan-Hellenic times and was the most important religious site for cult worship in ancient Aeolia, Thrace and Macedonia. Followers included the Spartan leader Lysander. The sanctuary grew during the Hellenistic era. Today, its remains include a cult initiation room and an amphitheatre.

Lésvos

6 The third-largest Greek island, Lésvos revolves around its capital, the elegant Mytilíni. Impressive churches and mansions line its harbourside. The town of Agiásos is considered the island's most picturesque and is famous for owning an icon believed to have been painted by St Luke. Villages of interest include Ypsiloú, situated near a fossilized forest and an extinct volcano. Lésvos, or Lesbos as it is often referred to, is best known for being the birthplace of Sappho, the ancient female poet who wrote erotic poems to other women. ◈ *Map Q1*

Límnos

7 In Greek mythology, Límnos was where Hephaestus, the god of metalworking, landed after being hurled out of Olympus (home of the gods) by his angry father Zeus. A volcanic island,

Límnos, or Lemnos, is largely flat with vineyards planted on lava-rich soil sloping towards wide, sandy beaches. Its capital is Mýrina, a town of Neo-Classical and Ottoman buildings and cobbled streets, dominated by its imposing Venetian *kástro* (castle). The island is known for its outstanding wine and herbal honey. ◈ *Map E1*

Ikaría

8 Ikaría is named after Icarus, the foolhardy son of ancient craftsman Daedalus. According to legend, Ikaros fell to his death after flying too close to the sun wearing artificial wings. The island has been inhabited since Neolithic times, and was part of the Genoese Aegean Empire and later the Ottoman Empire until its independence in 1912. Once a favourite haunt of pirates, evident in the defensive layout of its villages, Ikaría has rich soil

Volcanic landscape of Límnos

Hóra, Samothráki

which produces excellent wines. Its residents are known for their longevity. ◈ *Map F4*

9 Psará and Andípsara

Psará is best known for its heroic Freedom or Death flag, to which Psariots have been famously faithful in the face of battle. The most celebrated stance was in 1824 when, faced with the Ottoman invasion, residents blew both themselves and their invaders up with gunpowder. A poem, *The Destruction of Psará*, was written by Greek poet Dionýsios Solomós to mark the event. Psará's neighbour is the uninhabited Andípsara island. An important environmental and wildlife sanctuary, many interesting birds roost here, including Eleonora's falcon and the Mediterranean shearwater. ◈ *Off Híos • Map E3*

10 Samothráki

With the 1,600 m- (5,250 ft-) high Mt Fengári, hot thermal springs, olives groves, forests of oak and chestnut and two spectacular waterfalls, Samothráki has one of the most dramatic landscapes of all the East Aegean islands. At its heart is the capital Hóra, an elegant town of squares and cobbled streets. Nearby is the ancient capital of the island, Palaiópolis, and the remains of the Sanctuary of the Great Gods. ◈ *Map E1*

Day Trip to Foúrni

Morning

🕐 Foúrni can be reached easily by ferry from **Vathý** harbour or **Pátmos** harbour on Sámos and **Ágios Kírykos** on Ikaría. Foúrni Ferries and Greek Ferries are two of the companies serving the island. Departure and return times, as well as prices, vary, so do check in advance. After a hearty breakfast, head to the port of your choice. Most ferries leave between 9am and 10am and crossing times are short (under 20 minutes from Ikaría). Ferries pull into Foúrni's harbour, a lively place of working fishermen who mingle with visitors and local families going about their daily business. Promenade cafés offer the chance of a mid-morning coffee and snack. From here, head into Foúrni town, which centres around its main square, linked to the harbour by a single tree-lined street. Take time to admire the traditional Eastern Aegean architecture and shop along the agorá, known locally as the "shopping mile". Be sure to stop for lunch in one of the fish tavernas for which Foúrni is famous.

Afternoon

After lunch, take a short walk to **Kambí**, famous for its windmills, and **Psilí Ámmos**, where there are some fine beaches and bays to explore. Alternatively, head north by taxi or boat to the small, sleepy village of **Chrisomiliá**, where life has changed little in many decades, before heading back to the harbour for your return crossing.

Left **Mural detail, Moní Moúndon** Centre **Winnowing mastic, Olýmbi** Right **Painted house, Pýrgi**

Sights: Híos

1 Híos Town
With a history that has seen prosperity under the Genoese, a massacre by the Ottomans and huge earthquake destruction, Híos is now an attractive and modern capital. ☙ Map L5

2 Avgónyma
One of the most attractive hillside villages on the island, Avgónyma has elegantly restored houses and is home to many Greek-Americans. ☙ Map K5

3 Moní Moúndon
This 16th-century monastery is known for its well-preserved murals, including the famous Salvation of Souls on the Ladder. It is only open to the public for its festival every 29 August. ☙ Map K4

4 Volissós
This picturesque village, with restored stone houses arranged in amphitheatre-fashion around a mountain, is dominated by a ruined Byzantine castle. ☙ Map K4

5 Kámbos
Wealthy merchants and nobles once had summer mansions in Kámbos, before Híos' destruction in 1822. Citrus groves surround this popular area. ☙ Map L5

6 Vrontádos
Known for its landmark windmills, this village hugs the shore of a bay. Fishing boats line its quayside. Sights include the Moní Agíou Stefánou monastery. ☙ Map L5

7 Mastic Villages
Known as mastihohória or "mastic villages", these 20 or so fortified settlements, including Mestá, Pýrgi and Olýmbi, are so called due to the lucrative mastic gum industry. ☙ Map K6

8 Mestá
Mesta has one of the finest examples of the defensive architecture that characterizes the mastic villages. Its outer stone buildings join to create a wall. Its castle and churches are also worth visiting. ☙ Map K6

9 Pýrgi
Named after a medieval tower that stands here, the village of Pýrgi is best known for its painted houses. Façades are decorated with the grey and white geometric pattern known as xystá. ☙ Map K6

10 Olýmbi
With its fortress-like layout – whereby the whole village is contained within a wall, the only entrance being the Kato Porta watchtower – Olýmbi is a fine medieval monument. ☙ Map K6

Price Categories

For a three-course meal for one with half a bottle of wine (or equivalent meal), taxes and extra charges.	€ under €20
	€€ €20–€30
	€€€ €30–€40
	€€€€ €40–€50
	€€€€€ over €50

ft **To Tavernaki tou Tassou, Híos Town** Right **Chotsas Taverna, Híos Town**

10 Places to Eat and Drink: Híos

1 Mavrokordatiko Restaurant
oused in a beautifully restored 8th-century stone building, this staurant regularly hosts special vents, such as Greek nights. ine on Greek and international shes in the courtyard or inside. 1 Mitaráki, Kámbos • Map L5 22710 32900 • €€

2 Pýrgos Restaurant
One of the oldest tavernas Avgónyma, this family-run stablishment serves traditional shes. Try the spinach balls with reek salad. ◊ Avgónyma • Map K5 22710 42175 • €€

3 To Apomero
Dine at To Apomero for Greek shes with a modern twist. The cation offers fabulous views cross the Aegean to the Turkish oast. It gets busy at weekends. Kambos, Híos Town • Map L5 • 22710 9675 • €€

4 Chotsas Taverna
Known for the wine and úzo made by the proprietor, hotsas serves a choice of rilled and oven-cooked dishes. Georgíou Kondíou 3, Híos Town Map L5 • 22710 42787 • €€

5 Tzivaeri
The tempting dishes at this own centre ouzerí include fish r meat mezédes and shrimp ie. Oúzo and local wines are erved. ◊ 13 Neórion Street, Híos Town Map L5 • 22710 43559 • €€

6 Mesaionas Taverna
Afélia (pork) and kléftiko (lamb) are just two of the delicious oven-cooked dishes on the menu at this popular taverna. Wine is local and includes souma, which is produced in the village. ◊ Mestá • Map K6 • 22710 76050 • €€

7 Roussiko
Located in a wonderful stone building in the small village of Thymiana, Roussiko serves classic Greek food on a rooftop terrace. The speciality is lamb or pork kotsi (a shank cut). ◊ Thymiana • Map L5 • 22710 33352 • €€

8 Makellos
Makellos is a traditional taverna best known for its herísia (made by hand) dishes. These include dolmadákia or dolmádes (vine leaves stuffed with currants and rice) and macaroni. ◊ Pityós, central Híos • Map L5 • 22720 23364 • €€

9 Byzantio
The classic Greek dishes at Byzantio include plenty of vegetarian options. Try the beans, okra and aubergine cooked in oil. ◊ Afon Ralli Central Market, Híos Town • Map L5 • 22710 41035 • €€

10 To Tavernaki tou Tassou
With its brightly painted decor and tables overlooking the bay, this seafront taverna is popular with locals and visitors. Its menu features a selection of seafood. ◊ Livánou 8, Híos Town • Map L5 • 22710 27542 • €€

Left **Church interior, Pétra** Centre **Míthymna harbour** Right **Rooftop view of Agiásos**

🔟 Sights: Lésvos

1 Mytilíni Town
The capital of Lésvos, Mytilíni has a multicultural feel, with a selection of fine international restaurants, waterfront bars, museums, *belle époque* churches and Venetian and Ottoman mansions. ◈ *Map S2*

2 Míthymna (Mólyvos)
Dominated by its Byzantine castle, this village, locally known as Mólyvos, is characterized by its colourful stone houses and harbour. Míthymna is believed to be the birthplace of ancient poet Arion. ◈ *Map R1*

3 Moní Ypsiloú
Founded in the 12th century, this sprawling monastery sits on top of an extinct volcano, Mt Órdymnos. It has a superb collection of religious icons and an intricate wood ceiling in its *katholikon* (main church). ◈ *Map Q2*

4 Agiásos
Famous as a centre for pottery (still practiced today), this picturesque village is a labyrinth of tiny lanes lined with stone houses. Its church dates from the 12th century. ◈ *Map R2*

5 Sykaminiá
In this village of red and white houses, perched on Mt Lepétymnos' slopes, life revolves around its harbour. Strátis Myrivílis, author of the novel *The Mermaid Madonna*, which is set on Lésvos, was born here. ◈ *Map R1*

6 Sigrí
A quiet harbour, Sigrí boasts a petrified forest – fossils of trees buried under lava for three million years. ◈ *Map Q2*

7 Ándissa
An unspoiled village, Ándissa lies near the site of a city destroyed in 168 BC by the Romans. Life centres around its café-lined square. ◈ *Map Q2*

8 Mantamádos
This village of paved square and stone houses is famous for its pottery and a rare icon of the saint Taxiarch Archangel Michael displayed in its monastery, the Moní Taxiarchón. ◈ *Map S1*

9 Kalloní
Situated at the crossroads for routes to and from the main towns, this hillside village is famous for its sardines. ◈ *Map R.*

10 Pétra
A once sleepy village, Pétra is becoming a popular holiday spot due to its wide beach and shallow water. A volcanic monolith dominates its shore. ◈ *Map F*

The Captain's Table, Míthymna

Price Categories

For a three-course meal for one with half a bottle of wine (or equivalent meal), taxes and extra charges.

€ under €20
€€ €20–€30
€€€ €30–€40
€€€€ €40–€50
€€€€€ over €50

10 Places to Eat and Drink: Lésvos

1 Taverna Vafios

Greek gourmet-style dishes and the Lésvian dish of baked stuffed lamb with garlic can be enjoyed at this rural taverna. Produce is from its own gardens. ⊗ *Oikismós Vafiós, Vafiós • Map R1* • *22530 71752 • €€€*

2 Ramona Restaurant

The tables at the Ramona could not be closer to the sea, providing a great ambiance for enjoying traditional Greek cuisine and local wines. ⊗ *Mólyvos beach, Míthymna (Mólyvos) • Map R1* • *22530 71623 • €€*

3 Averof

One of the oldest and most traditional tavernas in Mytilíni, the Averof serves oven-baked dishes like *kléftiko* (lamb), *stifádo* (beef) and *afélia* (pork). It is inexpensive and ideal for a quick lunch. ⊗ *Ermoú Street, Mytilíni Town* • *Map S2 • 22510 22180 • €€*

4 Cavo d'Oro

The speciality of this super fish restaurant, close to where fishing boats unload their daily catch, is fish *mezédes*. ⊗ *Harbourside, Sigrí • Map Q2 • 22530 54221 • €€*

5 Thalassa

Located in a prime position on Petra's main promenade, Thalassa specializes in seafood dishes. The shrimp *saganáki (see p50)* is an unusual twist on a Greek favourite. ⊗ *Promenade, Petra, Lésvos • Map R1 • 22530 41366 • €€*

6 Aphrodite Hotel Restaurant

Open to non-residents, this hotel eatery is known for its "all-you-can-eat" buffet of traditional Greek and Lésvian dishes. Music is played most nights, while drinks comprise local wines and cocktails. ⊗ *Vaterá, near Mytilíni Town* • *Map S2 • 22520 61288 • €€*

7 Orizontas Café Restaurant

This restaurant, characterized by its colourful linens, cobbled terrace and palm trees, is right by the beach. It serves light snacks, traditional Greek meals and drinks. ⊗ *Mólyvos beach, Míthymna (Mólyvos) • Map R1 • 22530 71861 • €€*

8 Navagio Restaurant

Overlooking the sea, this elegant venue has a coffee house on the first floor and a restaurant on the second floor, where gourmet-style Greek dishes are served. It offers a fine wine list. ⊗ *Sappho Square, Mytilíni Town • Map S2 • 22510 21310 • €€€*

9 The Captain's Table

Fish features prominently on the menu at this village taverna. It is as popular with locals as it is with visitors. ⊗ *Míthymna (Mólyvos)* • *Map R1 • 22530 71241 • €€*

10 Triena Café Restaurant

Enjoy breakfast or lunch at this trendy café, along with romantic evening meals, looking out over the harbour. ⊗ *Mólyvos beach • Map R1 • 22530 71350 • €€*

Kokkári beach, Sámos

Islands, Bays and Beaches

Elínda Beach, Híos
This is a wonderful secluded beach of fine, golden sand and crystal-clear water within a deep bay. The surrounding hills protect the bay from strong winds. *West coast, near Anávatos • Map K5*

Mávros Gialós, Híos
Also known as Mávra Vólia, this beach lines a bay of turquoise waters. It has black pebbles, which were created by the lava of a nearby volcano and worn smooth by the sea over time. *South coast, near Emboreiós • Map K6*

Kokkári Beach, Sámos
Catching strong winds, Kokkári is one of the islands' best beaches for windsurfing. The pebbled beach lies next to a tourist resort, which has a variety of amenities. *North coast • Map F4*

Mykáli Beach, Sámos
Popular with locals, who can often be seen enjoying a picnic here, this white-pebble beach is one of the longest along this coastline. Mykáli beach is protected from the wind and has no amenities. *Southeast coast, near Psilí Ámmos • Map F4*

Foúrni Island
Once a haunt of pirates, this fishing island has some deep, protected bays, sheer cliffs and long sandy beaches. Its harbour is a bustling place, full of boats, tavernas, locals and visitors (see p119).

Alykí Bay, Thássos
Widely regarded as one of the most beautiful harbours in the Greek Islands, this richly forested bay of pine and olive trees has two sandy beaches, clear waters and unusual rock formations. *Southeast coast • Map E1*

Inoússes Island
Daily life on this charming, unspoilt island centres around its harbour, where a small museum tells the story of its maritime history. The landscape is dotted with olive groves and stone villages. *East of Híos • Map L4*

Psará Island
This unspoilt island is best known for the heroic but bloody stand it took against the Ottoman invasion of 1824. It is celebrated every year on 22 June. *Off Híos • Map E3*

Karfás Beach, Híos
The liveliest tourist beach on the island, Karfás has fine sand, gentle waters and amenities that include sunbeds, tropical-style umbrellas and nearby bars and cafés. Watersports are available *East coast, near Híos Town • Map L5*

Ánaxos Beach, Lésvos
Looking across the bay towards Mólyvos, this lively beach is long, sandy and lined with bars and tavernas. There are resorts nearby, making it popular with tourists. *Pétra • Map R1*

Price Categories

For a three-course
meal for one with half
a bottle of wine (or
equivalent meal), taxes
and extra charges.

€ under €20
€€ €20–€30
€€€ €30–€40
€€€€ €40–€50
€€€€€ over €50

Left **Klimataria Restaurant, Samothráki** Right **O Glaros, Límnos**

⁙⁰ Restaurants

1 Irodion Garden, Sámos
Housed in a stylish Neo-Classical villa, this restaurant has several terraces for alfresco dining. There's a broad menu with some unusual specials, such as spare ribs. ◈ *Aristarxou 34 • Map F4 • 22730 61642 • €€*

2 Marina Restaurant, Sámos
Enjoy local dishes such as stuffed *kalamári*, *stifádo* and *pastítsio (see pp50–51)* at this popular restaurant. You can dine on the terrace overlooking the gardens. ◈ *Potámi, Kokkári • Map F4 • 22730 92692 • €€*

3 Poseidon, Sámos
With tables set on a terrace right by the waterside and a menu of freshly caught fish, this is one of the most popular restaurants on the island. ◈ *Harbourside, Kokkári • Map F4 • 22730 61678 • €€*

4 O Glaros, Límnos
Known as much for its great views of the *kástro* (castle) as its super menu, this is a great place to enjoy fish. Try the lobster with spaghetti. ◈ *Harbourside, Mýrina Town • Map E1 • 22540 22220 • €€*

5 Klimataria Restaurant, Samothráki
Famous for its speciality dish, *gianiótiko* (baked pork with potato and eggs), this restaurant has a traditional and elegant feel. Wines and music are Greek. ◈ *Seafront, Hóra • Map E1 • 25510 41535 • €€*

6 Karnagio Taverna, Thássos
This *ouzerí*, built into rock on the seafront, has tables on the beach and a roof terrace with great views. Soft music and light Greek meals help make this a memorable place. ◈ *Seafront Liménas • Map E1 • 25930 23170 • €€€*

7 Anna's Restaurant, Ikaría
Overlooking the sea, this small fish restaurant has a good reputation for its imaginative menu. Be sure to try its lobster with lemon and stuffed *kalamári*. ◈ *Nas • Map F4 • 06932 149155 •€€*

8 Karydies, Samothráki
Delicious baked dishes such as *kléftiko (see p50)* with bread, are cooked in traditional wood ovens at this popular taverna. ◈ *Ano Meria 21 • Map E1 • 25510 98266•€€*

9 Taverna Steki, Thássos
Enjoy international cuisine as well as local Greek dishes made by the owner, Katerina, at this family-run taverna. Most of the vegetables come straight from her garden. ◈ *Potamiá • Map E1 • 25930 61009 • €€*

10 Tavern Zorbas, Thássos
Close to the village centre and the beach, this traditional taverna serves a wide range of grills, local dishes like *afélia* (pork), *souvláki (see p50)* and desserts. Local wines and beers are a speciality. ◈ *Skála Prínou • Map E1 • 25930 71483 • €€*

Left **Old truck, Évvia** Centre **Waterfront market, Évvia** Right **View of Skýros Town**

The Sporádes and Évvia

THE SPORÁDES, GREEK FOR "SCATTERED", *dot the Aegean Sea in an irregular fashion. Although some isles were inhabited in antiquity, they only really came to the fore in modern times as a haunt of the rich and famous. There are 24 islands, of which four are inhabited. These are Skiáthos, which became legendary in the 1960s for the stories of celebrities seen partying on expensive yachts, the holiday island of Skópelos and the quieter Skýros and Alónissos. All four islands are famous for their beaches and vineyards. Huge and unspoiled, Évvia has a long maritime history. In fact, its ports were among Greece's wealthiest in the 19th century.*

 Sights

1 Skiáthos	6 Patitíri
2 Skiáthos Town	7 Skýros
3 Skópelos	8 Skýros Town
4 Skópelos Town	9 Évvia
5 Alónissos	10 Peristéra

Left **Skópelos port** Right **Beach sign, Skiáthos**

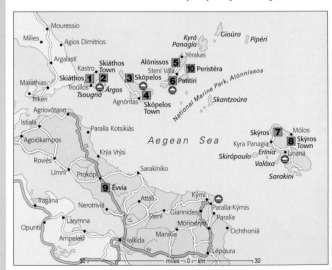

Preceding pages **Skópelos Town**

Picturesque Skiáthos Town

Skiáthos

The island's 44 km (30 mile) coast is lined, almost exclusively, with soft sandy beaches that have made it a popular holiday destination. The most famous beach is Koukounariés, where luxury yachts are moored. A good range of hotels, restaurants and bars has steadily grown to cater to visitors, especially in the south, but despite this the Skiáthos has managed to retain its rural charm. Inland, it has forests of pine, olive groves and mountains, with rural villages, churches and deserted monasteries dotting the landscape. ◈ Map M1

Skiáthos Town

The main port and capital of Skiáthos island, this bustling place still retains a timeless quality. Its restaurants and bars have somehow managed to blend in with their surroundings of red-roofed stone buildings, churches, cobbled lanes and courtyards. The town's harbour, once an important shipbuilding centre, lies between two hills. At its entrance is a pine-covered peninsula. The skyline of Skiáthos Town is dominated by churches, including the island's Cathedral of Trión Lerarchón. Be sure to see the old quarter of Limniá, with its period merchants' houses. ◈ Map M1

Skópelos

Lush pine forests cover the island's two peaks, Délfi and Paloúki, and valleys of citrus groves, orchards and endless vineyards yield the delicious fruits and wines the island is famous for. Skópelos has many bays and fabulous sandy beaches, including the stunning beach of Limnonári. The main communities are located in Skópelos Town, Glóssa and the small port of Agnóndas. There are also hamlets with enchanting farmhouses known as *kalývia*. ◈ Map M1

Skópelos Town

The capital of Skópelos and its main port, Skópelos Town lies in a deep bay with traditional mansions and more than a hundred churches built in amphitheatre style. They, and the town's cobbled lanes, ascend to a hilltop *kástro* (fortress). The view from this Venetian castle is spectacular. The town is also the commercial hub of the island, its fishing harbour a hive of activity. It is known for having some of the best fish restaurants on the island. ◈ Map M1

Wild flowers in a grove, Skópelos

Aléxandros Papadiamántis
One of Greece's most famous writers, Aléxandros Papadiamántis (1851–1911) was born on Skiáthos. His works, written in the country's then official language of Katharevousa, feature Skiáthos as their backdrop. They include the acclaimed *The Murderess* and the serialized *Merchants of the Nations*. He died a recluse on the island.

Peaceful beach, Skýros

5 Alónissos
Alónissos, the third largest of the Sporádes, is relatively untouched by tourism. Its 3,000 or so residents live in or around Patitíri and Paleá Alónissos, with only a handful living in the more rugged interior. Life here revolves around farming and working the vineyards. The island is known for its marine park, which offers protection to rare and endangered animal species, including the monk seal *(see p45)*. The isle's craggy limestone coastline and nearby islets are a natural habitat for the seal. 🔊 *Map N1*

6 Patitíri
Patitíri is the capital and main port of Alónissos, replacing the nearby old capital, known as Hóra. Its picturesque lanes are lined with traditional white houses that have red roofs and courtyards. Patitíri was built after Hóra was destroyed in the 1965 earthquake. The town radiates

Boats moored in Patitíri harbour

from the harbour, where tavernas line the seafront, fishing and pleasure craft bob in the water and ferries leave from the quayside to nearby islands. 🔊 *Map N1*

7 Skýros
A dramatic rock formation, its slopes covered in white houses, greets you on approaching Skýros. The largest of the Sporádes, the Island has mythological links to Achilles and King Theseus. It was colonized by Athenians, conquered by Macedonians and Romans and used as a place of exile in Byzantine times. It is now famous for its own pony breed, the Skýros pony, and for furniture craftsmanship. It is a traditional, peaceful haven. 🔊 *Map P2*

8 Skýros Town
Crowned by a part-Byzantine part-Venetian fortress, known as the Castle of Lykomedes, which stands on the site of an ancient acropolis, Skýros Town is one of the prettiest capitals in the Sporádes. The town's arched lanes lined with white-washed cube houses bear a striking simiarity to those seen in Cycladic villages. Around the town are chapels and churches, some with blue painted domes. There are museums, including the Archaeological Museum,

The Skýros pony, considered endangered, is believed to have been brought to the island of Skýros in the 8th century BC.

where displays from Neolithic times can be seen.
⊗ *Map P2 • Archaeological Museum: Platía Brooke; 22220 91327; open 8am–3pm Tue–Sun; adm*

9 Évvia

The fascinating archaeological site of Erétria, one of the city-states of ancient Évvia, is a must for visitors to the island. The other was Chalcis, which stood on the site of the island's modern capital, Halkída. Other places to visit include the scenic village of Prokópi and the ports of Kárystos and Kými, along with the largest spa town in Greece, Loutrá Edipsoú *(see pp28–9)*.

Port town of Kárystos, Évvia

10 Peristéra

Peristéra is one of several smaller isles and islets that lie off Alónissos, and like Skantzoúra, Pipéri and Gioúra, which are home to rare wildlife, it is now uninhabited by humans. A rugged place separated from Alónissos by just two narrow stretches of water, it is popular with sailing enthusiasts who anchor off its shores. It has sandy beaches, plus the remains of an old castle to explore.
⊗ *Map N1*

Day Trip to Alónissos

Morning

🕐 A great day out from **Skiáthos** or **Skópelos** is to take a ferry or hydrofoil to nearby **Alónissos**. Both the scenery and the pace of life are quite different here. Departure times vary according to the day and season, so check in advance the destination boards on the quayside marked to **Patitíri**, Alónissos. Most boats depart from 9:30 to 10:30am, so head for the quayside after a good breakfast. Boats leave from **Skiáthos Town** and take from 50 minutes to more than 2 hours to reach Patitíri, depending on the kind of boat. From Skópelos the journey takes only around 25 minutes.

On board the boat, enjoy the coastal scenery before disembarking at Patitíri. Check the time of your return ferry or hydrofoil as timetables do change. At Patitíri you can enjoy coffee or an early lunch before exploring the island. You can take a bus (timetables at the stop opposite the quay), or hire a taxi, car or bike. There are beach-hopping water taxis available too.

Afternoon

After lunch explore the port town of Patitíri before heading west to the old capital, **Paleá Alónissos**, perched precariously on a clifftop. Head north to the seaside village of **Steni Vála**, where you can enjoy a bite to eat at one of its tavernas. From here a road snakes towards the remote village of **Yérakas** *(see p134)*. Retrace your steps back to Patitíri for your return journey.

Left **Koukounariés beach, Skiáthos** Right **Stáfylos beach, Skópelos**

Best of the Rest

1 Megáli Ámmos Beach, Skiáthos

This fine sandy beach stretches around a large bay and lies adjacent to hotels, restaurants and bars. Amenities include sun beds, umbrellas and watersports. ◈ *East coast, Skiáthos Town • Map M1*

2 Koliós Beach, Skiáthos

Popular with watersports enthusiasts, Koliós is a long sandy beach that sweeps around a semi-circular bay. Sailing and paragliding are on offer. ◈ *South coast • Map M1*

3 Troúlos Beach, Skiáthos

This sandy beach has a gentle slope into the sea, making it ideal for families, while more secluded coves can be found around the headlands on either side. It has a choice of tavernas and bars. ◈ *South coast • Map M1*

4 Koukounariés Beach, Skiáthos

With its pine forest backdrop and fine white sands, this beach is one of the most beautiful natural bays in Greece. A popular holiday spot, it has restaurants and hotels nearby. ◈ *South coast • Map M1*

5 Limnonári Beach, Skópelos

Known for its white beach of tiny pebbles and its clear blue water, Limnonári is surrounded by pine forest and is one of the prettiest beaches on Skópelos. It has its own taverna. ◈ *South coast • Map M2*

6 Stáfylos Beach, Skópelos

This beach is named after the ancient Cretan king who, according to Greek mythology, landed here to found a colony on Skópelos. The picturesque Stáfylos village is nearby. ◈ *Southeast coast • Map M2*

7 Stení Vála, Alónissos

The small coastal village of Stení Vála is a popular holiday spot, with traditional tavernas and a handful of hotels. Nevertheless, its beaches, including picturesque Glýfa, remain uncrowded. ◈ *East coast • Map N1*

8 Mólos Resort, Skýros

Scenic Mólos and its neighbour Magaziá are two of the holiday resorts on Skýros. Their beaches, including sandy Mólos and more tranquil and natural Karefloú, are the closest to Skýros Town. ◈ *East coast • Map P2*

9 Pouriá, Skýros

Pouriá is a traditional coastal village known for the unusual rock formations that lie just off its shoreline. A haven for snorkellers, fish can be seen swimming through the sea-worn arches. ◈ *East coast • Map P2*

10 Yérakas, Alónissos

This small village lies on the largely undeveloped northern-most tip of the island. Its natural beaches are best known as a refuge for the protected monk seal. ◈ *North coast • Map N1*

Left **Sweets at Zaniakos Bakery, Évvia** Centre **Galerie Varsakis, Skiáthos** Right **Colourful ceramics**

🔟 Places to Shop

1 Rodios, Skópelos
This shop sells everything from antique furniture and local artifacts to works of art, ceramics from the island's villages and local handicrafts such as woven rugs and embroidered linen. ❧ *Skópelos Town • Map M1 • 24240 22924*

2 Karamouza, Évvia
Jewellery with an emphasis on modern design, including some unusual and witty pieces, can be found here, as well as ornaments and souvenirs. ❧ *Kotsika 2, Kárystos • Map E3 • 22240 26938*

3 Galerie Varsakis, Skiáthos
This old and respected art and antiques shop displays icons, embroidery, textiles and jewellery. The basement resembles a traditional kitchen, with antique pots. ❧ *Papadiamánti Street, Skiáthos Town • Map M1 • 24270 22255*

4 Gray Gallery, Skópelos
With its displays of acrylic paintings, watercolours and prints, this gallery is a good place to buy souvenirs. It has a fine selection of contemporary works, too. ❧ *Skópelos Town • Map M1 • 24240 23943*

5 Monogramma, Skópelos
From the jars of Skópelos conifer and wild flower honey to textiles, beads and ceramics in bold colours, this shop near the harbour is a great place to find a gift. ❧ *Élios • Map M1 • 24240 34081*

6 Archipelagos Gallery, Skiáthos
Housed in a traditional building, this gallery specializes in Greek folk art, woodcarvings, icons and ceramics, along with antique and modern gold and silver jewellery. ❧ *Papadiamánti Street, Skiáthos Town • Map M1 • 24270 22585*

7 Zaniakos Bakery, Évvia
Zaniakos bakes its own cakes, pastries – such as the sweet baklava – and confectionery. Do try its *glyká koutalioú* (candied fruit). ❧ *Kárystos • Map E3 • 22240 24456*

8 Símos Jewellery, Skiáthos
This elegant shop specializes in 14- and 18-carat yellow and white gold jewellery in modern or traditional designs. Many of the pieces are made by the owner. ❧ *Papadiamánti Street, Skiáthos Town • Map M1 • 24270 23777*

9 Sentefi Jewellery, Skópelos
One of the best jewellery shops on Skópelos, Sentefi offers gold and silver pieces in contemporary and traditional designs, along with watches and gifts. ❧ *Skópelos Town • Map M1 • 24240 22523*

10 Manos Ceramics, Skýros
This super shop in the heart of town has a display of vases, plates and bowls in various colours, and in contemporary and traditional designs. ❧ *Skýros Town • Map P2 • 22220 92877*

Left **Rock and Roll Bar, Skiáthos** Centre **Oionos Blue Bar, Skópelos** Right **Platanos Bar, Skópel**

TOP 10 Bars and Cafés

1 Platanos Jazz Bar, Skópelos
With dark and elegant decor, a range of sophisticated cocktails and live music from jazz to Latin American and blues, Platanos is frequented by locals as well as visitors. ✆ Platía Plátanos, Skópelos Town • Map M1 • 24240 23661

2 Karyakis Bar Restaurant, Skópelos
A happy hour every night and great views of Skópelos Town make this a good place for evening cocktails. ✆ On the road to Agia Barbara Monastery • Map M1

3 Pillows Cocktail Bar, Skiáthos
This bar serves generous cocktails at reasonable prices. The owner, Panos, organizes music and dancing in the evenings. ✆ Old Port, Skiáthos • Map M1 •06987 411711

4 Panorama Pizza, Skiáthos
A great hilltop pizzeria where delicious pasta, handmade pizzas with varied toppings, garlic bread and speciality coffees can be enjoyed while looking out over Skiáthos Town. ✆ Kastro, Skiáthos Town • Map M1 • 69441 92066

5 Mercurious Bar, Skópelos
With a terrace overlooking the harbour, this trendy bar is known for its creative cocktails and music and cultural events. ✆ Harbourside, Skópelos Town • Map M1 • 24240 24593

6 Kavos Café Bar, Skyros
Set right on the harbourside of Linaria village, Kavos couldn't offer a better spot to linger. Enjoy local wines, cocktails and snacks on its terrace. ✆ Linaria harbour • Map P2 • 22220 93213

7 Rock and Roll Bar, Skiáthos
Known for its cushioned seating for music lovers in a courtyard overlooking the harbour, this bar plays rock, dance and Latin music. Drinks include cocktails, beer and local spirits. ✆ Old Port, Skiáthos Town • Map M1 • 24270 22944

8 Eretria Village Resort, Évvia
With amenities such as bars, a café and restaurant, this popular complex also has tennis courts, swimming pool and special events. ✆ Erétria-Alivéri Road • Map L • 22290 41000

9 Nikos Café-Bar, Skiáthos
Serving breakfast, a grill and salad lunch and an evening menu of Greek classics, Nikos has a good choice of vegetarian dishes as well as a special children's menu. ✆ Papadiamánti Street, Skiátho Town • Map M1 • 24270 23430

10 Oionos Blue Bar, Skópelos
An atmospheric lounge bar With a heady mix of ethnic music jazz, blues and soul. Light meals, beer, cocktails, wine and whisky are served here. ✆ Off Platía Platano Skópelos Town • Map M1 • 69424 06136

During the winter months, some restaurants and cafés may close on certain days.

Price Categories

For a three-course	€	under €20
meal for one with half	€€	€20–€30
a bottle of wine (or	€€€	€30–€40
equivalent meal), taxes	€€€€	€40–€50
and extra charges.	€€€€€	over €50

Left **Windmill Restaurant, Skiáthos**

10 Restaurants

1 Garden Restaurant Alexander, Skópelos
Located in the main square, this restaurant is known for its garden. Enjoy a meal of classic local dishes and wine, while listening to Greek music. ◈ Skópelos Town • Map M1 • 24240 22324 • €€€

2 Astron, Évvia
This popular restaurant serves seafood, local meat and vegetarian dishes and home-made desserts and offers wines from around the world. ◈ Limni • Map D2 • 22270 31487 • €€€

3 Infinity Blue Restaurant, Skiáthos
Swordfish, sea bream and lobster are some of the seafood dishes offered at this elegant restaurant. Classic Greek starters, mains, desserts and more than 50 wines add to the experience. ◈ Harbourside, Koliós • Map M1 • 24270 49750 • €€€€

4 Tavern Glystéri, Skópelos
This taverna serves cool drinks, local dishes and flavoured saganáki (fried cheese). ◈ Glystéri beach, near Skópelos Town • Map M1 • 69443 54705 • €€

5 Windmill Restaurant, Skiáthos
Housed in a restored 19th-century windmill, this romantic restaurant serves fine local dishes on its terraces overlooking the harbour. ◈ Harbourside, Skiáthos Town • Map M1 • 24270 24550 • €€€€

6 Korali Restaurant, Skópelos
This beachside taverna has a magical setting and its menu is classic Greek. Mains include afélia and kléftiko (see pp50–51). ◈ Agnóndas • Map M1 • 24240 22407 • €€

7 Moschokarydo, Évvia
This traditional taverna is known for its mezédes, along with its well-presented fish dishes. Dine on the terrace overlooking the bay. ◈ Harbourside, Karystos • Map E3 • 22240 22441 • €€€

8 Agnanti Restaurant, Skópelos
Founded in 1953 and one of the best known tavernas in town, Agnanti serves classic Greek dishes with a contemporary twist, using fresh and organic produce. ◈ Glóssa • Map M1 • 24240 33606 • €€€

9 Anemos Restaurant, Skiáthos
The harbour view is spectacular from here, especially at night. The oldest taverna in town, Anemos offers a Greek menu with fine local wines. ◈ Harbourside, Skiáthos Town • Map M1 • 24270 21003 • €€€€

10 Restaurant Terpsis, Skópelos
Meaning "pleasure" in Greek, Terpsis was founded in 1965 and is famous for its spicy chicken stuffed with walnuts from the trees in its garden. Greek music plays as you dine. ◈ Stáfylos beach • Map M1 • 24240 22053 • €€€

Left **Banana beach, Skiáthos** Right **Velanió beach, Skópelos**

TOP 10 Best Beaches

Mandráki beach, Skiáthos

1 Banana Beach, Skiáthos
Sweeping around a large bay, this beach has amenities that include tavernas and watersports. A nudist beach, Little Banana, lies behind the rocks at one end. ✆ *South coast, near Koukounariés • Map M1*

2 Mandráki Beach, Skiáthos
This beach lies in a series of secluded coves known as Eliá, Mandráki and Angistrós bays. It is a very isolated spot. ✆ *West coast, near Mandráki • Map M1*

3 Lalária Beach, Skiáthos
Known for its unusual rock formations, sheer white cliffs and fine white sand, this beautiful beach can be reached only by boat. ✆ *North coast • Map M1*

4 Adrína Beach, Skópelos
Head along the path from Pánormos village or by boat to get to this deserted shingle beach, which is enclosed by a pine forest. ✆ *Adina, Pánormos • Map M1*

5 Glystéri Beach, Skópelos
This fine shingle beach lies in a small cove off a bay that protects it from strong winds. It

is good for swimming and there are tavernas here. ✆ *North coast near Skópelos Town • Map M1*

6 Velanió Beach, Skópelos
A beach of fine golden sand lapped by crystal-clear waters, Velanió is reached by a sign-posted path. Its beauty is that it is undeveloped and secluded. It is an official nudist beach. ✆ *Southeast coast, near Stáfylos • Map M.*

7 Yérakas Beach, Alónissos
This often desolate beach is home to a research centre of the Hellenic Society for the Study and Protection of the Monk Seal. ✆ *North coast • Map N1*

8 Ágios Pétros Beach, Skýros
A pretty, rocky beach surrounde by cedar trees, Ágios Pétros lies in a small bay. It is a popular sailing spot with locals. ✆ *Atsítsa, north coast • Map P2*

9 Palamári Beach, Skýros
This beach is located next to the remains of the ancient town of Palamári. Quiet and peaceful, it has golden sand, clear water and a few sleepy tavernas nearby. ✆ *North coast • Map P2*

10 Ochthoniá Beach, Évvia
Usually deserted, this wild and exposed beach lies near the rocky cliffs, rich vegetation and windswept trees of Cape Ochthoniá. ✆ *Northeast coast • Map N3*

Left **Boats anchored by Kyrá Panagía island** Right **Boat moored at Árgos island**

Islands and Islets

Peristéra Island
This small island is one of several that lie off Alónissos and are part of the Sporádes Marine Park. Its sandy coves attract the endangered monk seal *(see p45)*. ✎ *Off Alónissos • Map N1*

Valáxa Island
This uninhabited island and its neighbouring Skyrópoulo and Erínia islets attract yachtsmen because of their sheltered coves. They are accessible by boat from Péfkos. ✎ *Off Skýros • Map P2*

Petáli Island
This rugged island is said to have been owned by royalty and several celebrities, including the Spanish painter Pablo Picasso, whose house still stands in the forest near the beach. ✎ *Off Évvia • Map M2*

Dýo Adélfia
The twin islets of Mikró and Megálo Adélfia are known for their scuba-diving spots. However, the sport is strictly controlled as the islets lie in the Sporádes Marine Park. ✎ *Near Alónissos • Map N1*

Pipéri Island
Covered by pine forest, this island lies in the Sporádes Marine Park. It is home to rare flora and fauna, including the endangered Eleonora's falcon *(see p45)*. Disembarking here is prohibited, but you can view the wildlife from a boat. ✎ *Near Alónissos • Map P1*

Skantzoúra
This small archipelago of six islets is known for its beautiful cedars and its sacred monastery, the Moní Evangelístria, which lies on its main island. Hellenistic remains suggest ancient occupation. ✎ *Near Alónissos • Map N2*

Kyrá Panagía Island
This tiny island has the remains of a settlement, which is believed to be ancient Alónissos. Today there are just a handful of residents, who have built a community administered from Alónissos. ✎ *Off Alónissos • Map N1*

Gioúra Island
Uninhabited and part of the Sporádes Marine Park, this small, rugged island has archaeological remains that suggest it was inhabited as far back as Neolithic times. ✎ *Off Alónissos • Map N1*

Árgos Island
Árgos can only be reached by private boat and is a popular anchorage for yachts sailing around the Sporádes. The views of Skiáthos Town from the island's shores are outstanding. ✎ *Off Skiáthos • Map M1*

Tsougriá Island
Along with its islet, Tsougriáki, this richly forested island has a couple of sandy beaches within protected bays and is a popular day-trip destination for visitors staying in Skiáthos. ✎ *Off Skiáthos • Map M2*

Left **Temple of Poseidon's ruins** Centre **Cathedral, Égina Town** Right **View of Égina from Póros**

The Argo-Saronic Islands

COMPRISING THE MAIN ISLANDS of Égina, Salamína, Póros, Spétses and Ýdra, with the traditionally Ionian Kýthira further south, the Argo-Saronics stretch some 200 km (125 miles) from Piraeus in Athens to the Peloponnese coast. Both Égina and Salamína were famous for their maritime activities, while Póros and Spétses are better known for their bustling modern capitals, ceramics and pine forests. Ýdra is cosmopolitan and remote Kýthira is one of the candidates for the birthplace of Aphrodite, the goddess of love. Smaller islets, such as Angístri, Moní, Trikéri and Spetsopoúla beg to be explored. The archipelago has a refined feel in many of its towns, and yet by contrast, small sailing caïques and mules form the only means of transport on some islands.

Castle overlooking Kýthira town

🔟 Sights

1. Égina
2. Angistri
3. Salamína
4. Moní Faneroménis, Salamína
5. Póros
6. Temple of Poseidon, Póros
7. Spétses
8. Ýdra
9. Ýdra Town
10. Kýthira

Temple of Aphaia, Égina

Égina
1 Famous as the place where the world's first ever coins were minted in 700 BC and home to the impressive Temple of Aphaia *(see pp26–7)*, Égina is a pine-covered island with picturesque bays and beaches. Égina Town, its capital, hugs a natural harbour and multiple ferries from Athens arrive here daily. The island has enjoyed a lively past and much prosperity as a major maritime trading centre. Today, life quietly revolves around the production of pistachio nuts, considered the best in Greece. ◎ *Map L1*

Angístri
2 With a timeless charm and verdant landscape of pine trees, Angístri lies a short distance to the southwest of Égina and is a popular summer haunt of Athenian weekenders. Its main port is Skála, where there are a handful of hotels and restaurants, and the island's best beach, which runs along the coast from its church. In the past, the island enjoyed reflected glory and wealth from Égina, and excavations at the sites of Megarítissa, Apónissos and ancient Metochí have revealed many valuable treasures. ◎ *Map J2*

Salamína
3 The largest of the Saronic Gulf islands and separated from mainland Greece by a 2 km- (1.3 mile-) wide strait, crescent-shaped Salamína is most famous for being the site of the historic Battle of Salamis in 480 BC. The battle between the victorious Greek fleet and the Persian Empire was fought in the strait, with the Salaminians playing a key role. The island's capital, Salamína Town, lies in a deep bay to the west while Ágios Nikólaos is its most popular holiday spot. To the north is the base of the Hellenic Navy. The island is the legendary birthplace of the god Ajax. ◎ *Map D3*

Moní Faneroménis, Salamína
4 The 17th-century Moní Faneroménis is located on the north coast of Salamína on the spot where a preserved 18th-century icon, known as the Noefaneísis Panagía, was discovered by St Lauréntos. It depicts the *Last Judgement*. The monastery was used during the War of Independence (1821–9) as a hospital and refuge for women, children and Greek freedom fighters. In 1944, it was converted into a convent. Today, it is a popular attraction for visitors and the nuns host a festival every year on 23 August in honour of the Virgin Mary. ◎ *Salamína • Map D3 • 21046 81861 • Open 7am–12:30pm and 3:30pm– sunset daily • Donation*

Shrine opposite Moní Faneroménis

Ajax

A mythological Greek hero, Ajax was made famous in Homer's *Iliad* and *Odyssey*, two poems about the Trojan War. Ajax is said to have been born at Kanákia on the island of Salamína. The King of Salamis, Ajax was, according to legend, a man of great strength and a fearsome warrior, like his cousin Achilles.

Boats moored at Spétses port

5 Póros

Póros lies a short distance from Galatás in the Peloponnese and is made up of two islands: the richly forested but almost uninhabited Kalávria to the north and Sfairiá to the south. They are connected by a causeway. Its harbourside capital, Póros Town, lies on Sfairiá and despite the rapid growth of its tourism industry has managed to retain its massive charm. Tiny streets, lined with pastel-coloured 19th-century houses clinging to the hillside, give the town its character. ✎ *Map K3*

6 Temple of Poseidon, Póros

Ceramics sold in Póros

Heading inland from the Moní Zoödóchou Pigís, near the coast in the heart of Kalávria, are the ruins of the Temple of Poseidon. Believed to have been constructed around 520 BC, the structure was a refuge for Kalavrian tribes. Built in Doric style, it would originally have had 12 columns along its longer sides and 6 along its shorter sides. The site is said to have been where in 322 BC the orator Demosthenes poisoned himself rather than be captured by the Macedonians.
✎ *Kalávria • Map K3*

7 Spétses

Spétses is characterized by the scent of the pine forest that was planted in the early 1900s. The interior is dotted with holiday homes. Spétses Town, its capital, is the largest community and spreads along the eastern coastline for 2 km (1 mile). Here, life revolves around Dápia quay, where fashionable tavernas look out over the bay. The Ágios Nikólaos church and 19th-century mansions give a hint of the town's past wealth, largely made from shipbuilding. Archaeological finds suggest the island has been occupied since ancient times.
✎ *Map D4*

8 Ýdra

A once sleepy island, Ýdra rose to fame in the 1960s when two films were shot here: *Boy on a Dolphin* starring Sophia Loren and the comedy *Island of Love*. The glamour has remained ever since. Pretty whitewashed mansions belonging to artists, writers and the Athenian elite cling to the hillside, which rises steeply from the harbour. Ýdra has chic tavernas and a few beaches accessible only by yacht. Road-free, it is regarded as an exclusive holiday destination. ✎ *Map D4*

Ýdra Town

Ýdra Town, capital of Ýdra, is a charming mix of harbourside tavernas, frequented by a chic clientele, and elegant pastel-coloured homes. Built by mariners who had amassed wealth during the Napoleonic Wars by building blockades, these early 19th-century mansions, known as *archontiká*, are built of local stone. The are mostly private homes, but one mansion houses a marine academy and one a school of fine arts. Ýdra is known for the smart yachts that line its harbour. ◈ *Ýdra • Map D4*

Kýthira

Arriving on Kýthira island feels like stepping back in time. Tiny lanes flanked by dry-stone walls link dozens of hamlets with traditional blue and white homes, many showing elements of Venetian architecture. Kýthira lies south of the Peloponnese and was once governed by the Venetians and British as part of the Ionians, but is now an Argo-Saronic island. Many of its residents are returning Australian Kythirans who have, in turn, given the island a distinctive character. Its way of life is slow and the tourism low-key. ◈ *Map C5*

view of Kýthira's landscape

Day Trip from Égina to Angístri

Morning

Many ferries run between the northern Argo-Saronic islands daily, with one of the most popular day trips being between **Égina** and **Angístri**. Start your day with a good breakfast and head to the harbourside at **Égina Town**. The harbour is easy to find and big boards detail the ferry departure times. Look out for the one marked Skála, Angístri Island. The first ferry leaves at about 9:30am and then every couple of hours, but times do vary so be sure to check. Caïques also ply the waters at irregular times. The ferry crossing takes about 20 minutes. Look out for **Moní island** to your left and **Metopí islet** to your right, and then look ahead to catch your first glimpse of picturesque **Skála**. Once you have disembarked, stop for coffee before making your way to the beach. You can also hire a scooter or bike to explore the island. If you are lucky, you may be able to catch one of the infrequent buses that run from Skála to **Limenária** via the small port of **Mýlos**, all of which have tavernas for lunch.

Afternoon

On the steep hillside above Skála, **Metochí** provides a sense of the island's history and breathtaking views. Retrace your steps back to Skála in time to catch a return ferry. They leave around 5:40pm, but check as times can vary. Arriving back in Égina you can enjoy a delicious evening meal at one of the harbourside restaurants.

Left **Kamíni beach, Ýdra** Right **Fortified islet of Boúrtzi, Póros**

TOP 10 Best of the Rest

1 Sárpa Bay, Égina
With crystal-clear waters, this bay, off the road to Pérdika, is one of the capital's best. It has a café and golden sand dotted with tropical-style umbrellas. ◈ *Égina Town • Map K1*

2 Souvála, Égina
Famous for its mineral-rich springs, the once sleepy fishing village of Souvála is now Égina's second port. Ferries arrive here from Athens. It is a picturesque spot with tavernas lining its esplanade. ◈ *Near Vathý • Map L1*

3 Megalochóri, Angístri
The capital of Angístri island, Megalochóri (Mýlos) is an unspoilt coastal village of blue and white stone houses. These cluster along tiny streets that give no hint of this village's former historic importance as a key naval base. ◈ *Map J2*

4 Kamíni, Ýdra
Known as Mikró Kamíni, for its diminutive nature, this picturesque little fishing harbour has its own castle, a collection of traditional tavernas and a quiet beach. ◈ *Map D4*

5 Vlychós, Ýdra
A tiny village that revolves around its enchanting blue and white church, Vlychós has a pretty beach dotted with tropical-style sun umbrellas. A handful of tavernas and a small resort are close by. ◈ *Map D4*

6 Bísti Bay, Ýdra
Bísti bay, with its pebbly beach and safe water, is a lovely spot, especially for watersports. Kayaking, snorkelling and scuba diving trips are available. ◈ *Map D4*

7 Zogeriá Bay, Spétses
This bay, the most beautiful on Spétses, is the island's best-kept secret. It lies in a small cove surrounded by a dense, scented pine forest. Its beach is sandy and water sapphire blue. ◈ *Map L*

8 Ambelákia, Salamína
This is the oldest village on the island, and is famous as the site of the Battle of Salamis *(see p141)*. It boasts a citadel, a port and the ancient ruins of an acropolis. ◈ *Map D3*

9 Boúrtzi, Póros
A tiny fortified island, Boúrt has a chequered past. Under th rule of Basil I the Macedon (AD 812–886), it was the scene of battles against the Saracens and was later used by the Germans as a refuge during WWII. ◈ *Map K3*

10 Venetian Castles, Kýthira
Kýthira has several fortifications, including a mighty Venetian castle that stands on rocks overlooking its capital. Nearby are the ruins of the Kato Hora castle with its well-preserved Lion of St Mark statu and the Avlémonas bastion.

Left **Ceramics at Stoa, Póros** Right **Speak Out, Ýdra**

10 Places to Shop

1 Stoa, Póros
Stoa sells leather bags and belts, acrylic paintings of local scenes, statuettes and pottery pieces, many crafted by local artisans. ◎ *Póros Town beach* • *Map K3* • *22980 26761*

2 Dia Xeiros, Égina
Local crafts, including brightly coloured plaques, vases and bowls, along with holiday essentials like sunglasses, are available at this shop. ◎ *Near the harbour, Égina Town* • *Map K1* • *22970 27505*

3 Kalezis Bookshop, Égina
This attractive little bookshop, overlooking the harbour, has a wide range of novels and guides to help you around the island. It also sells Greek and international newspapers. ◎ *Harbourside, Égina Town* • *Map K1* • *22970 25956*

4 Gion, Póros
Gion stocks designer beachwear, sportswear with names like Nike and Timberland, and holiday accessories for men, women and children. ◎ *Harbour, Póros Town* • *Map K3* • *22980 24158*

5 Exantas, Salamína
This shop is a veritable Aladdin's cave of unusual souvenirs. Small items of handcrafted furniture sit alongside metal lanterns, children's toys and colourful ceramics. ◎ *Papaníkoloaou Evangélou 6* • *Map D3* • *21046 51886*

6 Anne-Marie's, Ýdra
Anne-Marie's is a supermarket-cum-gift shop where everything from local fruit and vegetables to barbecues can be purchased in addition to local treats like *glyká* confectionary. ◎ *Ýdra Town* • *Map D4* • *22980 54064*

7 Trendy Ethnic, Salamína
Colourful dresses, beachwear and sandals, along with scented candles and pretty bead necklaces are some of the items sold at this store. ◎ *Salamínas 222* • *Map D3* • *21046 50165*

8 Anchor, Égina
Easy to find on the seafront and housed in an attractive stone building, Anchor offers the chance to buy an elegant evening outfit or more casual clothing as well as accessories. ◎ *Harbourside, Égina Town* • *Map K1* • *22970 26422*

9 Koukiaris Konstantinos, Spétses
This elegant shop sells intricate gold and silver jewellery for which Spétses is well known. ◎ *Spétses Town* • *Map D4* • *22980 29467*

10 Speak Out, Ýdra
Housed in a period property along Ýdra Town's seafront, this boutique is full of eclectic fashion goods that vie for attention with its *objects d'art*. Glittery sandals and colourful dresses are among the tempting items. ◎ *Harbourside, Ýdra Town* • *Map D4* • *22980 52099*

Left **Church in Kypséli** Centre **Fisherman, Perdika harbour** Right **A villa in Agía Marína**

Sights: Égina

1 Égina Town
Neo-Classical buildings in pastel shades, often occupied by a fish taverna selling the catch of the day, line this town's hugely picturesque harbour. Fishing boats crowd its waterside, while landmarks include the ruins of the Temple of Apollo. ® *Map K1*

2 Temple of Apollo
Just one column is left of this great 6th-century BC temple built in honour of Apollo, prompting it to be known as Kolóna ("The Column"). ® *Map K1*

3 Temple of Aphaia
This well-preserved temple of goddess Aphaia is more than 2,500 years old *(see pp26–7)*.

4 Monastery of Agios Nektários
This monastery houses one of the largest Greek Orthodox cathedrals in the world. It was built in the early 1900s by the patron saint of the island, Nektários, who is buried here. ® *Map K1*

5 Pérdika
The quaint fishing harbour of Pérdika is a gem. It is lined with fish tavernas where you can sit and watch fishing vessels and yachts. Surrounded by nature, it is a walker's paradise. ® *Map K2*

6 Paleohóra
For around 1,000 years until the early 19th century, this deserted village was Égina's capital. It is said that its inhabitants were forced into slavery by pirates. Visitors can see the remains of churches here. ® *Map L1*

7 Mesagrós
Known for its ceramics, this mountain village is a popular tourist spot. It has traditional 19th century houses and the pretty church of Polítissa. ® *Map L1*

8 Kypséli
Pistachio plantations stretch along the Kypséli plateau, producing the island's biggest export. It is the fastest-growing business district of Égina. ® *Map K1*

9 Agía Marína
This cosmopolitan holiday resort has hotels, tavernas and a sandy beach. It takes its name from the little church that stands in the bay. ® *Map L1*

10 Pahiá Ráhi
This rural village on the slopes of Mt Óros is home to the Hellenic Wildlife Hospital of Égina, a refuge for sick animals. ® *Map L2* • www.ekpazp.gr

Price Categories

For a three-course meal for one with half a bottle of wine (or equivalent meal), taxes and extra charges.

€ under €20
€€ €20–€30
€€€ €30–€40
€€€€ €40–€50
€€€€€ over €50

Agora Tavern, Égina Town

Restaurants: Égina

1 Morfonios Restaurant
Serving *mezédes* of dips, local meat and fish dishes and salads, along with seafood and international cuisine like steak with fries, this resort restaurant looks out over the beach and bay. ✪ *Agía Marína • Map L1 • 22970 32312 • €€€*

2 Adonis Fish Tavern
Enjoy fresh fish dishes at this appealing taverna – the octopus cooked with tomatoes is especially good. Dine on the terrace to appreciate the views of Pérdika's harbour ✪ *Pérdika • Map K2 • 22970 61443 • €€€*

3 Babis
Nostalgic images adorn the walls of this great taverna overlooking the bay. Dine inside or on the terrace. The menu is classic Greek with a contemporary twist. ✪ *Aktí Tóti Xatzí, Égina Town • Map K1 • 22970 23594 • €€*

4 Remetzo Taverna
The delicious menu at this harbourside restaurant features octopus to start, followed by the speciality, lobster with pasta. Fine wine completes the meal. ✪ *Pérdika • Map K2 • 22970 61658 • €€€*

5 Agora Tavern
This chic little restaurant is popular with locals. Octopus, sea bream and shrimp are prominent on the menu. Try the prawns in tomato sauce. ✪ *Fish market, Égina Town • Map K1 • 22970 27308 • €€*

6 Nontas
This pretty little taverna has terraces right next to the fishing harbour. Greek dishes, along with mouthwatering seafood caught fresh that day, feature on the menu. Try the shrimps in garlic. ✪ *Pérdika • Map L1 • 22970 61233 • €€*

7 Flisvos
Known for its shellfish and fresh fish dishes, this restaurant lies on the water's edge, looking out over the bay. Its selection of wines and beers feature local brews. ✪ *Leofóros Kazantzáki, Égina Town • Map K1 • 22970 26459 • €€*

8 O Skotadis Restaurant
This seafront taverna offers an extensive selection of salads and starters, followed by meats and seafood such as anchovies, squid and sardines. Watch the boats in the bay as you dine. ✪ *Paralía Egínas, Égina Town • Map K1 • 22970 24014 • €€*

9 Plaza Café-Restaurant
Enjoy fantastic sunsets while dining at this restaurant right by the beach. There are seafood specials and a wide range of organic wines. ✪ *Kazantzaki 4, Égina Town • Map K1 •22970 26017 • €€*

10 Costantonia
A lively restaurant and bar, Costantonia offers breakfast, coffee and evening dining delicacies such as grills with homemade dips and *mezédes*. ✪ *Agía Marína • Map L1 • 22970 32192 • €€€*

Left **En Plo, Égina** Right **Yacht Club Panagakis, Égina**

Bars, Cafés and Clubs

1 Remvi, Égina
Open all day and night, and located right on the harbour, this is the place to enjoy coffee, drinks and snacks during the day and cocktails and music until the early hours. ❧ *Near the harbour, Égina Town • Map K1 • 22970 28605*

2 Big Banana, Égina
A lively café-cum-taverna with an open-air terrace, the Big Banana is open for breakfast, coffee and juices through the day, along with informal meals. ❧ *Agía Marína • Map L1 • 22970 32859*

3 Barracuda Beach Bar, Égina
Serving colourful cocktails, light snacks and American-style waffles, this beach bar is a great place for a bite. ❧ *Agía Marína • Map L1 • 22970 32095*

4 To Rodon ton Anemon, Spétses
Known as The Rose of the Winds, this sophisticated music bar has subtle lighting, stone walls and wood panelling. It serves cocktails, and guests can dance to a mix of music genres. ❧ *Paleó Limáni • Map D4 • 22980 74244*

5 En Plo, Égina
Serving waffles and crêpes with a range of beverages, this lively café is right by the harbour. Open for breakfast, lunch and informal dinners. ❧ *Harbourside, Égina Town • Map K1 • 22970 26482*

6 Club Stavento, Spétses
With its indie, garage and hip hop sounds, this lively night-club is popular with the young and trendy. DJs and live bands play into the night. ❧ *Old Harbour, Spétses Town • Map D4 • 22980 75245*

7 Inn on the Beach, Égina
This long-established café-bar on Panagitsa Beach has a beach-side terrace on which coffee, cocktails, ice creams and snacks are served. Nightly entertainment is provided by a resident DJ. ❧ *Égina Town • Map L1 • 22970 25116*

8 Mourayo Music Bar, Spétses
Housed in a 19th-century building, Mourayo has been at the heart of Spétses nightlife since 1975. Enjoy drinks and music on the large open-air terrace. ❧ *Old Harbour, Spétses Town • Map K1 • 22980 73700*

9 Yacht Club Panagakis, Égina
This stylish seafront café-bar serves coffee with sweet and savory crêpes and grills and pizzas. Its bar has an extensive cocktail menu. ❧ *Dimokratías 20, Égina Town • Map K1 • 22970 26654*

10 Dionysos Café Bar, Póros
Open all day for snacks and drinks, the Dionysos is a welcoming café-bar. R&B and the latest pop tunes are played into the night. ❧ *Póros Town beach • Map K3 • 22980 23511*

Price Categories

For a three-course
meal for one with half
a bottle of wine (or
equivalent meal), taxes
and extra charges.

€	under €20
€€	€20–€30
€€€	€30–€40
€€€€	€40–€50
€€€€€	over €50

Akroyialia Restaurant, Spétses

⁰₁⁰ Restaurants

1 Tavern Karavolos, Póros
With nostalgic artifacts adorning its blue and white walls, this attractive little taverna serves classic Greek dishes. Try its *mezédes*, some of the best in Póros. You can dine inside or in the courtyard. ✎ *Harbour, Póros Town • Map K3 • 22980 26158 • €*

2 Patralis Fish Tavern, Spétses
Dating back to 1935, this taverna was established by a local fisherman. To this day it specializes in fresh fish dishes. Try the mussel rice, a tasty dish with garlic and tomato. ✎ *Kounoupitsa seafront • Map D4 • 22980 75380 • €€*

3 Akroyialia Restaurant, Spétses
Dining on the beachside terrace of this popular restaurant is magical. Some of the tables are set right on the beach. ✎ *Kounoupitsa seafront • Map D4 • 22980 74749 • €€*

4 Christina's Taverna, Ýdra
Grilled seafood dishes are the speciality here. If you feel adventurous, try the scorpion fish. Dining is on a lovely rooftop terrace. ✎ *Spilios Charamis, Ýdra Town • Map D4 • 22980 53516 • €€*

5 Kodylenia Taverna, Ýdra
This charming taverna, a few steps from the water's edge, is owned by a fisherman. He makes the daily catch, which is then beautifully prepared. ✎ *Seafront, Kamínia • Map D4 • 22980 53520 • €€*

6 Taverna Kathestos, Póros
The owner of this traditional taverna, with bright-blue painted chairs and a marine decor, prides himself on using organic fruit and vegetables for cooking delicious meals. ✎ *Póros beach • Map K3 • 22980 24770 • €€*

7 Toxotis Taverna, Angístri
Serving both Greek and international dishes, and a good selection of vegetarian options, this charming taverna is centrally located. Local wines served. ✎ *Skála crossroad, Skála • Map K2 • 22970 91283 • €€€*

8 Sunset Restaurant, Ýdra
As its name suggests, diners at this restaurant, perched on the edge of the harbour, enjoy stunning sunsets. Its menu is traditional Greek with a contemporary twist, and is accompanied by a fine wine list. ✎ *Harbour, Ýdra Town • Map D4 • 22980 52067 • €€€*

9 Garden of Taste, Ýdra
With vines providing plenty of shade, the courtyard of this taverna is ideal for a memorable meal. A highlight of the Greek menu are the sweet and savoury *saganáki (see p50).* ✎ *Ýdra Port • Map D4 • 22980 53705 • €€*

10 Taverna Rota, Póros
With tables set under canopies, this pleasing restaurant serves breakfasts and classic Greek meals. ✎ *Harbour, Póros Town • Map K3 • 22980 25627 • €€*

Left **Cloud-shrouded Moní island** Right **Spetsopoúla island**

Islands and Islets

Moní Island
Reached from Pérdika by boat, this peaceful, pine-covered island – inhabited only by deer and goats – is popular with day-trippers who flock to its beaches.
◈ *Between Égina and Angístri • Map K2*

Trikéri and Spetsopoúla Islands
Lying off the coast of Spétses, the tiny, somewhat barren island of Trikéri and the privately owned Spetsopoúla island are popular landmarks with sailors. Although there are no public moorings, yachts often sail in their waters.
◈ *East of Spétses • Map D4*

Metopí Islet
This little islet, dominated by its church, offers tranquility and just nature for company. It has some fine beaches and moorings, making it a popular day-trip destination from Égina or Skála.
◈ *Between Égina and Angístri • Map K2*

Dokós Island
Inhabited since Neolithic times and with valuable Hellenic and Byzantine archaeological remains, this remote island is now home to Orthodox monks.
◈ *North of Ýdra • Map D4*

Alexandros Island
Often known as Platoníssi Nisída, Aléxandros is one of the many islands lying to the south of Ýdra. Quiet and undeveloped, it has pretty coves and beaches.
◈ *Southwest of Ýdra • Map D4*

Petássi Island
Popular with yachtsmen, this small island offers a few safe anchorages in the sheltered Bísti bay. There are also many coves along its indented coastline.
◈ *Northwest of Ýdra • Map D4*

Elafónissos Island
Its sand dunes, stretching as far as the eye can see, attract visitors from the Peloponnese, who make a short sea crossing to reach this almost barren island. Its main settlement is the small port. ◈ *North of Kýthira • Map C5*

Andikýthira Island
This isolated little island has a population of around 50, all of whom live in the three villages of Potamós, Galaniána and Harhaliána. Fishing and farming are its only industries. ◈ *South of Kýthira • Map D5*

Nafítilos Islet
Nafítilos, along with a cluster of other tiny islets, including Psíra, Poretí, Thérmones and Póri, lie off Kýthira's coast. All are uninhabited and are popular with day-trippers due to their glorious beaches. ◈ *South of Kýthira • Map D4*

Makroníssi Island
Reached by a causeway from Diakófti, this relatively flat island has rich vegetation, lots of birdlife, sandy beaches and is popular with walkers. Its small port is extremely picturesque.
◈ *Off Diakófti • Map D4*

Left **Agía Paraskeví beach, Spétses** Right **Ágii Anárgyroi beach, Spétses**

🔟 Best Beaches

1 Agía Marína Beach, Égina
This small, bustling resort, popular with wind surfers and sailing enthusiasts, is picturesque with its whitewashed houses, tavernas and fabulous beach.
❧ *Agía Marína • Map L1*

2 Marathónas Beach, Égina
Busy yet scenic, the beach alongside the fishing village of Marathónas is known for its excellent selection of fish restaurants. With sun umbrellas, snorkelling and diving available, it is a popular spot.
❧ *South of Égina Town • Map K1*

3 Aiginítissa Beach, Égina
Quieter than its neighbour, Marathónas, this beach has shallow, crystal-clear water ideal for children. Sun loungers and shades are available. ❧ *South of Égina Town • Map K1*

4 Skála Beach, Angístri
The longest stretch of beach on the island and its sandiest, Skála attracts both locals and day-trippers from Égina. It runs along the coast from the town's Ágii Anárgyroi church. ❧ *Map K2*

5 Neórion Beach, Póros
Sandy and surrounded by tall pine trees, this is one of the most picturesque beaches on the island. Sometimes known as Mikró Neório, it has a good selection of tavernas as well as watersports to enjoy. ❧ *Northwest of Póros Town • Map K1*

6 Russian Bay, Póros
Taking its name from when it harboured the Russian ships that supported the Greek fleets during the revolution of the 1820s, this sheltered bay has golden sand and a handful of tavernas.
❧ *Northwest of Póros Town • Map K1*

7 Agía Paraskeví Beach, Spétses
The beautiful church of Agía Paraskeví lends its name to this long stretch of sand and pebble enclosed within a cove. Fragrant pine trees provide it with shelter.
❧ *Near Dápia • Map D4*

8 Ágii Anárgyroi Beach, Spétses
Of the many good beaches in the Argo-Saronics, the Ágii Anárgyroi is the largest. Lying in a cove, this popular sandy beach has shallow waters for safe swimming. ❧ *Near Dápia • Map D4*

9 Agía Marína, Spétses
Famous as much for its beauty as for the remains of an Early Bronze Age civilization, this beach has watersports and sun beds. Inland is a chapel of the same name. ❧ *Near Dápia • Map D4*

10 Palaiópoli Beach, Kýthira
Kýthira's largest beach and, according to folklore, where the goddess Aphrodite was born, Palaiópoli has sun umbrellas, tavernas and watersports. It is on the site of the ancient city of Scandeia. ❧ *East coast • Map D5*

STREETSMART

GREEK ISLANDS' TOP 10

Left **Holidaymakers** Centre **Information office and church** Right **A view of Santoríni**

TOP 10 General Information

1 When to Go
The Greek Islands are primarily a summer destination, but the mild winter months are also great for an activity holiday. In the cooler months (December–February) snow can fall in the mountains. Average temperatures are around 26°C (79°F) in summer and 10°C (50°F) in winter.

2 Where to Go
The larger islands, such as Corfu and Kefalloniá in the Ionians, Rhodes and Kos in the Dodecanese, Mýkonos and Santoríni in the Cyclades and Crete are ideal for beach holidays, while the smaller, rural islands, offer a more relaxed pace.

3 Tourist Offices
There are tourist and tourist police offices in most main towns on the islands, but they would prefer you telephone with your enquiry rather than walking in. The exception is the airport desks, where information on hotels, car hire and attractions is available. The tourist police number for all islands is 171.

4 Passport and Visas
EU citizens visiting the Greek Islands need only a valid passport and can stay for an unlimited period. Most other visitors, including citizens of the USA, Canada, New Zealand and Australia, can stay for up to 90 days without a visa. Other, non-EU citizens should consult the Greek embassy in their home country before departure, to be sure of having the correct documentation.

5 Customs
Duty-paid goods such as alcohol and perfumes for personal use are no longer subject to official limits within the EU, and there is no restriction on the amount of money you can bring in for holiday use. However, please declare large sums. The removal of archaeological artifacts is strictly prohibited. Non-EU citizens may be spot checked.

6 Currency
The currency of the Greek Islands is the euro. It comes in denominations of 1, 2, 5, 10, 20, 50 cents and 1 and 2 euro coins, and banknotes of 5, 10, 20, 50, 100, 200 and 500 euros. Visitors may bring in an unlimited amount of foreign currency, but large sums should be declared on arrival.

7 What to Take
If you take prescribed medicines, carry enough for your stay, along with a doctor's note. In terms of clothes, the islands have a relaxed way of life so take beachwear for resort-style holidays, casual wear for evenings, sports clothing and a jumper for cool evenings. Do pack sunscreen, aftersun and a sun hat.

8 Electricity
The standard current throughout the islands is 230V AC (50Hz). The plugs are two round pin variety, or three round pin for some appliances. Adaptors for British and transformers for some American appliances may not always be available, so carry what you need.

9 Children
The islands are family-orientated, with most attractions, hotels and restaurants providing amenities for children. Take care to prevent sunburn and when on beaches, be aware that there are often strong sea currents. Products like nappies are available in supermarkets, but if travelling with a baby on formula food, be sure to pack plenty, as the same brand may not be available.

10 Weddings
There's nothing more romantic than a wedding on a Greek Island beach. The procedure for civil marriages is straightforward, although church wedding formalities vary between the islands. Couples need to present the correct documentation before the big day. Many hotels have dedicated wedding planners.

Left **Ferry to Límnos** Centre **Yachts at an anchorage** Right **Road signs in Greek and English**

TOP 10 Getting There and Around

1 Package Holidays

Most visitors arrive on a package organized by a holiday company that includes inward and outward flights, accommodation and transfers to and from the airports. Package holidays tend to be beach or resort orientated, but specialist walking, sailing, diving and wedding packages are also available.

2 By Scheduled Flight

The Greek Islands are served directly by many European airlines and by intercontinental companies via domestic connections from the Elefthérios Venizélos international airport in Athens. Most flights arrive at the main airports, such as Corfu, Kefalloniá and Zákynthos in the Ionians, Chaniá and Iráklio on Crete, Rhodes, Kos, Sámos and Skiáthos. Domestic flights link the islands.

3 By Charter Flight

Tour operators specializing in beach and resort holidays, weddings and activity holidays fly charter flights into the main airports of the Ionians, Cyclades, Aegean, Dodecanese and Crete from key locations around Europe. Some fly throughout the year, while others offer a limited service in winter.

4 By Boat

The island groups are well served by ferries. Many routes start in Athens and the city's Piraeus Port has dozens of boats leaving for Crete, the Cyclades, the Dodecanese, the North and South Aegean, and the Saronic Gulf, while other ports such as Igoumenítsa, Pátra and Kyllíni serve the Ionians.

5 By Yacht

There is a wide choice of marinas and anchorages for yachtsmen to disembark and come ashore. Among them are the Gouviá Marina and Limín Kérkyra Marina on Corfu, the Kos Marina, Ágios Nikólaos at Lassíthi on Crete, the Marina Mandráki on Rhodes and the marinas at Skiáthos and Sýros.

6 By Cruise Ship

The islands appear on many cruise ship itineraries. These floating hotels can often be seen anchored a little way off Corfu Town's coastline or at the harbour of Zákynthos. Other popular ports of call include Rhodes and Pátmos in the Dodecanese, Santoríni and Mýkonos in the Cyclades and Crete.

7 Car Hire

All airports, resorts and many smaller towns have car hire company offices. You can hire a 4WD if planning to explore off-road, or a minibus if travelling with a group. Family cars are also available. A full driving licence held for at least a year is required. US licence holders must have an International Driving Permit.

8 Rules of the Road

Driving is on the right, with priority from the right at junctions. Observe speed limits and be especially careful while driving in mountainous areas or villages. Highways tend to be in good order. Children under 12 must not travel in the front.

9 By Bus

Most bus services are operated by local companies. Town harbours usually house bus stations. A journey can feel a little like stepping back in time, as many vehicles are older models. There are intercity buses linking major island capitals to Athens, which include the cost of the ferry.

10 By Taxi

It is generally easy to find a taxi on any of the islands. The main towns have taxi ranks and even the smallest villages have a vehicle available to hire. Taxis are metered and inexpensive, but if hiring a taxi for a day's sightseeing, it is a good idea to negotiate a fixed price beforehand.

Fly during the summer months for a wider choice of flights to the Greek Islands.

155

Left **Family enjoying a meal** Centre **Children at the beach** Right **Supermarket signage**

Special Concerns

1 Sight and Hearing Difficulties

Few archaeological sites or museums around the islands provide their guides in a Braille format or have them adapted to audio for visually impaired visitors, or even versions of their narratives to assist those with hearing difficulties. However, the Greek Tourist Organization is keen to reverse this.

2 Wheelchair Access

Hotels and restaurants are now introducing ramps and bathroom facilities suitable for accommodating wheelchairs, but public buildings, museums and especially archaeological sites where the ground is uneven still present a problem for users. The Greek Tourist Organization has a leaflet designed to assist wheelchair users.

3 Travelling With Children

Children will adore the Greek Islands, especially if they are keen on sailing, snorkelling or playing on the beach, but care should be taken to avoid sunburn and accidents in strong sea currents. Supermarkets and pharmacies generally stock medicines, nappies and food, although in case of any special dietary needs, do carry what you require, as the same brands may not always be available.

4 Senior Citizens

Greek people are especially respectful of older folk and it is not uncommon to see all generations of a family dining together in a restaurant. Risks are few but can include heat exhaustion and dehydration, so wear a hat and drink lots of water.

5 Women Travellers

While Greece and its islands are generally safe for women travelling alone or in a group, some incidents have been reported, so normal care should be taken. It is advisable to avoid walking alone at night and accepting lifts from strangers. Ensure someone is always aware of your plans.

6 Gay and Lesbian Travellers

Many of the laid-back islands, such as Rhodes, Mýkonos and Santoríni, are open-minded when it comes to homosexuality. No longer considered an illegal relationship, homosexual couples are generally accepted, and some beaches, clubs and boat charter companies are now exclusively gay.

7 Special Diets

The Greek diet largely comprises meat, fish, vegetables and fruit, but dairy products such as yoghurt and nuts are often used in dishes too. Visitors with diabetes, lactose or gluten intolerances, nut allergies, or those following a vegetarian or vegan diet need to exercise care. Some restaurants have vegetarian options and, with advance notice, will cater for special diets.

8 Student Travellers

The Greek Islands are popular with students and many companies specialize in student travel. Concessions are not usual for ferry, train or bus travel, but some museums and sites offer discounts, or even free admission, on production of a student identity card.

9 Travelling With Pets

There are strict rules on bringing pets into Greece and its islands. A pet must be micro-chipped and have an up-to-date rabies vaccination record. If travelling from another EU country it is possible to apply for a pet passport and some airlines will carry animals, but pets may have to be quarantined on arrival.

10 Smoking

Greeks are a nation of smokers and measures introduced by the government to ban smoking in public places are often ignored, or observed with reluctance. Restaurants may provide a smoking area, but in public buildings you will see no-smoking signs.

Left **Palace of Knossos** Centre **Picturesque Santoríni** Right **Boats at Égina Town harbour**

🔟 Specialist Holidays

1 Archaeology
The fabulous palaces of Knossos and Phaestos on Crete, Paleókastro on Kefaloniá and the ruined temples on Corfu's Mon Repos Estate are some of the places that appear on holiday tour itineraries. In addition, the island of Delos is one of Greece's most important archaeological sites.

2 Island Hopping
The island groups lend themselves to hopping from one port to another. Numerous ferries ply between the islands. For example, in the Ionians it is easy to reach Paxí from Corfu, or from Nydrí on Lefkáda to Fiskárdo on Kefaloniá, or to Frikes on Itháki, while in the Cyclades you have the choice of visiting all the islands.

3 Wildlife
The islands and islets provide an ecosystem for many flower varieties as well as wildlife and bird species that can be seen on specialist holidays. The Aegean alone has some 80 indigenous plants, including the *pancratium maritimum* or sea daffodil, and some 300 resident and migratory birds, including the endangered Bonelli's eagle.

4 Walking and Hiking
While the hilly landscape can present challenges to the novice hiker, there are designated trails – from long, difficult routes to small ones over flat terrain. Many take in sights too. For example, the Paleohóra to Vathý route on Itháki is a 4-km (3-mile) walk with a break at the Melissáni cave.

5 Cruising and Sailing
With a good choice of ports, marinas and anchorages, a mild climate with moderate winds most of the time, and tide movements that change by just a little each day, the waters around the Greek Islands are ideal for cruising and sailing holidays. Harbourside tavernas add to the charm of the experience.

6 Cooking
Greeks are famous for their love of food and some of their most delicious recipes are steeped in tradition. Covered by vineyards, the islands are known for their wine. The advent of cuisine-themed holidays is new to the isles but they are gaining popularity. Wine tours are also becoming common.

7 Painting
Specialist companies and individuals offer painting holidays, but this is one of the easiest types of break to do alone. The landscape of flowers and trees, tiny villages of whitewashed, red-roofed stone buildings, harbours full of boats and crystal-clear turquoise seas make this an enchanting place to capture on canvas.

8 Horse Riding
It is magical to take a trek through olive groves or farmland in the early morning or mid-evening. Centres under the Hellenic Equestrian Federation dot the isles. They include the Range Rodeo Riding Club, Corfu, Kos Riding Club and Rodo Riding Club Kadmos, Rhodes. ◈ *Hellenic Equestrian Federation • 22990 49350 • www. equestrian.org.gr*

9 Golf
There aren't too many good international standard courses to choose from. Two of the largest are the Corfu Golf Club and the Crete Golf Club, both 18-hole courses. They have the usual hire facilities, a driving range and Pro Shop. The Hellenic Golf Federation controls the sport. ◈ *Hellenic Golf Federation • 21089 41933 • www.hgf.gr*

10 Diving and Snorkelling
Seeing the underwater beauty of the islands has long been a popular holiday choice for many diving and snorkelling enthusiasts. Government schools can be found in all the major coastal towns, each offering dives for novices and experienced divers.

Left **Public phone** Centre **ATM** Right **Letter box**

Banking and Communications

Currency
The islands adopted the euro in 2001, replacing the long-standing drachma. The euro comes in eight coins of 1, 2, 5, 10, 20, 50 cents, and 1 and 2 euros, and banknotes in 5, 10, 20, 50, 100, 200 and 500 denominations. Changing money to euros is quite easy, even in smaller towns.

Banks
The opening hours of the islands' banks are 8am through to 2pm on each weekday except Friday when they close at 1:30pm. Banks are generally closed in the afternoons and on Saturday, although in major tourist areas some stay open later, especially during the summer months.

ATMs
Smaller towns and even villages are catching up by having their own ATMs, but still these machines are usually only found in the main towns and in tourist areas. Operating round the clock and dispensing local currency, the ATMs generally accept all major cards.

Credit Cards
Visa, Mastercard, Diners Club and American Express credit cards, as well as major debit cards, are almost always accepted by hotels, larger restaurants and shops in main towns, but cash is preferred in smaller establishments. Most village stores and tavernas only accept cash.

Language
Like the rest of Greece, islanders use modern Greek, which is derived from the ancient language used in the classical era and the New Testament of the Christian Bible. It uses the Greek alphabet, which has 24 letters from Alpha through to Omega. However, English is widely spoken because most Greeks have studied it to some extent.

Telephones
The Greek telecommunications company, Organismós Tilepikoinoníon Elládos (OTE), provides good service, although prices can vary with local calls being inexpensive and calls to neighbouring islands or international calls being quite expensive. Towns have telephone booths, as do some villages. Phonecards are available at kiosks.

Post Offices
Opening times are from around 7:30am to 2pm on weekdays, although larger post offices often stay open later and on Saturday, especially in holiday resorts. All major towns and most of the villages have post offices, which are easily identified by the blue and yellow signs that read *tahydromío* (post office). Letter boxes are bright yellow.

Internet
The fast-moving world of technology hasn't bypassed the islands. Many hotels now offer guests Internet facilities and every town and most villages have at least one Internet café.

Newspapers and Magazines
British and European newspapers are usually available in kiosks, supermarkets and hotel foyers the day after publication, although the mark up can be substantial. English and Greek language local publications, which tend to focus on current news and events, are available too, along with international magazines.

Television and Radio
Greece has public television and radio stations that are broadcast around the islands. There are also several privately owned stations which provide a glimpse of local culture. Hotels tend to have satellite television installed for a choice of international news and lifestyle channels.

Left **Ambulance** Centre **Medical centre** Right **Police officer**

ⁱ⁰10 Security and Health

1 Emergency Numbers

In the event of an emergency dial 100 for police, 166 for an ambulance and 199 to alert the fire department. Dial 107 to find out the opening times of the nearest pharmacy. The coastguard can be called by VHF radio or by telephone on 108. Response times to emergency calls are generally good.

2 Police

There are two divisions of police in the Greek Islands: the tourist police, who monitor hotels, restaurants and venues catering to tourists, and the regular police, who handle incidents of crime. The tourist police can be contacted by dialling 171. English is widely spoken.

3 Ambulance

Medical facilities are generally good in the major towns, although less so in the villages. Ambulance response times are good, but, as few roads have names, be prepared to give details of sights when giving directions. Telephone 166 for an ambulance in the event of a medical emergency.

4 Fire

Like residents, visitors should look out for and report any fires. They ignite with some regularity in the height of summer and because of the tinder dry landscape flames can spread rapidly. For emergencies, call 199.

5 Health Insurance

Citizens of the EU are entitled to free emergency medical care as reciprocal arrangements are in place with Greece and its islands. Before travelling, visitors should obtain a European Health Insurance Card (EHIC), available from the Department of Health. The EHIC does not replace health insurance. Non-EU citizens should always have insurance.

6 Hospitals

Greek National Health Service facilities can be limited on the islands, although the larger towns have modern hospitals with accident and emergency departments. Staff usually speak English. Air ambulances are available, if necessary, to fly serious cases to the state-of-the-art hospitals in Athens.

7 Doctors

As with dentists, doctors' private fees are payable immediately on treatment and a receipt is given for insurance purposes. Emergency medical situations should always be referred to a hospital, rather than a practitioner. Hotels can recommend local doctors who can assist with minor medical problems. Most will speak English well.

8 Dental Care

Dental practices are run on a private basis, with fees for emergency treatment payable immediately. Receipts are given for insurance purposes. Dentists have usually trained in Athens or further afield like the UK and, as such, the standard of knowledge and care throughout the islands is high.

9 Pharmacies

Pharmacists are highly trained and can advise on ailments as well as prescribe and dispense certain medicines. Identified by a green cross, pharmacies stock a large range of medication, although it is wise to carry prescribed drugs sufficient for your stay. Telephone 107 for information on timings for pharmacies.

10 Crime

The crime rate is especially low in the islands, although reports of theft and assaults tend to occur more frequently in the tourist areas than in the villages. It is wise to take sensible precautions, such as ensuring you do not keep all your documents or money together, watching your valuables and locking your car.

Tap water in the Greek Islands conforms to international hygienic standards and is safe to drink.

Left **Spring flowers** Centre **Locals dancing** Right **A camp site in a forest**

🔟 Budget Tips

1 Travelling Off-Season

Autumn, winter and spring in the Greek Islands can be glorious. Taking a package holiday during off-season is often much cheaper and offers an opportunity to explore the islands minus the crowds. Enjoy the beautiful autumn colours or spring flowers and take walks in pleasant temperatures.

2 Cheap Flights

Explore the possibility of booking a low-cost flight and then accommodation separately. If you can be flexible on dates, you are likely to pay a lot less. Check the Internet or ask your agent for any last-minute deals, which can often be much cheaper than booking from a brochure months in advance.

3 Discounts

If planning ahead, check if the company offers discounts for early booking. It can amount to substantial savings. If you are a senior citizen or a student, do not forget that you may get a discount on entry charges to museums and archaeological sites with proof of age.

4 Self-Catering

Staying in self-catering accommodation can be cost-effective and lots of fun. It means you can experience the lively atmosphere of a local market, buy fresh produce and eat at home or head off into the forest for a barbecue like the locals. You also have the flexibility to try out the local tavernas.

5 Hostels

The islands have a long tradition of being an island-hopping, backpackers' paradise and a selection of hostel-style accommodation has developed. Although not luxurious and rarely offering a range of facilities, hostels are usually comfortable and can be a good place to stay for anyone on a budget.

6 Picnics

Picnics are a favourite summer Sunday event for Greek families. You will see all generations laughing and eating together in designated picnic spots that often overlook beaches or are located in pine forests. Fun to prepare with fresh, inexpensive produce from local markets, picnics are cheap and may even mean you can mingle with the locals.

7 Free Entertainment

Impromptu festivals with music and dancing or more organized open-air concerts are commonplace in towns and village squares throughout the islands. Many celebrate religious milestones, such as Easter or Lent, or derive from traditions such as when a successful harvest is gathered in. Visitors are always welcome to join in.

8 Camping

There are some great, inexpensive camp sites, many with restaurants, showers, supermarkets and, in some cases, leisure facilities such as a swimming pool. The most popular are those next to beaches, in forests or olive groves. In high summer you will need to book in advance.

9 Working Holidays

Holiday work tends to revolve around tourist areas and working as a holiday rep, in a restaurant or bar, or driving public vehicles, provided you have the right qualifications, are all possibilities. EU citizens do not need a work permit, although they should register for residency after 90 days. Nationals of other countries need a work permit.

10 Hitchhiking

Hitchhiking is a good way to get around for travellers on a budget, and is generally accepted as a way of life here. In fact, it is a great way to meet locals, who tend to be generous in giving lifts and information on what to do and where to go. Women travelling alone should exercise the usual caution.

Left **Sign prohibiting photography** Centre **Children in a pool** Right **Chilled cola**

Things to Avoid

1 Military Zones
Army, navy and air force military zones and bases tend to be clearly signposted and it is best to avoid them in case your actions are misunderstood. Do not photograph any military personnel, or any building, vehicle or place that appears to be military, without permission.

2 Photography
Along with military premises and personnel, do not take photographs inside churches or monasteries as it is considered disrespectful. If you are planning to take pictures in a museum, a privately owned attraction or an archaeological site, always check if photography is allowed. Sometimes it is but without flash. Video equipment is treated the same.

3 Offending your Host
Greek people are extremely sociable and will often extend an invitation to you to dine with their family. Consider this an honour and expect a large gathering. Always take flowers, wine, chocolate or pastries for the host. Dress smart-casual unless dining in a top-notch restaurant.

4 Sunburn
Prolonged exposure to the sun should be avoided. Always apply plenty of high-factor sun-

protection cream, especially if swimming, and wear sunglasses and a hat. Fair-skinned people and children are particularly vulnerable to sunburn. Heat exhaustion is a serious affliction; take adequate precautions.

5 Dehydration
Always drink plenty of water to avoid dehydration. Carry water when visiting archaeological sites and outdoor attractions in particular, as drinking water is not always available. Bottled water is available from all supermarkets and kiosks. If you do get dehydrated, seek medical help.

6 Mosquitoes
Mosquitoes do not carry serious diseases in Greece but they can leave a nasty bite. Some people may even get a reaction to a mosquito bite, in which case a pharmacy should be able to advise. Wear repellent, especially after dark or when near stagnant water, and invest in a plug-in deterrent device.

7 Scams
Scams and hard-sell schemes, such as property or boat timeshare schemes, although rare in the Greek Islands, do exist and tourists are often the victims. Take sensible precautions and be on your guard. If you are offered an opportunity that sounds too good to

be true, it probably is. Read the small print before signing anything.

8 Crime
Always take care when carrying valuables, especially in crowded areas, and be sure to securely lock your vehicle or accommodation when leaving personal items behind. Crimes such as pick-pocketing, theft from cars and burglaries are rare but again, sensible precautions should be taken. Violent crime is extremely rare.

9 Drugs
The authorities have a zero-tolerance policy when it comes to the use or dealing of drugs, and as a result the consumption of such substances is relatively low. Carrying drugs into the country can result in serious consequences. Take a note from your doctor if carrying prescribed drugs.

10 Dubious Clubs
Some of the larger resorts like to cater for all types of visitors and as such a selection of late-night clubs are available. Some are advertised as "adults only". The authorities regularly monitor such venues to ensure they conform to strict guidelines but visitors wishing for a milder form of evening entertainment might do best to avoid them.

Left **Interior of a bar, Crete** Centre **Traditional taverna, Lésvos** Right **A typical menu**

Dining Tips

1 Restaurants
The Greek Islands offer a fabulous choice of places to satisfy your tastebuds, from traditional tavernas to French, Italian, Oriental and even Mexican restaurants. However, do look out for restaurants in tourist areas that advertise "international" cuisine and have what appears to be an endless menu; chances are the food will be microwaved.

2 Tavernas
Look out for family-owned tavernas that have local specialities on the menu. Dishes, such as *kléftiko* (lamb slow-cooked with herbs in a special domed oven), will almost certainly be freshly prepared. A stay in the islands wouldn't be complete without a meal at a traditional taverna.

3 Cafés and Snack Bars
Every village, however small, will have at least one café. These *kafenías* are an institution throughout the islands and act as the central point of a community. Generally, they serve just coffee, water and spirits, but some also serve sandwiches or light meals and are more akin to a snack bar.

4 Fast Food
American-style hamburger restaurants, pizza parlours and ice-cream shops have made their mark on the Greek Islands and can be found in most major towns. The local equivalent is a *souvlatzídiko*, which sells delicious *souvláki* (chunks of pork or chicken chargrilled with herbs). Look out for bakeries offering freshly made pastries.

5 Vegetarians
Dishes such as vegetable *moussakás* appear on many taverna menus, although few restaurants are exclusively vegetarian. Greeks are a nation of meat lovers but because many fast for Lent as part of the Greek Orthodox tradition, recipes for fruit and vegetable dishes have been handed down through the generations.

6 Local Beers and Spirits
A range of excellent beers are brewed in Greece, such as the famous Mythos brand, while popular spirits include *tsíbouro*, made from grape pulp, and the aniseed-flavoured *oúzo*, which turns white when water is added. There are local versions of white rum, brandy and other spirits, while Greece's traditional wine is *retsína*.

7 Water
It is completely safe to drink tap water in the Greek Islands. However, on some islands the water has a slightly brackish taste as a result of the desalination process. Beware of restaurant staff pushing bottled water on you by claiming the mains supply is undrinkable or unsafe. While bottled water is available everywhere, filling up from the tap for excursions saves the use of excess plastic bottles.

8 Soft Drinks
A wide range of internationally known soft drinks, plus a selection of locally produced alternatives in bottles and cartons, can be found in supermarkets and kiosks. Fruit juices can be purchased in large cartons or smaller versions. Restaurants and bars will always have soft drinks.

9 Menus
Menus are usually written in Greek and English, although in smaller village tavernas they may be in Greek only. Some may not have a menu at all. Often diners are invited into the kitchen to choose their meal or are advised as to what is being cooked that day. Check the price before ordering.

10 Service Charges
A service charge is included in the price of meals on the menu. However, if the service you received was good then you might like to consider rounding up the bill or adding up to 10 per cent as a tip.

A great way to sample local dishes is to order mezédes.

Left **Rural villas** Centre **Signage for apartment rental** Right **Holiday apartments**

🔟 Accommodation Tips

1 High and Low Season
Most hotels in the Greek Islands will have at least two sets of rates, one for the high season (around June to September) and one for the low season (October to May). The exception will be the Christmas, New Year and Easter holiday periods, when prices rise accordingly.

2 Package Holidays
The Greek Islands are a popular package-holiday destination. Normally including flights, accommodation, transfers to and from the airport and sometimes car hire and child care, a package can be less expensive and is a convenient way to arrange a holiday, especially for families.

3 Reservations
The easiest way to reserve accommodation is via the Internet. Almost all accommodation providers can be contacted via e-mail and there are many booking websites. Due to Greece's debt crisis, many hotels are offering good-value deals. Prices change frequently and may differ from the price bands given in this guide.

4 Booking Before You Go
While there are many hotels, resorts and villas of all star ratings on the islands, they can get booked well in advance by the big tour operators. It is therefore wise to book ahead in high season, or if you wish to stay at a particular location or have specific requirements.

5 Booking When You Get There
Some visitors might prefer the spontaneity of island hopping and selecting accommodation on arrival. Airports and ports generally have tourist information offices listing local hotels, resorts, villas and camp sites and can assist you in your search for a place to stay. On some islands, proprietors still meet ferries.

6 Tipping
It is generally unnecessary to tip if a hotel employee has shown you to your room, although if the person has been particularly helpful or you are staying in a five-star hotel with porters, then you might like to tip a few euros. Chamber staff would also appreciate a few euros for their services.

7 Hotel Grading
Greek Island hotels and tourist accommodation is monitored by the Greek National Tourist Organization. It regularly monitors establishments to ensure its strict guidelines for facilities and services are met, and implements a grading system. Grades range from A for the best to E, plus an L grade for luxury hotels.

8 Apartments
Apartments designated for tourists come under the same Greek National Tourist Organization's classification system as hotels, irrespective of whether they are private or in a resort-style complex. Grades, and in turn prices, are dependent on the facilities offered, such as a communal swimming pool, a maid service and the number of bedrooms.

9 Villas
A villa holiday can be a good option for visitors keen on flexibility. Ranging from two-bedroom villas to large, luxurious residences. Always check if they come fully equipped. Most will include the use of a swimming pool with sun loungers. Like apartments, villas are graded and can be located in town centres or the countryside.

10 Rural Properties
A great way to sample local life is to stay in a private rural villa or in a villager's own home. Villas, which come under the grading system if designed for tourists, are often advertised privately or are available through a specialist company, while rooms can be found simply by asking at the local coffee shop.

Streetsmart

Left **Bella Venezia, Corfu** Right **Paxos Beach Hotel, Paxi**

10 Luxury and Mid-Range Hotels

1 Divani Corfu Palace

This luxurious hotel by the sea offers swimming pools, a fitness suite, a children's playground and beautifully presented rooms with satellite television. The gardens are designed to echo the tone of the surrounding hillside forests, citrus groves and olive trees. 🕲 *Kanóni, Corfu Town • Map B5 • 26610 38996 • €€€€ • www.divanis.com*

2 Marbella Corfu

A five-star hotel with well-appointed rooms, the eco-friendly Marbella Corfu boasts a concert hall, a spa and fitness centre and restaurants, including La Terrazza, which looks out over the beach. 🕲 *Agios Ioánnis • Map B6 • 26610 71183 • €€€€ • www.marbella.gr*

3 Pelecas Country Club, Corfu

The restoration of a mansion and its outbuildings, including the stables and summer house, created this luxurious club. Occupying a private estate from the 18th century, it offers glamourous suites and studios, a swimming pool, tennis courts and a dining hall. 🕲 *Pélekas • Map A5 • 26610 52918 • €€€ • www.country-club.gr*

4 Grecotel Corfu Imperial

Gourmet restaurants, elegant rooms, a spa and berthing for yachts are just some of the super facilities offered at the five-star Grecotel Corfu Imperial. The hotel stands on a stunning peninsula overlooking the bay of Corfu, and has Italianate-style gardens and decor. 🕲 *Komméno • Map B5 • 26610 88400 • €€€€€ • www.corfuimperial.com*

5 Corfu Palace

Set in subtropical gardens overlooking the Garitsa bay, the deluxe Corfu Palace has well-equipped rooms with marble baths and sea views, restaurants such as the respected Scheria, pools, and a spa offering seawater treatments. 🕲 *Leoforos Dimokratias 2, Corfu Town • Map B5 • 26610 39485 • €€€€ • www.corfupalace.com*

6 Gelina Village, Corfu

Classical Corfiot and Byzantine themes in the decor of Gelina Village make it a refreshing stay for a holiday. Its amenities include a restaurant, spa, history museum, water-park and sports centre. 🕲 *Acharávi • Map A4 • 26630 64000 • €€€ • www.gelinavillage.gr*

7 Iberostar Kerkyra Golf, Corfu

Ideal for an activity-filled holiday, Iberostar Kerkyra Golf has tennis courts, restaurants and a nearby 18-hole golf course. For children, there is a mini club and playground, plus a family entertainment programme. 🕲 *Alykés Potamoú • Map B5 • 26610 24030 • €€€ • www.louishotels.com*

8 Bella Venezia, Corfu

A town-centre hotel in an apricot-coloured Neo-Classical mansion, Bella Venezia offers elegance and seclusion. Dining in the courtyard garden is a memorable experience. 🕲 *Zambéli 4, Corfu Town • Map B5 • 26610 46500 • €€€ • www. bellaveneziahotel.com*

9 Cavalieri Hotel, Corfu

Occupying a centrally located, tall Venetian townhouse, the Cavalieri Hotel has uninterrupted sea views. Refurnished in a country-home style, it has well-equipped rooms and a roof garden 🕲 *Kapodistríou 4, Corfu Town • Map B5 • 26610 39041 • €€€ • www. cavalieri-hotel-corfu-town. com*

10 Paxos Beach Hotel, Paxi

Made of local stone, with bungalows dotted amongst terraces of olive trees, this hotel overlooks a pretty bay and has a private beach. There is also a swimming pool, a playground and a restaurant serving local dishes. 🕲 *Gáios • Map B2 • 26620 32211 • €€€ • www.paxosbeachhotel.gr*

It is mandatory for all hotels to display their licence from the Greek National Tourist Organization in a prominent place.

Price Categories

For a standard, double room per night (with breakfast if included), taxes and extra charges.

€	under €50
€€	€50–100
€€€	€100–200
€€€€	€200–300
€€€€€	over €300

ft **Dionysus Camping Village** Right **The Pink Palace**

🔟 Budget Stays and Camping: Corfu

Fundana Hotel
Full of character, the Fundana Hotel is housed in a pink-washed, 17th-century Venetian mansion that stands in terraced gardens full of hibiscus and olive trees. The rooms and suites are stylish and welcoming. There are sun terraces round the pool and a small terrace for alfresco dining. ⬊ *Odysséos 1, Paleokastrítsa, Corfu • Map A5 • 26630 22532 • €€ • www.fundanavillas.com*

Casa Lucia
Set in the countryside, Casa Lucia comprises former olive-press buildings that have been remodelled into self-catering cottages. Many date to the Venetian period and feature vaulted ceilings. On offer are painting, yoga and T'ai Chi classes. ⬊ *Sgómbou, Corfu • Map A5 • 26610 91419 • €€ • www.casa-lucia-corfu.com*

The Pink Palace
A lively hotel and hostel, the beachside Pink Palace complex has a host of leisure activities from table tennis, volleyball and basketball to rock climbing, snorkelling and safari. It even has a nightclub. ⬊ *Agios Górdios Beach, Sinarádes • Map B5 • 26610 53103 • € • www.thepinkpalace.com*

Anemona Studios
A building of ten apartments, some with private balconies, the Anemona Studios lies on Paleokastrítsa resort's periphery, with amenities nearby. Guests can also use the nearby Phivos Studios' swimming pool and bar. ⬊ *Paleokastrítsa, Corfu • Map A5 • 26630 41101 • €*

Hotel Bretagne
Renovated into a charming establishment with a homely feel, the Hotel Bretagne offers guestrooms and restaurants within easy reach of Corfu Town's airport and main attractions. ⬊ *K Georgáki 27, Corfu Town • Map B5 • 26610 30724 • €€*

Hotel Avrilios
With its rural location and easy distance to one of the longest and prettiest beaches on Corfu, the Hotel Avrilios offers a taste of local life and yet has amenities nearby. The hotel has self-catering apartments, a restaurant, a swimming pool and sun terraces. ⬊ *Kávos Lefkímmis • Map B6 • 26620 61262 • €*

Dionysus Camping Village
One of Corfu's oldest camp sites, the Dionysus Camping Village is set amid gardens and forest. It welcomes caravans and camper vans, and has bungalows and tents for hire. On-site are shower blocks, a laundry, a supermarket, and a restaurant. ⬊ *Danílas Bay, Dasiá, Corfu • Map B5 • 26610 91417 • € •www.dionysuscamping.gr*

Paleokastritsa Camping
Shower blocks, electricity, a children's play area, and the use of a swimming pool in its sister holiday complex, are just some of Paleokastritsa Camping's facilities. Set in shady olive groves, this site is open to caravans, camper vans and visitors with tents. ⬊ *Paleokastrítsa, Corfu • Map A5 • 26630 41204 • € • www.campingpaleokastritsa.com*

Hotel Zafiris
This modern two-star hotel comprises studios and apartments laid out around gardens and walkways. Amenities include the Waterfalls restaurant, which uses vegetables from its own organic garden, and Saxophone cocktail bar. ⬊ *Melitsa Perouládes, Corfu • Map A4 • 26630 95086 • € • www.zafirishotel.gr*

Thekli-Clara Studios
An attractive group of stylish and well-equipped white-washed studios in the centre of Gáios. Many have balconies with great views ideal for relaxing and watching the local life. There are harbourside taverns close by. ⬊ *Gáios, Paxí • Map B2 • 26620 32313 • € • www.theklis-studios.com*

Left **Ionian Blue**, Lefkáda Right **Caravel Zante**, Zákynthos

TOP 10 Luxury and Mid-Range Hotels

1 Ionian Blue, Lefkáda
Set on a hillside with panoramic views of the sea, the Ionian Blue is one of the island's fore-most hotels. Luxurious and elegant, it provides all amenities including a spa, swimming pools, restaurants and an inti-mate gourmet restaurant. ॐ *Nikiána • Map H1 • 26450 29029 • €€€€ • www.ionianblue.gr*

2 Armonia, Lefkáda
A modern hotel with traditional architecture, Armonia offers well-furnished rooms, some with vaulted ceilings and sea views. Amenities include a pool and cocktail bar. The restaurant's terrace looks out over the bay. ॐ *Megálo Avláki, Nydrí • Map G1 • 26450 92751 • €€€ • www. hotel-armonia-lefkas.com*

3 Grand Nefeli Hotel, Lefkáda
A four-star hotel, Grand Nefeli offers an array of facilities, including a child-ren's playground, swim-ming pool, terraces and gardens. It has its own windsurfing tutors. Rooms also have climate control. ॐ *Póndi, Vasilikí • Map G1 • 26450 31378 • €€€ • www.grandnefeli. com*

4 Mareblue Apostolata Resort & Spa, Kefalloniá
This four-star hotel is among the finest on the island. It has a spa and several restaurants, including the Sea Pearl and Sunrise, serving buf-fets and à la carte cuisine. Tennis and volleyball are available. ॐ *Skála • Map H3 • 26710 83581 • €€€€*

5 Trapezaki Bay Hotel, Kefalloniá
Positioned on a hilltop, this adults-only hotel offers dramatic views, peace and tranquillity. All of the 33 rooms are comfortably furnished and the restaurants offer some of the best Greek food to be found on the island. ॐ *Trapezaki, Kefalloniá • Map G3 • 26710 31502 • €€€ • www.trapezakibay hotel.com*

6 Cephalonia Palace, Kefalloniá
A choice of room types, including family rooms, are available at this mod-ern four-star resort. Relax around its freshwater pool, lounge on its ter-races or try horse riding, sailing or scuba diving. Children have their own pool and playground. ॐ *Xi Lixourioú • Map G3 • 267 10 93112 • €€€€ • www. cephaloniapalacehotel.com*

7 Mabely Grand, Zákynthos
Understated elegance is the byword for this hotel. Lavish guestrooms, a massage studio and library lounge are just some of the facilities this five-star establishment offers.

Choose from the seafront à la carte restaurant or try local dishes in Byzantine, its own taverna. ॐ *Kambí • Map H4 • 26950 41302 • €€€€ • www.mabely.gr*

8 Hotel Palatino, Zákynthos
This seafront four-star hotel is ideal for a holiday or business stay. Trinity restaurant serves both Greek and international cuisine, and the Palatino Café & Cocktail Bar is welcoming. Amenities include tennis courts. ॐ *Kolokotróni 10, Zákynthos Town • Map H • 26950 27780 • €€€€ • www.palatinohotel.gr*

9 Astir Palace, Zákynthos
This modern resort-style hotel has gardens, a swimming pool and child-ren's play area. The 120 air conditioned rooms have balconies overlooking the sea. The restaurant serve international cuisine. ॐ *Laganás beach • Map H4 • 26950 53300 • €€€€ • www.astir-palace.com*

10 Caravel Zante, Zákynthos
This medium-size hotel enjoys an idyllic location, surrounded by olive groves and overlooks the beach. It has a Fun Park on-site, along with restau-rants and a theatre. Rooms offer sea views. ॐ *Plános, Tsiliví • Map H4 • 26950 45261 • €€€€ • www.caravelzante.gr*

The Greek National Tourist Organization sets prices for all grades of hotels each year, with the exception of luxury hotels

Price Categories

For a standard, double room per night (with breakfast if included), taxes and extra charges.	
€	under €50
€€	€50–100
€€€	€100–200
€€€€	€200–300
€€€€€	over €300

left **Odyssey Apartments, Itháki**

10 Budget Stays and Apartments

1 Ostria Hotel, Lefkáda
Decorated in a traditional Greek style, this small pension-style hotel is set on a hillside overlooking the bay. Each of its 12 rooms has a balcony. The owners are keen chefs and use local ingredients to prepare classic Greek cuisine served in its restaurant. ✪ *Agios Nikítas • Map G1 • 26450 97483 • €*

2 Arion Hotel, Lefkáda
A few minutes' walk from the beach, this small hotel of 12 apartments and studios is built in a traditional style with white-washed walls and set in 1.2 ha (3 acres) of gardens and olive groves. There are panoramic views from the terrace. ✪ *Ligia • Map H1 • 26450 71260 • €*

3 Bel Air Hotel, Lefkáda
An attractive terracotta and cream complex, the Bel Air Hotel is located minutes from the beach. It has 33 air-conditioned apartments, swimming and spa pools, plus a children's pool. It also has bars and an alfresco dining terrace. ✪ *Nydrí • Map G1 • 26450 92125 • €€ • www.hotel-belair.gr*

4 Odyssey Apartments, Itháki
This complex is a find for those on a budget. Situated minutes from the beach and town centre, it comprises studios and apartments with balconies and kitchens, all decorated in a fresh colour scheme. Breakfast is served on a terrace with views over a pool. ✪ *Vathý • Map H2 • 26740 33400 • €€ • www.odyssey apartments.gr*

5 Allegro Hotel, Kefalloniá
Located near Argostóli's central square, this is an ideal hotel for guests wishing to explore the capital. The air-conditioned rooms have music systems. This two-star hotel has a taverna with great bay views. ✪ *A Hoidá 2, Argostóli • Map G3 • 26710 22268 • €€*

6 Linardos Apartments, Kefalloniá
This white-washed hotel is an integral part of the scenery around the picturesque bay at Ássos. Stylishly decorated, air-conditioned studios and a two-storey apartment designed for up to six people come complete with an equipped mini kitchen and a daily maid service. ✪ *Ássos • Map G2 • 26740 51563 • €€ • www.linardos apartments.gr*

7 Grivas Gerasimos Apartments, Itháki
A modern building overlooking Vathý bay, the Grivas Gerasimos comprises two and three bedroom apartments with a balcony or terrace. Air-conditioning and an equipped kitchen are among the facilities, plus there is a daily maid service provided. Nearby is a good choice of tavernas and shops. ✪ *Vathý bay • Map H2 • 26740 33328 • €€*

8 Leedas Village, Zákynthos
A super collection of villas built in traditional style using local stone, this self-catering complex is well priced. The decor is stylish. Features include stone walls and timber ceilings, a garden, barbecue area, children's play area and communal pool. ✪ *Lithákia • Map H4 • 26950 51305 • €€ • www.leedas-village.com*

9 Albatros Apart-Hotel, Zákynthos
Comprising 35 tastefully furnished 2 and 3 bedroom apartments with a kitchen, balcony and music system, this modern "aparthotel" revolves around its ground floor taverna. ✪ *Laganás • Map H4 • 26950 51139 • €€ • www.albatroshotel.gr*

10 Astoria Hotel, Zákynthos
A long-established family-run hotel, the Astoria is right next to the beach. It provides stylish guestrooms, plus a lounge bar, shop and a restaurant serving traditional Greek dishes using local produce. ✪ *Alykés bay • Map H4 • 26950 84059 • €€ • www.astoriazante.com*

Left **Harmony Boutique Hotel** Centre **Mýconian Ambassador** Right **Mediterranean Royal**

🔟 Luxury and Mid-Range Hotels

1 Mediterranean Royal, Santoríni

Designed to harmonize with the local architecture, this hotel stands in huge gardens next to a private beach. Its traditional taverna is on the beach, plus it offers guests a gym, spa, watersports and a children's playground. ◎ *Agía Paraskeví • Map V2 • 22860 31167 • €€€ • www. mediterraneanbeach.gr*

2 Harmony Boutique Hotel, Mýkonos

A boutique hotel with elegant decor, the Harmony offers rooms designed to capture traditional Mýkonian styling, with features including designer toiletries. Its à la carte restaurant uses mainly organic produce, while services include beauty treatments. ◎ *Mýkonos Town • Map P6 • 22890 28980 • €€€€ • www.harmonyhotel.gr*

3 Mýconian Ambassador, Mýkonos

Overlooking the town and its beach, this five-star hotel has elegant, themed rooms, including Arabian, Mýkonian and Asian. Its spa, a choice of restaurants, cocktail bar, pools and a diving centre are on site. ◎ *Platýs Gialós, Mýkonos Town • Map P6 • 22890 24166 • €€€€ • www. myconianambassador.gr*

4 Astir of Paros, Páros

Standing in a large garden full of date palm trees and hibiscus, this luxury seafront complex resembles a traditional Cycladic village. Mediterranean and Chinese-themed restaurants, an art gallery, pools and a fitness suite are some of the facilities. ◎ *Náoussa • Map E4 • 22840 51976 • €€€€ • www.astirofparos.gr*

5 Dolphin Bay, Sýros

This four-star hotel has 140 rooms with a range of amenities and views of the bay. Meals are served in a restaurant and traditional taverna. In the grounds is a half Olympic-size pool, and a children's playground. ◎ *Galissás • Map M6 • 22810 42924 • €€€ • www.dolphin-bay.gr*

6 Yria Hotel Resort, Páros

A member of the Small Luxury Hotels group, this is a Cycladic-style resort of 67 low, whitewashed buildings set around a pool. Rooms are lavish and well-equipped, and guests can dine in the dining hall or relax in the library lounge or spa. ◎ *Parásporos bay, Pároikia • Map E4 • 22840 24154 • €€€€ • www.yriahotel.gr*

7 Cavo Tagoo, Mýkonos

Built into a rock face, this luxurious hotel is a landmark in the capital. Its decor is minimalist and rooms are well-appointed, some have private pools. It has a spa, fitness suite and gourmet restaurant. ◎ *Mýkonos Town • Map P6 • 22890 20100 • €€€€€ • www.cavotagoo.gr*

8 Faros Hotel, Sýros

Housed in white and blue buildings, this four-star hotel comprises studios, apartments and suites, all with sea views. They surround a swimming pool. A mini shopping mall, hairdresser and fitness suite are available for guests. ◎ *Azólimnos • Map N6 • 22810 61661 • €€€ • www.faros-hotel.com*

9 Ostraco Suites, Mýkonos

A boutique-style retreat, the Ostraco overlooks the sea. Sun terraces around a swimming pool, a spa pool and a cocktail bar are among its amenities. The hotel's 21 rooms are well equipped. ◎ *Mýkonos • Map P6 • 22890 23396 • €€€€ • www.ostraco.gr*

10 Aphrodite Paradise Beach, Mýkonos

This lively resort has its own nightclub with events such as retro discos and Greek music nights. Facilities include a boutique, mini-market, bars and a restaurant. ◎ *Kalafáti beach • Map P6 • 22890 71367 • €€€ • www. aphrodite-mykonos.com*

Price Categories

For a standard, double room per night (with breakfast if included), taxes and extra charges.

€	under €50
€€	€50–100
€€€	€100–200
€€€€	€200–300
€€€€€	over €300

Left **Helmos Hotel** Right **Paradise Beach Resort**

🔟 Budget Stays and Camping

1 Paradise Beach Resort, Mýkonos

This popular resort with a camp site offers accommodation in tents and simply furnished cabins, apartments and rooms. Located on the beach, and one of the liveliest in Mýkonos, the camp site has a restaurant, snack bar and Internet station, plus lots of watersports. ◈ *Paradise beach • Map P6 • 22890 22852 • € • www.paradise-greece.com*

2 Acropolis Hotel, Íos

Guestrooms have private bathrooms, air conditioning, a fridge and views of the beach. This simply furnished, value-for-money hotel has private parking and a bar, while nearby is a choice of tavernas. ◈ *Mylopótas beach • Map E5 • 22860 91303 • € • www.hotelacropolis.gr*

3 Adonis Hotel, Náxos

This appealing white and blue-painted hotel lies in the centre of a village, near the beach. Its 23 rooms are attractively furnished. The restaurant serves breakfast, lunch and Greek dishes for dinner. ◈ *Apóllon • Map H4 • 22850 67060 • € • www.naxos-hotel-adonis.com*

4 Aegean Village Georgy, Páros

Standing in a lemon orchard, this small complex of pretty, white stone cottages looks out over the bay. Comprising six apartments, each with air conditioning and kitchen, it is located in the old town near beaches, tavernas and the port. ◈ *Pároikia • Map E4 • 22840 23187 • €*

5 Madoupa Hotel, Mýkonos

With a choice of rooms from single to quadruple, each with amenities that include climate control, this traditional 22-roomed hotel lies minutes from sandy beaches and the town centre. Breakfast is served on the terrace. ◈ *Vrýssi village • Map P6 • 22890 22635 • €€*

6 Mare-Monte Hotel, Íos

Close to a golden-sand beach and fish tavernas, this blue and white hotel offers air-conditioned studios that overlook the harbour. A swimming pool, sun terrace and bar are on offer. ◈ *Seafront, Gialós • Map E5 • 22860 91585 • €€*

7 Helmos Hotel, Náxos

With Mediterranean colours and extras like fluffy towels and Internet connection, this town centre hotel makes a charming and good-value place to stay. It is close to the Áyios Geórgios beach and nearby tavernas. ◈ *Náxos Town • Map Q4 • 22850 22155 • €€ • hotelhelmos.com*

8 Studio Eleni, Mýkonos

Boasting charming Mýkonian architecture, this studio complex is in the heart of town near tavernas, bars and clubs. The town's famous windmill is minutes away. Each studio is nicely furnished, air-conditioned, has Internet access and a kitchen with fridge. ◈ *Agías Paraskevís 22, Mýkonos Town • Map Q4 • 22890 22806 • € • www.studioeleni.com*

9 Agali Houses, Santoríni

A collection of beautifully furnished studios and apartments, all with a central location and views of the caldera, Agali Houses is a gem. Equipped with air conditioning, kitchen and television in each room, as well as a pool and breakfast room on site, it is a good base for exploring the island. ◈ *Firostefani • Map U2 • 22860 22811 • €€€ • www.agalihouses.gr*

🔟 Avra Studios, Mýkonos

Characterized by chic, bold furnishings, the colour-themed air-conditioned studios in this traditional Mýkonian country house come complete with satellite television, stereo and Internet. They also have a modern kitchen and an area for dining alfresco. ◈ *Tourlos Bay • Map P6 • 22890 27247 • €€*

Streetsmart – Accommodation in the Cyclades

The prices for camp sites include a pitch with electricity and on-site facilities.

Left **9 Muses, Pátmos** Centre **Palazzo del Mare, Kos** Right **Irene Palace, Rhodes**

🔟 Luxury and Mid-Range Hotels

1 Oceanis Hotel, Rhodes

Overlooking the Ixiá beach, this luxurious modern hotel offers guests well-equipped rooms, a swimming pool with its own "island" bar, restaurants, entertainment lounge and numerous sports ranging from tennis to watersports. ◎ Ixiá • Map V4 • 22410 24881 • €€€ • www.hoteloceanis.eu

2 Irene Palace, Rhodes

This family-orientated hotel provides activities that include treasure hunts and crafts workshops for children, while parents can enjoy the fitness and health suite, and golf nearby. Its restaurant serves Rhodian fare. ◎ Kolýmbia • Map V5 • 22410 56202 • €€€ • www.irenepalace.gr

3 Kalderimi Hotel, Astypálea

This luxurious hotel is housed in a traditional village cottage complex complete with arches, exposed brickwork and whitewashed walls with blue paintwork. Homemade breakfast is served on a beachside terrace. ◎ Livádi • Map F5 • 22430 61120 • €€€ • www.kalderimi.gr

4 Rodos Park Suites, Rhodes

Timeless elegance is the term that best describes this hotel. Super guest-rooms, a spa and fitness suite and a brasserie and bistro that serve exquisite dishes combine to provide guests with a memorable place to stay. ◎ 12 Ríga Feréou Street, Rhodes Town • Map V4 • 22410 89700 • €€€€ • www.rodospark.gr

5 Konstantinos Palace, Kárpathos

Set around its own pool and gardens close to the beach, and with amenities that include a sports complex and à la carte and buffet restaurants this is a top-end family hotel. Rooms feature lots of extras, such as a music system. ◎ Pigádia • Map Y6 • 22450 23401 • €€€€ • www.konstantinospalace.gr

6 Arkasa Bay Hotel, Kárpathos

Built in a style in keeping with its surroundings, this hotel offers everything for a pleasant stay. It has swimming pools, a children's playground, fitness suite and restaurants that serve Greek and international dishes. ◎ Arkása bay, Arkása • Map X6 • 22450 61410 • €€€€ • Disabled Access • www.arkasabay.com

7 Palazzo del Mare, Kos

Besides richly appointed rooms, this luxury hotel has both an indoor and outdoor pool, Jacuzzis, a gym and an amazing spa. There's a good Italian restaurant, and a number of bars offering snacks and drinks. ◎ Palatsida S.A., Palazzo del Mare, Marmari • Map X1 • 22420 42320 • €€€ • www.bluelagoongroup.com

8 Continental Palace, Kos

Ideally situated for exploring Kos Town and close to the marina, this modern hotel caters for families. Services includ babysitting, children's pools and a playground. Most guestrooms have sea views and are well presented. ◎ Georgíou Papandréou Street, Kos Town • Map Y1 • 22420 22737 • €€€€ • www.continentalpalace.com

9 9 Muses, Pátmos

An eye-catching collection of holiday cottages presented in a traditional style, the 9 Muses has a swimming pool, bar and gardens. The gourmet dinners are delivered by a waiter to your own private terrace ◎ Sapsíla bay • Map F4 • 22470 34079 • €€ • www.9musespatmos.com

10 Petra Hotel & Suites, Pátmos

Stunning views across Grikos Bay can be enjoyed from the large and very comfortable rooms here. There is excellent dining and a range of spa treatments. ◎ Grikos • Map F4 • 22470 34020 • €€€ • www.petrahotel-patmos.com

Price Categories

For a standard, double room per night (with breakfast if included), taxes and extra charges.

€	under €50
€€	€50–100
€€€	€100–200
€€€€	€200–300
€€€€€	over €300

Amarylis Hotel, Kárpathos

Budget Stays

1 Sea & Sun Studios, Rhodes
Offering good value, this modern complex of air-conditioned and well-equipped holiday studios overlooks a quiet, sandy beach. Each studio has a private terrace or balcony to enjoy the view. There are tavernas nearby. Special deals are available on longer rentals. ◊ Kiotári beach • Map U5 • 69813 77108 • €€ • www.kiotari.gr

2 Skala Hotel, Pátmos
Set in a garden full of bougainvillea and tropical shrubs, this traditional Pátmos-style hotel offers guests a quiet and relaxing place to stay. Facilities include attractive rooms, sun decks, a conference suite and restaurant. ◊ Skála • Map F4 • 22470 31343 • €€ • www.skalahotel.gr

3 Hotel Camelia, Kos
An attractive three-star hotel in the centre of Kos Town, Hotel Camelia has 22 air-conditioned rooms. Each room has its own balcony, bathroom, television and kitchen, as well as internet access. A daily maid service is provided. There is a TV lounge, bar and café on site. Private parking is also available. ◊ 3 Artemisías Street, Kos Town • Map Y1 • 22420 28983 • € • www.camelia-hotel.com

4 Asteri Hotel, Pátmos
Close to Skála's sights, this appealing hotel boasts traditional Pátmos architecture and is built from local stone. Guest-rooms have sea views and good amenities. There is also a breakfast terrace and gardens. ◊ Skála • Map F4 • 22470 32465 • €€ • www.asteripatmos.gr

5 Amarylis Hotel, Kárpathos
Close to Pigádia's shops, markets and tavernas, this pretty whitewashed hotel offers bright and airy furnished studios and apartments, each with a kitchen, private bathroom and balcony overlooking the gardens. ◊ Pigádia • Map Y6 • 22450 22375 • €€ • www.amarylis.gr

6 Australia Studios, Astypálea
With views of the castle and located just minutes from the beach, this modern complex offers simply furnished studios with kitchens. Its garden is a delight. There are tavernas nearby. ◊ Péra Gialós • Map F5 • 22430 61275 • €€

7 Hotel Philoxenia, Kálymnos
Located in gardens of tropical palm trees close to the beach, this inexpensive, family-run hotel makes a good base for budget-conscious visitors. It has its own bar and restaurant. ◊ Armeos • Map F4 • 22430 59310 • €€ • www.philoxenia-kalymnos.com

8 Galini Studios, Kálymnos
The island of Télendos can be seen from most of the studios in this charming pension-style guesthouse. Popular with climbers, it is close to many recognized climbing and trekking routes, as well as village tavernas. ◊ Masoúri • Map F4 • 22430 47193 • €€ • www.galinistudio.gr

9 Afendoulis, Kos
An inexpensive family-run hotel close to the marina and Kos Town centre, the Afendoulis has pleasingly presented air-conditioned rooms, with showers and Internet access. It has a jasmine-filled garden where breakfast is served. ◊ 1 Evripílou Street, Kos Town • Map Y1 • 22420 25321 • € • www.afendoulishotel.com

10 Hotel Rodon, Pátmos
The balconies of the attractive Hotel Rodon's well-equipped and air-conditioned guestrooms afford views of the harbour or St John's Monastery. The beach, as well as a number of restaurants, are located close by. ◊ Skála • Map F4 • 22470 31371 • €

Left **Lemnos Village Resort** Centre **Argentikon Hotel restaurant, Híos** Right **Filiopi Hotel**

Luxury and Mid-Range Hotels

1 Aeolian Village, Lésvos

This 84-room complex is ideal for families. Located near the beach, it offers a children's club and play area, along with pools, its own taverna and well-equipped guestrooms. Activities include Greek cooking lessons. 🕲 *Skála Eressoú • Map Q2 • 22530 53585 • €€€*

2 Varos Village, Límnos

Spread over six reconstructed traditional buildings, this hotel's rooms are well-equipped and it has its own taverna. The pool is the largest in the Aegean, and there is also a gym. 🕲 *Varos Traditional Settlement, Límnos • Map E1 • 22540 31728 • €€€*
• www.varosvillage.com

3 Kalidon Panorama Hotel, Sámos

Guestrooms at this attractive four-star hotel, built in an amphitheatre fashion around the pool, either look over its tropical garden or towards the sea. Guests can dine on classic dishes at its terrace restaurant. 🕲 *Kokkári • Map F4 • 22730 92800 • €€€ • www.kalidon.gr*

4 Grecian Castle Hotel, Híos

Combining medieval Híot and modern styling, this four-star hotel is full of character. Its guestrooms are luxurious, while facilities include the elegant à la carte Pirgos Restaurant, a cocktail bar and pool. 🕲 *Bella Vista beach, Híos Town • Map L1 • 22710 44740 • €€€*
• www.greciancastle.gr

5 Heliotrope Hotel, Lésvos

Built to reflect Aegean architecture and standing in beachside gardens full of palm trees, this hotel offers rooms with sea views and amenities such as a seawater pool and hydro massage. 🕲 *Vigla beach, Mytilíni • Map S2 • 22510 45857 • €€ • www.heliotrope.gr*

6 Argentikon Hotel, Híos

This complex of suites has been created within a 16th-century estate, where architectural details such as frescoes have been retained. From the restaurant and health suite to the guests' accommodation, the feel is one of total luxury. 🕲 *Kámbos • Map L5 • 22710 33111 • €€€€ • www.argentikon.gr*

7 Lemnos Village Resort, Límnos

This beachside holiday resort's rooms are split-level, luxuriously furnished and well-equipped. On site are pools, sports facilities, and chic restaurants serving international cuisine. 🕲 *Platý • Map E1 • 22540 23500 • €€ • www. lemnosvillagehotel.com*

8 Filiopi Hotel, Ikaría

A modern hotel built in a traditional Aegean style only a few minutes walk from the village centre, the Filiopi comprises studios with kitchen facilities and television. Breakfast and drinks are served on its attractive terrace. 🕲 *Ágios Kírykos • Map F4 • 22750 24124 • €€€*

9 Loriet Hotel, Lésvos

Housed in a beautifully restored 19th-century mansion, with many of its historic features preserved, this hotel is full of character. It has elegant guestrooms, a restaurant, a courtyard pool area surrounded by pine trees and a garden. The garden has a century-old tree-lined avenue that was once used by horse-drawn carriages. 🕲 *Variá, Mytilíni • Map S2 • 22510 43111 • €€€€ • www.loriet-hotel.com*

10 Kerveli Village Hotel, Sámos

The Kerveli is a luxurious hotel located in a bay famous for its sunrises. It has six buildings, surrounded by cypress and olive trees. Life revolves around its pool, elegant sun terraces and its à la carte restaurant, while guestrooms are tastefully decorated. 🕲 *Kerveli • Map F4 • 22730 23006 • €€ • www.kerveli.gr*

Price Categories

For a standard,
double room per
night (with breakfast
if included), taxes
and extra charges.

€ under €50
€€ €50–100
€€€ €100–200
€€€€ €200–300
€€€€€ over €300

Left **Anthemis Hotel, Ikaría** Right **Filoktitis Hotel, Límnos**

Budget Stays and Camping

1 Filoktitis Hotel, Límnos

An inexpensive family-run hotel within easy reach of the Rihá Nerá beach and the town centre, the Filoktitis is charming. It has its own restaurant, bar and car parking.
◈ Rihá Nerá, Mýrina • Map E1 • 22540 23344 • €€
• www.hotelfiloktitis.gr

2 Hotel Cohyli, Sámos

Enjoy breakfast on the terrace of this small family-run hotel while listening to the sound of the lapping waves. Attractively decorated guestrooms, the superb Garden Restaurant and Greek hospitality make this a memorable place.
◈ Seafront, Iréon • Map F4 • 22730 95282 • €
• www.hotel-cohyli.com

3 Anthemis Hotel, Ikaría

This two-star hotel offers super guestrooms that come complete with air conditioning, a dining terrace and fridge. Room service is offered. The hotel lies close to the beach and the village centre. ◈ Thermá • Map F4 • 22750 23156 • €€

4 Agia Sion Hotel, Lésvos

Housed in a period building amid the cobbled streets of the village centre, this small hotel offers visitors the chance to experience rural island life. Its rooms are well-equipped, while the hotel facilities include a garden restaurant. ◈ Agiássos, near Mytilíni • Map S2 • 22520 22242 • €

5 Chíos Camping, Híos

With facilities that include a restaurant, shops and a launderette, this is one of the more organized camp sites on Híos. It has electrical hook-up and children's play areas, and occupies a fantastic waterside location. ◈ Ágios Isidóros-Sykiáda • Map K5 • 22710 74111 • €

6 Lymberis Apartments, Límnos

A great place to stay for anyone on a budget, these air-conditioned apartments are close to the beach and harbour. They come complete with a kitchen and a minibar, and there is a breakfast terrace on site. ◈ Mýrina • Map E1 • 22540 23352 • €

7 Plaka Studios, Híos

Offering great value, Plaka Studios occupy a new, stone-built complex that stands in gardens overlooking the sea. The 10 studios are air-conditioned and have modern, well-equipped kitchens, a fridge and satellite television. ◈ Karfás • Map L5 • 22710 32955 • €€ • www.plakastudios.gr

8 Dionyssos Campsite, Lésvos

This camp site offers pitches for tents and caravans right near the popular beach at Vaterá. On-site facilities include electrical hook-up, water coolers and showers. There is a designated building for cooking and a laundry is also available. Nearby there are tavernas, bars and shops. ◈ Vaterá • Map R3 • 22520 61151 • €

9 Zorbas Apartments, Híos

Run by Yiannis Zorbas and his family, this long-established complex of apartments is a gem. The studios are beautifully clean and stylish, have TV, Internet access and are air conditioned. The meals are classic local dishes and are taken with the family. All the apartments have fully-equipped kitchens and bathrooms with showers. ◈ Volissós • Map K4 • 22740 21436 • €€ • www.chioszorbas.gr

10 Anthemis Apartments, Sámos

This modern complex of apartments is a short walk from the beach and the village centre with its shops and tavernas. Each apartment has a kitchen with fridge, telephone and balcony. ◈ Kalami • Map F4 • 22730 28050 • € • www.samos-apartments.com

➤ The prices for camp sites include a pitch with electricity and on-site facilities.

Left **Aegean Suites Hotel, Skiáthos** Right **Apollon Suite Hotel, Évvia**

Top 10 Luxury and Mid-Range Hotels

1 Atrium Hotel, Skiáthos

This 75-room luxury hotel is built of natural stone in amphitheatre style on a hillside overlooking Agía Paraskeví beach. Its many amenities include chic, well-equipped guestrooms, a taverna serving home-made local dishes, swimming pools, a spa and ball sports. ✆ *Agía Paraskeví, Plataniás • Map M1 • 24270 49345 • €€€ • www.atriumhotel.gr*

2 Esperides Hotel, Skiáthos

A modern hotel with 180 rooms and a suite, the Esperides is a beachside complex within easy reach of the town centre. It is family orientated, with special play areas and menus for small appetites. Its restaurant serves Mediterranean cuisine. Facilities include a swimming pool and Internet. ✆ *Skiáthos Town • Map M1 • 24270 22245 • €€€ • www.esperidesbeach.gr*

3 Skiáthos Palace Hotel, Skiáthos

With views of the famous Koukounariés beach, this five-star hotel is one of the most luxurious on the island. Its 258 rooms are tastefully decorated and the roof garden restaurant is known for its creative cuisine. It also has tennis courts and children's play areas. ✆ *Koukounariés • Map M1 • 24270 49700 • €€€ • www.skiathos-palace.gr*

4 Aegean Suites Hotel, Skiáthos

A five-star boutique hotel, the Aegean oozes understated luxury. From lavish fabrics to individual music centres, the guest-rooms are outstanding. Amenities include a gourmet restaurant, gym and holistic beauty centre. The hotel is exclusively for adults and teenagers. ✆ *Megáli Ámmos • Map M1 • 24270 24066 • €€€€ • www.aegeansuites.com*

5 Apollon Suites Hotel, Évvia

This four-star complex of 36 sea-view suites is minutes from the beach and the harbour, and not far from the centre of town. The guestrooms are well-equipped. There is an á la carte restaurant, sports amenities and a children's playground on site. ✆ *Kárystos • Map D3 • 22240 22045 • €€€ • www.apollonsuiteshotel.com*

6 Pleoussa Studios, Skópelos

The Pleoussa Studios is a collection of 10 luxury studios built with paved areas and arches to reflect the architecture of Skópelos. Each suite has a pleasing decor, air conditioning and a kitchen. Internet access is provided. Each unit enjoys panoramic views of the bay. ✆ *Skópelos Town • Map M1 • 24240 23141 • €€€ • www.pleoussa-skopelos.gr*

7 Almira Mare Hotel, Évvia

The Almira is a modern four-star hotel with a children's playground and pool, adult's pool, sports amenities and restaurants. All rooms have Internet and air conditioning. ✆ *Ágios Minás, Halkída • Map M3 • 22210 97100 • €€€*

8 Pelagos Hotel, Évvia

The amenities at the luxurious Pelagos include a fitness suite, badminton and tennis courts, a spa and swimming pools. Its 119 tastefully decorated rooms have a music system and satellite television. ✆ *Ágios Minás, Halkída • Map M3 • 22210 99310 • €€€€ • www.hotelpelagos.gr*

9 Adrina Beach Hotel, Skópelos

A four-star hotel, the Adrina is close to the beach. Features include a spa pool that overlooks the sea and an elegant terrace taverna serving Greek dishes. ✆ *Pánormos • Map M1 • 24240 23373 • €€€ • www.adrina.gr*

10 Hotel Nefeli, Skýros

A sense of luxury envelops you as you step into this eco hotel. Nefeli is built around a sea-water swimming pool and elegant sun terraces. It has an á la carte break-fast bar and taverna. ✆ *Skýros Town • Map P2 • 22220 91964 • €€€ • www.skyros-nefeli.gr*

Price Categories

For a standard, double room per night (with breakfast if included), taxes and extra charges.

€ under €50
€€ €50–100
€€€ €100–200
€€€€ €200–300
€€€€€ over €300

Left **Sign for a camp site** Right **Rovies Camping, Évvia**

10 Budget Stays and Camping

1 Aegeon Hotel, Skópelos

This 15-room, two-star modern hotel, built in traditional style, is covered in bougainvillea and stands on a hillside overlooking the bay. The rooms are simple, well-equipped and have a balcony, air conditioning and television. There is a children's playground too. ⊗ *Skópelos Town • Map M1 • 24240 22619 • €€*

2 Karakatsanis Nikos Rooms, Alónissos

This collection of rooms makes a good, inexpensive base from which to explore the island. Each has a fridge, private bathroom and balcony. There is a community kitchen and a courtyard dining area. All rooms have glorious sea views. ⊗ *Vótsi • Map N1 • 24240 66188 • €*

3 Valledi Village Hotel, Évvia

A swimming pool with attractive sun terraces and a breakfast lounge are just two features of this modern two-star apartment-style hotel overlooking the bay. Rooms have kitchens and are stylishly decorated. ⊗ *Kými • Map N3 • 22220 29150 • €€ • www.valledivillage.gr*

4 Rovies Camping, Évvia

This camp site opened in 1985 and has a loyal following. It is located amid gardens and trees at the foothills of Mt Telethrion and right next to the beach. Amenities include plots for tents and caravans, a supermarket, launderette, café and children's playground. ⊗ *Rovies, near Límni • Map D3 • 22270 71120 • €*

5 Pension Maria, Alónissos

Surrounded by pine trees and close to the bustling harbourside, this collection of studios offers great views and good amenities. Each studio has its own kitchen with fridge, a private bathroom and a balcony. There are tavernas, bars and restaurants nearby. ⊗ *Patitíri • Map N1 • 24240 65348 • € • www.alonnisos-maria.com*

6 Hotel Pothos, Skiáthos

A small, attractive hotel in the heart of Skiáthos Town, the Pothos stands in mature gardens of palms and red hibiscus. Rooms are pleasingly furnished, with air conditioning and balconies that look out over the gardens. ⊗ *Skiáthos Town • Map M1 • 24270 22694 • € • www.pothos-skiathos.com*

7 Koukounariés Camping, Skiáthos

This popular camp site can be found just off the beach and has a restaurant, supermarket and children's play areas. A launderette is on site, as are showers. There are designated plots under the canopy of the camp's mature trees. ⊗ *Koukounariés beach • Map M1 • 24270 49250 • €*

8 Karystion Hotel, Évvia

Tastefully decorated, this two-star hotel represents good value. It stands on a peninsula with great views of the bay. You can dine inside or on its "wrap-around" terrace and relax in the coffee bar. Rooms are air conditioned. ⊗ *Kárystos • Map E3 • 22240 22391 • €€ • www.karystion.gr*

9 Pandora Studios, Skiáthos

The beautifully presented apartments and studios here have sea views and are equipped with a kitchen, satellite television, Internet access and air conditioning. Located in gardens with palm trees near the village centre and beach. ⊗ *Koliós • Map M1 • 24270 49272 • € • www.skiathospandora.gr*

10 Hotel Regina, Skópelos

Although the amenities of this two-star hotel are basic, it has a great side street location looking over the bay. There is a charming breakfast room, while its 11 modern bedrooms have air conditioning and fridges. ⊗ *Skópelos Town • Map M1 • 24240 22138 • €€*

The prices for camp sites include a pitch with electricity and on-site facilities.

175

Left **Hotel Brown, Égina** Centre **Hotel Angelica, Ýdra** Right **Economou Mansion, Spétses**

🔟 Luxury and Mid-Range Hotels

1 Sto Roloi Hotel, Póros

Housed in a beautifully renovated 19th-century Neo-Classical building, Sto Roloi, meaning "At the Clock Tower", is a collection of luxurious apartments and a suite. Elegantly furnished with antiques, the rooms have features such as massage showers. The hotel is close to the harbour. ✪ *Kostelénou 34-36 • Map K3 • 22980 25808 • €€ • www.storoloi-poros.gr*

2 Zoe's Club Hotel, Spétses

Close to the beach and the port of Dápia, this charming complex of apartments and maisonettes has been built around a pool and sun terrace. The luxury guests' accommodation has every amenity, from bathrobes to DVD players and Internet access. Babysitting services are available. ✪ *Harbourside, Spétses Town • Map D4 • 22980 74447 • €€€ • www.zoesclub.gr*

3 Economou Mansion, Spétses

This 19th-century former naval master's mansion has period architecture and antiques. The luxurious studios and suites have air conditioning and Wi-Fi. Some have private terraces with sea views. ✪ *Harbourside, Spétses Town • Map D4 • 22980 73400 • €€€ • www. economouspetses.gr*

4 Mistral Hotel, Ýdra

A luxury hotel in a country mansion-style building, the Mistral offers 18 individually designed rooms with quality bathrooms and features like satellite television. Breakfast is served in the garden and includes home-made bread. ✪ *Harbour, Ýdra Town • Map D4 • 22980 52509 • €€€ • www.hotelmistral.gr*

5 Orloff Resort, Spétses

Chic, minimalist decor, handmade furniture, crisp linens and marble bathrooms are some of the features of the suites and maisonettes at this resort. It uses natural materials to reflect traditional architecture. ✪ *Old Harbour, Spétses Town • Map D4 • 22980 75444 • €€€ • www.orloffresort.com*

6 Hotel Angelica, Ýdra

This boutique hotel is housed in an old mansion. Its original architecture of stone walls, wooden beams and arches gives its well-decorated rooms much character. Among its features are a sauna, pool and business suite. ✪ *Andréa Miaoúli 43, Ýdra Town • Map D4 • 22980 53202 • €€€€ • www.angelica.gr*

7 Vasilis Bungalows, Kýthira

A collection of 12 bungalows built among mature olive trees, this complex is ideal for exploring Hóra. The bungalows are air conditioned and have a private patio. Guests can enjoy breakfast on the terrace. ✪ *Kapsáli • Map C5 • 27360 31125 • €€€ • www. kythirabungalowsvasili.gr*

8 Bratsera, Ýdra

Named after a local ship used by sponge divers and housed in a charming restored 19th-century sponge factory, this hotel is luxurious. The spectacular lobby leads through gardens to the pool, restaurant and 26 rooms. ✪ *Hóra, Ýdra Town • Map D4 • 22980 53971 • €€€ • www. bratserahotel.com*

9 Leto Hotel, Ýdra

A total of 21 rooms, including four that are interconnected and one with wheelchair access, are offered at this family-orientated luxury hotel. A lounge, gym and garden provide perfect places to unwind. ✪ *Ýdra Town • Map D4 • 22980 53385 • €€€ • www.letohydra.gr*

10 Hotel Brown, Égina

The 19th-century sea sponge factory that was transformed into Hotel Brown is a landmark. This elegant hotel comprises 28 rooms, with views of the bay, and a collection of bungalows dotting the garden. ✪ *Égina Town • Map K1 • 22970 22271 • €€ • www.hotelbrown.gr*

Price Categories

For a standard, double room per night (with breakfast if included), taxes and extra charges.

€	under €50
€€	€50–100
€€€	€100–200
€€€€	€200–300
€€€€€	over €300

Delfini Hotel, Ýdra

🔟 Budget Stays

1 Hotel Plaza, Égina
This small, welcoming hotel looks out over the harbour. Its guest studios each have a kitchen with fridge for self-catering, air conditioning and television, while a whole raft of tavernas, bars and shops are within walking distance. There is also a laundry room on site. 🅂 *Égina Town • Map K1 • 22970 25600 • €€*

2 Pension Erofili, Ýdra
A whitewashed stone cottage minutes from the harbourside, this pension is a convenient base for exploring Ýdra. It offers 11 tastefully decorated and air-conditioned rooms and one suite. The courtyard is surrounded by bougainvillea. 🅂 *Ýdra Town • Map D4 • 22980 54049 • €€ • www.pensionerofili.gr*

3 Pension Electra, Égina
Despite its location in the centre of town, this family-run pension is quiet and relaxing as well as clean and comfortable. First-class studios have sea views, and each has a private terrace or patio area. 🅂 *Égina Town • Map K1 • 22970 26715 • € • www.aegina-electra.gr*

4 Kamares Apartments, Kýthira
This complex of 10 apartments is located in an 18th–19th-century rural house, whose stone arches give it plenty of character. Amenities include air conditioning, parking and private kitchens. Great views of the surrounding countryside. 🅂 *Aroniádika • Map C5 • 27360 33420 • €*

5 Margarita Hotel, Kýthira
The elevated location of this hotel ensures it has panoramic views from almost every room. Housed in a 19th-century mansion, it offers good value with 12 air-conditioned rooms and a terrace where breakfast is prepared by the French owners. 🅂 *Hóra • Map C5 • 27360 31711 • € • www.hotel-margarita.com*

6 Hotel Liberty 2, Égina
Covered in bougainvillea and boasting traditional architecture, this attractive hotel is minutes from the beach. Its pleasing guestrooms look out over the bay, while facilities include a breakfast terrace, a gift shop and a satellite television lounge. 🅂 *Agia Marína • Map L1 • 22970 32105 • € • www.hotelliberty2.gr*

7 7 Islands Hotel, Spétses
On a hillside overlooking Spétses harbour, this Anglo–Greek-owned hotel is located 10–15 minutes' walk from the main town. It provides a peaceful setting for a stay in Spétses. 🅂 *Barbatsi, Spétses Town • Map D4 • 22980 73059 • €€ • www.7islands-spetses.com*

8 Villa Rodanthos, Égina
A Neo-Classical building comprising 10 self-catering studios, the Villa Rodanthos is minutes from the harbour, which is famous for fish tavernas. It has a breakfast lounge, bar and roof garden. Each studio is elegantly decorated and has a kitchenette and balcony. 🅂 *Pérdika • Map K2 • 22970 61400 • € • www.villarodanthos.gr*

9 Delfini Hotel, Ýdra
This small hotel lies in a cluster of traditional Hydran seamen's cottages overlooking the bay. Fully renovated, its rooms are spacious and well equipped, many boasting panoramic sea views. The terrace is a great place to watch the bustle of the harbour. 🅂 *Ýdra Town • Map D4 • 22980 52082 • € • www.delfinihotel.gr*

10 Hydroussa Hotel, Ýdra
The Hydroussa is a 40-room hotel, housed in a traditional mansion-style property within walking distance of the harbour. Guests can enjoy air-conditioned rooms and dine in the breakfast hall or relax in the drawing room or gardens. 🅂 *Platía Vótsi, Ýdra Town • Map D4 • 22980 53580 • €€ • www.hydroussa-hydra.gr*

Left **AKS Annabelle Beach Resort** Right **Istron Bay Hotel's pool**

TOP 10 Luxury and Mid-Range Hotels

1 AKS Annabelle Beach Resort

This five-star village hotel lies next to a Blue Flag beach and offers pools, watersports and a fitness centre with a sauna and treatment room. The 262 bungalow rooms are luxurious. ❧ *Seafront, Chersónissos • Map E6 • 28970 23561 • €€€ • www.akshotels.com*

2 Albatros Hotel

An attractive white-washed hotel standing in lush gardens of palm trees and tropical shrubs, the Albatros offers a choice of dining areas, including its super à la carte Daphne restaurant. On site are a children's club and pool, and a fitness suite. ❧ *Seafront, Chersónissos • Map E6 • 28970 22144 • €€€ • www.albatros.gr*

3 Hersonissos Palace

This hotel, with a mix of Greek Neo-Classical and contemporary styling, has 150 rooms, four suites and tennis courts. Mediterranean cuisine is served in its restaurant and poolside buffet. ❧ *Harbourside, Chersónissos • Map E6 • 28970 23603 • €€€€ • www.hersotels.gr*

4 Istron Bay Hotel

Overlooking a bay, this hotel has a warm and welcoming feel. Family run, it celebrates Cretan traditions with music evenings and Greek à la carte cuisine, while offering amenities such as watersports, tennis and aerobics. ❧ *Harbourside, Ístro, Agios Nikólaos • Map F6 • 28410 61303 • €€€ • www.istronbay.gr*

5 Anissa Beach Hotel

Guests can swim, enjoy watersports, play tennis and eat Mediterranean dishes in the La Pergola restaurant at this hotel overlooking the sandy beach of Anissáras. Its rooms are chic and well-equipped, with most having sea views. ❧ *Seafront, Anissáras, Chersónissos • Map E6 • 28970 23264 • €€ • www.anissabeach.com*

6 Kalimera Kriti Hotel

A luxurious beachside hotel with architecture influenced by the Minoan palaces of Crete, the Kalimera Kriti has amenities such as restaurants, a piano bar, pools and shops in its re-creation of a village square. ❧ *Sísi village • Map E6 • 28410 69000 • €€€€ • www.kalimerakriti.gr*

7 Angela Suites Boutique Hotel

Contemporary and stylish, this collection of suites lie just minutes from Sísi beach and close to the village. Individually designed rooms are chic and well-equipped, while facilities include fresh-water pools, a fitness and alternative therapy suite, cocktail lounge and an à la carte restaurant. ❧ *Sísi village • Map E6 • 28410 71121 • €€ • www.angelasuites.com*

8 Elounda Bay Palace

Surrounded by large gardens and with an infinity pool overlooking the sea, this hotel is a haven of peace. There is a water's edge restaurant, private gym and a spa. ❧ *Seafront, Eloúnda • Map F6 • 28410 67000 • €€€€ • www.eloundabay.gr*

9 Galaxy Hotel

One of the finest hotels on the island, the Galaxy is the last word in luxury. Amenities at this 127-room hotel include gourmet restaurants and a wellness centre with hammam and gym that is complimentary or guests. ❧ *Leofóros Dimokratías 75, Irákleio • Map E6 • 28102 38812 • €€€ • www.galaxy-hotel.com*

10 Fodele Beach and Water Park

This lively five-star resort has bungalow guest-rooms built in a style reminiscent of Venetian architecture. The Fodele has every amenity from restaurants serving European cuisine, bars and a children's club to sports, gym and water-park. ❧ *Irákleio • Map E6 • 28105 21251 • €€€ • www.fodelebeach.gr*

Price Categories

For a standard, double room per night (with breakfast if included), taxes and extra charges.	
€	under €50
€€	€50–100
€€€	€100–200
€€€€	€200–300
€€€€€	over €300

Hotel Kissamos

🔟 Budget Stays and Camping

1 Adelais Hotel
Built in the style of the local stone homes, this super hotel has rooms with a bright Mediterranean-themed decor, sun terraces, pools and a restaurant serving refined cuisine. There is a children's playground and pool. 🕲 *Tavronítis, Chaniá • Map D6 • 28240 22929 • €€ • www.adelais.gr*

2 Camping Sisi
The excellent facilities at this attractively located camp site include a swimming pool, Wi-Fi, laundry room and kitchen. It's a 15-minute walk to the pretty village of Sisi, and a 5-minute walk to the beach. 🕲 *Sisi, Lasithi • Map E6 • 28410 71247 • www.sisicamping.gr*

3 Lefkoniko Seaside Hotel
This complex of air-conditioned studios and apartments has sea views and is central for local amenities. Buffet and à la carte restaurants, bars and swimming pools are available at its nearby sister hotel, the Lefkoniko Beach Hotel. 🕲 *Sofoklí Venizélou 76 and Eleftherías, Réthymno • Map E6 • 28310 55326 • €€*

4 Hotel Castro Amoudára
This attractive hotel has 53 guestrooms, most of which have a balcony looking out over the swimming pool and gardens. Maxims, its own traditional-style taverna, serves Cretan cuisine and wine, while a pool bar serves cocktails. 🕲 *A Papandréou Street 301, Amoudára • Map E6 • 28108 22770 • € • www.castro-hotel.com*

5 Mirtilos Studios-Apartments
Located minutes from the sandy beach of Telonío, with views of Kíssamos bay, this complex of well-equipped studios and apartments is a good holiday base. It has gardens with sun terraces, a dining area and two large pools. 🕲 *Tzanakákis Square, Kíssamos • Map D6 • 28220 23079 • €€ • www.mirtilos.com*

6 Réthymno Youth Hostel
Housed in a Venetian stone building standing amid gardens in the heart of Réthymno, this youth hostel centres around its pretty patio. Dormitory rooms are basic but clean, and Internet and light meals are available. 🕲 *Tobázi Street 41, Réthymno • Map E6 • 28310 22848 • € • www.yhrethymno.com*

7 Hotel Kissamos
Comprising 24 rooms with private bathrooms, air conditioning and great views of Kíssamos bay, this hotel offers guests a home-from-home feel. There are some palm tree-shaded gardens and a swimming pool available for guests to use. 🕲 *Iroón Polytechníou 172, Kíssamos • Map D6 • 28220 22086 • €€ • www.hotelkissamos.gr*

8 Hotel Caretta Beach
Offering good value for money, these apartments are beautifully furnished and come with room service and Internet access. The hotel is surrounded by olive groves, and has a pool, restaurant and a beach. 🕲 *Geráni Kydonías, Chaniá • Map D6 • 28210 61700 • €€ • www.caretta-beach.gr*

9 Mithimna Camping
This large, shady camp site is well organized, with a restaurant serving Cretan dishes, a laundry, hot and cold water and electrical hook-up. A mini-supermarket is on site. Caravan and tent owners are welcome. 🕲 *Drapanías, Kíssamos • Map D6 • 28220 31444 • € • www.campingmithimna.com*

10 Youth Hostel Plakiás
Nestled in an olive grove with walking trails and beaches nearby, this hostel provides nicely furnished shared bungalows, inexpensive meals, drinks and Internet. It also hosts barbecues and party nights. 🕲 *Plakiás • Map E6 • 28320 32118 • € • www.yhplakias.com*

General Index

Index

Index

Acknowledgments

The Author
Carole French is an award-winning BBC-trained journalist, based in Cyprus and the UK. Her work has appeared in publications including *ABTA Magazine*, *Homes Overseas* and the *Daily Mail*. She has worked on travel guides for Michelin, Time Out and Thomas Cook, and provided expert consultation on the Greek Islands for television.

Photographers Tony Souter, Helena Smith
Additional Photography Peter Anderson, Joe Cornish, Ken Findlay, Geoff Garvey, Robin Gauldie, Michelle Grant, Paul Harris, Nigel Hicks, Rupert Horrox, Peter Jousiffe, Dave King, Ian O'Leary, Annabel Milne, David Murray, Brian Pitkin, Rob Reichenfeld, Clive Streeter, Robert Vente, Kate Whitaker, Linda Whitwam, Peter Wilson, Francesca Yorke
Consultant Nick Edwards
Fact Checker Anthony Clark

At DK INDIA
Managing Editor Aruna Ghose
Editorial Manager Sheeba Bhatnagar
Design Manager Kavita Saha
Project Editor Shikha Kulkarni
Project Designer Shruti Singhi
Assistant Cartographic Manager Suresh Kumar
Senior Picture Research Coordinator Taiyaba Khatoon
Picture Researcher Sumita Khatwani
DTP Coordinator Azeem Siddiqui
Proofreader and Indexer Andy Kulkarni

At DK LONDON
Publisher Douglas Amrine
List Manager Julie Oughton
Design Manager Mabel Chan
Project Editors Alexandra Whittleton, Dora Whitaker
Designer Tracy Smith
Cartographer Stuart James
DTP Operator Jason Little
Production Controller Danielle Smith
Revisions Team Namrata Adhwaryu, Ashwin Adimari, Claire Baranowski, Marta Bescos, Emer FitzGerald, Fay Franklin, Carole French, Paul Marsden, Rada Radojicic, Alice Saggers, Liz Sharp, Susana Smith

Picture Credits
Placement Key: a = above; b = below/bottom; c = centre; f = far; l = left; r = right; t = top.

Photography Permissions
Dorling Kindersley would like to thank the following for their assistance and kind permission to photograph at their establishments

9 Muses, Patmos; Aegean Suites Hotel, Skiathos; Agora Tavern, Egina; AKS Annabelle Village, Crete; Angelica VIP Boutique Hotel, Ydra; Aqua Plus Water Park, Crete; Aquarium, Rhodes; Benetos Restaurant, Patmos; Blue Lagoon Resort, Kos; Byzantine Museum, Rhodes; Chotsas Taverna, Hios; Christie, Crete; Cretaquarium, Crete; Esperos Village Resort, Rhodes; Figaro Art & Music Café, Crete; Greek Restaurant Museum, Kos; Heart Rock Café, Kos; Helmos Hotel, Naxos; Irakleio's Archaeological Museum, Crete; Irene Palace Hotel, Rhodes; Klik The Scandinavian Bar, Crete; Koo Club, Santorini; Levantis Restaurant Paros; Lido Waterpark, Kos; Manolis Taverna, Karpathos; Mediterranean Royal, Santorini; Monastery of St John, Patmos;

Jea Moni de Chios; Pacifae, Crete; Palada Taverna, Tinos; Papagalos Restaurant, Santorini; Paradise Beach Resort and Camping, Mykonos; Patsouras, Kefallonia; Pigadi Restaurant, Crete; Restaurant Drosia, Kalymnos; Santorini Kastelli Resort; The Windmill Restaurant, Skiathos; To Tavernaki tou Tassou; Viveur Wine Bar, Rhodes.

The publisher would like to thank the following individuals, companies, and picture libraries for their kind permission to reproduce their photographs:

4CORNERS IMAGES: SIME/Huber Johanna 128-129, /Simeone Giovanni 52-53.

ALAMY IMAGES: Gary Blake 139tl; Eyebyte 7cra; Stephen French 80tl; ML Image Group Ltd 105tl; imagebroker/Christian Handl 103tr; kpzfoto 105tr; LOOK Die Bildagentur der Fotografen GmbH Holger Leue 10cla; MARKA 56tl; Hercules Milas 40tr; Adrian Muttitt 139tr; Steve Outram 56tc; Terry Harris just greece photo library 56br; Marco Trajola 60tr; TTL Images 28-29c.

ARGENTIKON LUXURY SUITES: 172tc.

BLUE LAGOON GROUP: 170tc; BUON AMICI: 75tl; THE

BRIDGEMAN ART LIBRARY: © Ashmolean Museum, University of Oxford, UK Cycladic Figurine, Naxos, c.3000-2000 BC (marble), 32ca.

CAFE BAR MUSES: 78tl; COLORADO CLUB: 62bl; CORBIS: Bettmann 33cl; Vanni Archive 16-17c.

GETTY IMAGES: Brian Hagiwara 50br; Ingolf Pompe 11bc; THE GRANGER COLLECTION, NEW YORK: 32tl, 32tc.

KILMTARIA: 127tl

ODYSSEY APARTMENTS: 167tl

PHOTOLIBRARY: age fotostock/ Terrance Klassen 152-153; Imagestate/Christophe Bluntzer 57tl, /Barbara Heller 24bl, /CM Dixon 26c, 27tl, 27cra; LOOK-foto/ Ingolf Pompe 59cr; Mauritius/ Manfred Habel 10-11c; Robert Harding Travel/David Beatty 56tr, /Fraser Hall 30-31, /Sakis Papadopoulos 66-67, /Ellen Rooney 1c, /Marco Simoni 39tl, 94-95; PHOTOSHOT: TTL/Graham Bell 74tl.

SKANDINAVIAN BAR: 63br.

YACHT CLUB PANAGAKIS: 148tr.

All other images are © Dorling Kindersley. For further information see www.dkimages.com

Special Editions of DK Travel Guides

DK Travel Guides can be purchased in bulk quantities at discounted prices for use in promotions or as premiums. We are also able to offer special editions and personalized jackets, corporate imprints, and excerpts from all of our books, tailored specifically to meet your own needs.

To find out more, please contact:
(in the United States) SpecialSales@ dk.com
(in the UK) travelspecialsales@ uk.dk.com
(in Canada) DK Special Sales at general@tourmaline.ca
(in Australia) business.development@ pearson.com.au

Selected Map Index